TRANSLUCENCE

Religion, the Arts, and Imagination

edited by

CAROL GILBERTSON AND
GREGG MUILENBURG

Fortress Press
Minneapolis

TRANSLUCENCE
Religion, the Arts, and Imagination

Quote from "Luther" by W. H. Auden, Copyright © 1940 Christian Century Foundation. Reprinted with permission from the Oct. 2, 1940, issue of *The Christian Century.*

Quote from "For the Time Being," copyright © 1944 by W.H. Auden, from *For the Time Being* by W. H. Auden. Used by permission of Random House, Inc. and Faber & Faber Ltd.

Quote from "The Man Watching," from *Selected Poems of Rainer Maria Rilke,* edited and translated by Robert Bly, © 1981 by Robert Bly. Reprinted by permission of HarperCollins Publishers Inc.

Quote from "In Memory of W. B. Yeats," From *Another Time* by W. H. Auden, published by Random House. Copyright © 1940 W. H. Auden, renewed by the Estate of W. H. Auden. Used by permission of Curtis Brown, Ltd., Random House, and Faber & Faber Ltd.

Cover art: © Photonica
Cover design: Kevin Vanderleek
Interior design: Allan S. Johnson, Phoenix Type, Inc.

Library of Congress Cataloging-in-Publication Data
    Translucence : religion, the arts, and imagination / edited by Carol Gilbertson and Gregg Muilenburg.
        p. cm.
    Includes bibliographical references.
    ISBN 0-8006-6089-7 (alk. paper)
    1. Christianity and the arts—Congresses. I. Title.
    BR115.A8 T73 2004
    261.5/7 22
                                        2004014337

Manufactured in the U.S.A.

08   07   06   05   04   1   2   3   4   5   6   7   8   9   10

Contents

Editors' Preface

This volume results from an extended conversation that began in July 2001 at Harvard University during a two-week Lutheran Academy of Scholars Seminar focused on the public intellectual and the arts. A disparate group—clergy, theologians, visual artists, musicians, and poets, as well as scholars of literature, philosophy, and art—we were united in concern for the demise of effective academic voices in American public life. Reading widely about the modern and postmodern context, we observed that today's faculties have greater disciplinary specialization and a firmer dedication, even at small liberal arts colleges, to publishing scholarly work. But this specialized expertise is countered by a sense of inadequacy in extra-disciplinary discourse—a phenomenon that jeopardizes liberal arts education as much as it dilutes public discourse. We especially bemoaned the near silence of Lutheran voices in a public discourse where the term *Christian* has been almost completely co-opted by a politically active and adeptly organized Christian conservative movement.

Our task included learning about each other's institutions as well as disciplines. We are not all Lutherans, and only some were raised as Lutherans. Those of us who teach at Lutheran institutions recognize the colleges' very different relationships to the church and levels of willingness to engage in religious discourse. We needed to gain fluency in different vocabularies—the language of musical performance and musicology, art critical theory, abstract philosophical and theological discourse, literary theory and pedagogy—and we also needed to bridge gaps among traditional, modern, and postmodern assumptions.

In our residence hall and meeting room, we had animated conversations, periodically lubricated by good food and drink in Cambridge's ethnic restaurants. We became not only committed colleagues who nurtured each other's work but also great friends. This book results from discussions that continued online after that July seminar into the stunning autumn of September 11—including sharing our campuses' confused responses to that tragic event. In several post-seminar meetings over the next three years, we grew more excited about this book's purpose, and eventually eight of the eleven seminar members contributed chapters.

Our conviction is that there is indeed a deeply relevant phenomenon that imbues the many realms of human experience. Our focus is this profound sense that God's light shines through human art in multiple ways. Perhaps the most eloquent literary passage on such divine illumination comes in the invocation to Heavenly Light with which John Milton begins the third book of his seventeenth-century Christian epic, *Paradise Lost:*

> thou Celestial light
> Shine inward, and the mind through all her powers
> Irradiate, there plant eyes, all mist from thence
> Purge and disperse, that I may see and tell
> Of things invisible to mortal sight.[1]

Though Milton asks for a transparent, mist-free vision as he writes this poem, aiming to "justifie the wayes of God to men,"[2] the writers here acknowledge that longing for elusive transparency but in fact see the *mist* of each artistic medium as a beautiful *translucence*—in metaphor, text, drama, music, and the visual arts. This simultaneous balance of partial clarity and partial obscurity, which mirrors God's paradoxical disclosure and concealment to humans, is art's particular gift. Because it is deeply embedded in physicality and imagination's nonrational logic, art's

---

1. John Milton, *Paradise Lost,* in *The Riverside Milton,* ed. Roy Flannagan (Boston: Houghton Mifflin, 1998), 3:51–55.
2. Ibid., 1:26.

glass gives a radiantly filtered vision of God, a textured sense of divine presence.

We wish to note that our discoveries were catalyzed by the seminar's director, Ronald F. Thiemann, Professor of Theology and of Religion and Society at Harvard Divinity School, and its facilitator, L. DeAne Lagerquist, Professor of Religion at St. Olaf College. Both offered provocative critique, clarification, and deep encouragement, and DeAne graciously provided the volume's introduction. We are grateful to the Lilly Foundation, Lutheran Brotherhood (now Thrivent Financial for Lutherans), and the Evangelical Lutheran Church in America's Division of Higher Education and Schools for supporting the Lutheran Academy in its experimental stages. We are delighted that our intellectual exhilaration—as well as the fruitful conversations of three other seminars—has led to the creation of a permanent Lutheran Academy under DeAne's capable leadership and supported by Lutheran colleges and other funding agencies. As editors we thank our fellow writers for their continued commitment to the conversation despite their busy lives. And our own packed but rich lives, at two midwestern Lutheran colleges with supportive colleagues, include committed spouses—Mark Z. Muggli and Patricia Muilenburg—whose partnering made our individual and collaborative work more possible. For our respective children (Clara and Ellen Gilbertson Muggli, Megan and Benjamin Muilenburg), we wish a public discourse that includes their voices along with those of other informed, liberal Christians.

Contributors

Paul Beidler is Assistant Professor of English at Lenoir-Rhyne College in Hickory, North Carolina. He teaches British literature, literary theory, and linguistics, and has previously published on Laurence Sterne, Alfred Tennyson, Gerard Manley Hopkins, and Wallace Stevens.

Karen Black is Associate Professor of Music and College Organist at Wartburg College, Waverly, Iowa, where she teaches organ, church music, and music theory, serves as college organist, and conducts the Chapel Choir. Active as recitalist and clinician, she recently performed at the German Reformation sites of Neuendettelsau, Wittenburg, and Eisenach, and has been heard on Minnesota Public Radio's *Pipedreams*.

Kathryn Pohlmann Duffy is Professor of Music at Grand View College, Des Moines, Iowa, where she teaches music history and theory and directs the Grand View College Choir. In 2001 she received the Grand View College Faculty Recognition Award for teaching and mentoring. She is presently editing the liturgical music of Thomas Müntzer.

Carol Gilbertson is Professor of English at Luther College, Decorah, Iowa. She was the 2002–2004 Dennis M. Jones Distinguished Teaching

Professor in the Humanities, directing the Luther Poetry Project, designed to raise campus awareness of poetry's power and relevance. She has published poems and essays, as well as scholarly work on John Milton, T. S. Eliot, and Ezra Pound. She is working on a book of poems.

James S. Hanson is Associate Professor of Religion at St. Olaf College. His areas of teaching and research interest include the literary and theological interpretation of the Gospels, Jewish-Christian relations and dialogue, and religion and the arts. He is also an active participant in the arts, performing regularly as an actor and musician.

Bruce Allen Heggen serves as pastor of the Lutheran Campus Ministry at the University of Delaware and teaches in the writing program of the University's English Department. He earned his Ph.D. in Christian theology at McGill University, writing on the thought of Joseph Sittler, and has twice earned fellowship grants in poetry from the Delaware Division of the Arts.

L. DeAne Lagerquist is Professor of Religion at St. Olaf College, Northfield, Minnesota, as well as Executive Director of the Lutheran Academy of Scholars. Trained as a historian of Christianity, her scholarly work has focused upon women and Lutherans, primarily in the United States. *The Lutherans,* her narrative history of that tradition since the colonial era, was published by Greenwood in 1999.

Gregg Muilenburg is Professor of Philosophy at Concordia College, Moorhead, Minnesota. He has published in the areas of epistemology, metaphysics, faith and reason, and on the Cretan novelist Nikos Kazantzakis. He is presently editing a book on the nature of the public intellectual and finishing a book on metaphor.

Curtis L. Thompson is Professor of Religion at Thiel College, Greenville, Pennsylvania. He is the author of *Expecting and Exposing God: Biblical Theology for a Late Modern Age* (1998), the translator (with Paul Kangas) of *Between Hegel and Kierkegaard: Hans L. Martensen's Philosophy of Religion* (1997), and co-author of *Science and Our Global Heritage: Multidisciplinary Perspectives on Sustainability* (2004).

Introduction

L. DEANE LAGERQUIST

Conversation derives etymologically from a "turning together" and even hints at the life-altering turns we know as conversion. This volume aims to draw readers into a vital, even urgent, conversation about religious dimensions of the intellectual and artistic life and their relevance to our life together in academy, church, and nation.

Tertullian in the third century probed the possibility of religion and philosophy's talking together productively. His question—What has Athens to do with Jerusalem?—is the classic Christian articulation of a more general question: What has reason to do with faith? Though Tertullian answered, "Nothing," his overly simple formulation has stimulated much exploration. Recently it has informed, though not determined, vigorous discussion of religion and higher education.[1]

When the discussion moves from general issues and becomes disciplinary, the dialogue of science and religion is frequently raised as the hard case on the assumption that natural science relies upon objective reason antithetical to religion, which is based upon faith. Indeed the

---

1. For a particularly insightful reading of Tertullian and his contemporary Clement on this question, see Nicholas Wolterstorff, "Tertullian's Enduring Questions," *The Cresset* 62/7 (June/July 1999): 5–16.

tense relationship of science and religion is a major focus of contemporary scholarship. In contrast, the conversation about art and religion appears to assume a fundamental similarity between the two: put too neatly, both are subjective rather than objective, emotive rather than rational, a matter of personal opinion rather than of public argument. Therefore it seems that the two must live together more harmoniously than do science and religion. Yet, careful attention to art and religion, such as is given in this volume, reveals the rich complexity and power in their turning together.[2]

With Augustine the authors of these contributions allow that "corporal and temporal things," such as the words of a poem printed on a page or the notes of a chorale sung in a concert hall, are a means of comprehending things "eternal and spiritual." Also like Augustine they take care to distinguish one sort of thing from the other even as they tease out the dynamics of the turning or join in the dance. Work such as theirs produces valuable insights about the larger issues of human knowledge, religious life, and education. These authors offer *translucence* as a metaphor for the interactions of art and religion; they posit that while art provides access to profound truths central to religion (to Christianity in particular), at the same time art distorts or conceals. This metaphor emerged from conversations begun in a seminar sponsored by the Lutheran Academy of Scholars in 2001. The seminar intentionally included artists and the arts in its discussion of faith and reason, of religion and higher education.[3] The seminar also pursued the Lutheran Academy's intention to cultivate Lutheran theological insights into these matters. Seminar participants found that characteristic Lutheran themes, such as sacramental sensibility and awareness of divine self-revelation simultaneous with God's continued hiddenness, are well suited to con-

---

2. Among such treatments is George Dennis O'Brien, *The Idea of a Catholic University* (Chicago: University of Chicago Press, 2002). O'Brien fruitfully includes science and art in his examination of the nature of religious truth. He cautions against too close an association of religion with the truth of art. For a study focused more narrowly on a single art, see Jeremy S. Begbie, *Theology, Music and Time* (Cambridge: Cambridge University Press, 2000).

3. The topics of these contributions are determined by the composition of that group. In addition to the authors, it included Kathryn Ananda-Owens (St. Olaf College), Tim Schmidt (Waldorf College), and Cassandra Tellier (Capital University). Ronald F. Thiemann (Harvard University) was the seminar leader.

sideration of the arts; moreover, they discovered that the arts provide a particularly valuable opportunity for exploration of Lutheran resources for the work of higher education.[4]

Like *Scholarship and Christian Faith: Enlarging the Conversation,* this work offers an alternative to the prevalent integrationist model of Christianity and scholarship.[5] While Douglas Jacobsen and his Messiah College colleagues probe Anabaptist traditions, these authors respond to calls for greater attention to Lutheran resources, calls issued by non-Lutherans Richard T. Hughes and Mark Noll. In a recent essay Noll named exemplary figures from Lutheran history—"the penetrating vision of Luther, the scholarly aplomb of Melanchthon, the irenic efficiency of the Concord formulators, the surging brilliance of Bach, the passionate wisdom of Kierkegaard, or the heroic integrity of Bonhoeffer"—and then noted the surprising fact that Lutherans have been a "relatively inconspicuous presence" in the United States.[6] Although his essay concerns public life broadly construed, the characteristics listed as the basis for Lutheran contribution are applicable to higher education as well: an "understanding of the labyrinthine depths of human evil

---

4. Other considerations of Lutheran contributions to higher education include: Ernest L. Simmons, *Lutheran Higher Education: An Introduction for Faculty* (Minneapolis: Augsburg Fortress, 1998); *Called to Serve: St. Olaf and the Vocation of a Church College,* ed. Pamela Schwandt, Gary DeKrey, and L. DeAne Lagerquist (Northfield, Minn.: St. Olaf College, 1999); *The Lutheran Reader,* ed. Paul J. Contino and David Morgan (Valparaiso, Ind.: Valparaiso University, 1999); and Tom Christenson, *The Gift and Task of Lutheran Higher Education* (Minneapolis: Augsburg Fortress, 2004). In addition, see these shorter pieces: Richard Solberg, "What Can the Lutheran Tradition Contribute to Christian Higher Education?" in *Models for Christian Higher Education: Strategies for Success in the Twenty-First Century,* ed. Richard T. Hughes and William B. Adrian (Grand Rapids: Eerdmans, 1997), 71–81; L. DeAne Lagerquist, "What Does This Mean? Lutheran Higher Education," *Lutheran Education* (March/April 2000): 184–98; idem, "The Vocation of a Lutheran College in the Midst of American Higher Education," *Intersections: Faith + Life + Learning* (Summer 2001): 11–19; Mark U. Edwards Jr., "Characteristically Lutheran Leanings?" *dialog* 41/1 (Spring 2002): 50–62; and Mark R. Schwehn, "Lutheran Higher Education in the Twenty-first Century," in *The Future of Religious Colleges,* ed. Paul J. Dovre (Grand Rapids: Eerdmans, 2002), 208–23; Robert Benne, "Integrity and Fragmentation: Can the Lutheran Center Hold?" in *Lutherans Today: American Lutheran Identity in the Twenty-First Century,* ed. Richard Cimino (Grand Rapids: Eerdmans, 2003), 206–21.

5. Douglas Jacobsen and Rhonda Hustedt Jacobsen, eds., *Scholarship and Christian Faith: Enlarging the Conversation* (Oxford: Oxford University Press, 2004).

6. Mark Noll, "American Lutherans Yesterday and Today," in Cimino, *Lutherans Today,* 19.

and the majestic power of God's grace in Christ," appreciation of the objective character of divine salvation, the notion that the church is more than a collection of like-minded people, and "the Lutheran gift for ambiguity." Acknowledging the difficulty of marketing this latter trait to prospective college students, Hughes concurs that a gift for ambiguity is particularly valuable for sustaining the life of the mind and informing the work of education.[7] Indeed, precisely this affinity for ambiguity stands behind this volume's title and its contentions about the productivity of conversation between art and religion.

Curtis Thompson helpfully examines *translucence:* the word and the metaphor. His exposition of this "shining through" need not be rehearsed here. But his assertion that what shines is glorious is worth noting, particularly in a volume that claims to mine Lutheran resources. Worshippers sing about "the beauty of the earth" or the change "from glory into glory," but seldom has anyone pointed out that a theologian of the cross's commitment to call a thing what it is may require calling it beautiful. Despite Martin Luther's appreciation for the loveliness of a rose or the splendor of music, Lutherans generally guard against false confidence in earthly things by emphasizing imperfections, suffering, and brokenness. Thompson's theology of glory does not advocate pride or some sort of triumphalism; to the contrary, encounter with such shining glory—whether beautiful or ghastly—evokes awe, humility, and relinquishment of credit and control. Karen Black describes this response when she recalls her experience singing Bach's *St. Matthew Passion.*

Again following Augustine, Thompson contrasts two-eyed interpretation of such an experience, indeed of all art, with an opaque reading that focuses upon the corporal surface and misses the eternal. This is not, however, permission to squint in such a way that one sees only the spiritual and ignores the temporal. Neither faith nor imagination benefits from ignorance or inattention to the world. Kathryn Pohlmann Duffy reminds us that neglect of details such as the specific style and construction of a musical work (an assumption of transparency, if you will) impoverishes the hearer as well as the interpretation. A modern listener, intent upon gaining a glimpse of the glory shining through it, may be tempted to ignore the particularity of the composer's craft. Duffy

---

7. Hughes, "Introduction," 6–7. See also his *How Christian Faith Can Sustain the Life of the Mind* (Grand Rapids: Eerdmans, 2001), 85–94.

demonstrates that informed, considered attention to these details can enhance the hearer's understanding of the work as well as contributing to her apprehension of the spiritual.[8]

Here translucence is cast as a metaphor. Translucence is not merely a physical quality of a rice-paper screen that allows one to see a human form on the other side without identifying the person. It is also a quality of art. The metaphor of translucence requires us to notice both the thin alabaster slices of a lampshade and the light shining through that stone; it requires us to notice both the paint perfectly applied to the canvas and the spiritual dimension that the pigment imperfectly conveys. Beyond its suggestions about art, metaphorical translucence suggests something about metaphors and the subtle yet powerful way that they work. In his essay Gregg Muilenburg, having read Cretan novelist Nikos Kazantzakis as well as classical and modern philosophy, notes that a metaphor's effectiveness relies upon our startled perception of a similarity between two things that are not the same. He posits that metaphors point toward knowledge by diverting attention away from themselves. In this assertion Muilenburg seems to depart from Kazantzakis, who anticipates matter being transubstantiated into the spiritual rather than pointing to it or allowing its glory to shine through. The simultaneous disjuncture and harmony, this "preposterous falseness" of metaphor, provokes struggle that does not guarantee either full or clear cognitive understanding. Still, encounter with metaphor offers a sort of knowledge that can change a person and even move that person to action. Art, including realistic, representational painting or photography, shares in this metaphorical quality. While referring to something actual, temporal, even corporal—perhaps a person, a landscape, an emotion, or an event—the work of art is not that thing but rather the painting, the poem, or the performance itself. The work of art may also allow some Other, perhaps the Holy, to shine through its translucent slices of stone or its carefully constructed counterpoint.

---

8. The kind of analytical attention Duffy gives to music is identified as *considered* in Susanna Bede Caroselli, "Instinctive Response as a Tool for the Scholar," in Jacobsen and Jacobsen, *Scholarship and Christian Faith*, 135–49. Caroselli offers *instinctive response* as a complement to that approach and applies both to interpretation of a fifteenth-century altarpiece. The importance of this partnership of approaches is implied by Black, Gilbertson, and Hanson as well as by Duffy. In his discussion of art as *signatured* truth, O'Brien provides helpful analysis of the interplay of the historical particularity of a piece of art that is part of a tradition and its potential to convey universal truth (*The Idea*, 39).

The similarity between this quality of metaphor and Lutheran teaching about sacrament is significant.[9] The elements of the Eucharist remain what they are—bread and wine—and yet they are infused with (under, in) the real presence of Christ: consubstantiation rather than the Roman Catholic notion of transubstantiation that Kazantzakis translated to *metousiosis* and applied widely. Bread and wine are not flesh and blood, but faith perceives divine presence and receives forgiveness. Lutheran theologians would quickly point out that what transpires at this meal is not metaphorical, neither is it a memorial or a miracle. But the experience of eating this meal and thinking about it in terms that affirm both the elements' earthly reality and Christ's divine reality in them can nurture a sensibility attuned to the metaphorical and to art. Such a sensibility is willing to acknowledge that there is true and reliable knowing that is not based upon objective rationality. Even granting, with Noll, that awareness of the objective nature of God's action is a crucial feature in their teaching about the sacraments, most Lutherans recognize that there are subjective components in their perception of grace at the Lord's table. And at the same time Lutheran children learn from the Small Catechism that in baptism it is not water alone that conveys divine grace; it is water and the Word (of God). As these teachings insist upon both the corporal reality of the elements and the eternal benefits they convey, so too repeated participation in these rituals involves subjective human reception of objective divine gift. Their participation in and interpretation of the sacraments should predispose Lutherans to appreciate ambiguity and prepare them for interpretation of art that reveals while it also conceals or even distorts.

This sacramental sensibility is shaped by the sacraments' ritual and narrative context, which informs and limits. The Word active in baptism is the incarnate Word, Jesus, as well as the gospel message. The eyes of those who see glory shining through water, wine, and bread have been prepared by the witness of the Bible and of the community of faith. This seeing is not merely a matter of imagination, but also a matter of informed faith. The faith is a gift from God; its Christian training is the human work of education. In that work Christians give special priority to the Bible—the written Word, itself both human artifact and divine

---

9. For an explanation of these teachings attuned to their consequences for faithful life, see Bradley Hanson, "Meeting God in Physical Symbols," in *A Graceful Life: Lutheran Spirituality for Today* (Minneapolis: Augsburg Books, 2000).

message. The Bible instructs faith's imagination. How and where is a concern of James Hanson's contribution. Drawing on his training as a biblical scholar and an actor, Hanson argues for the spiritual value of experiencing the Bible as oral, performed art rather than only as words on a page, even authoritative, sacred words. In this setting both actor and audience are interpreters of the text. Departing from the volume's focal metaphor, Hanson asserts that the actor strives to be transparent, putting her own experiences and scholarly preparation in service of the word. Perhaps this transparency is something like the *metousiosis* of matter into spirit that Kazantzakis anticipates. For actor and audience immediate encounter depends upon and produces a different knowledge from that cultivated by historical, literary, or theological study. While it may include clarification of baffling passages, this knowing is also transforming and can move one to action.

When the focus shifts from the sacraments and the Bible to art, the partnership of faith, imagination, and learning continues. These contributions suggest that faith and imagination are sympathetic while maintaining that they are not equivalent. Bruce Allen Heggen points to Martin Luther's deep appreciation of poetry and music and reminds readers that Luther nonetheless gave priority to faith and salvation. That neither art nor imagination is saving does not render them unimportant; however, it does place them among temporal and corporate things rather than among those that are eternal and spiritual. Remember that in Augustine's scheme the temporal and corporate mediate the eternal and the spiritual. Paul Tillich, as Heggen notes, asserted that art provides occasions for encounter with the Holy. Contemporary usage tends to identify anything that does this as itself spiritual. The danger in this identification is the possible collapse of two interacting elements into one that confuses them: anything that moves a viewer becomes spiritual and is thus about the Holy.

Aware of this danger, Heggen draws on Tillich's distinction between religious content and religious style in his own effort to determine what makes art not only religious or spiritual, but Christian.[10] His position,

---

10. Contemporary usage makes distinguishing what is spiritual from what is religious, what is generally religious or spiritual from what is specifically Christian, a thorny task. For a helpful three-tiered definition of spirituality, see Joann Wolski Conn, "Toward Spiritual Maturity," in *Freeing Theology: The Essentials of Theology in Feminist Perspective,* ed. Catherine Mowry LaCugna (San Francisco: HarperSanFrancisco, 1993), 236–37. Spirituality, Conn notes, currently refers to: (1) "a general human capacity for

that religious style is more likely to transform nonreligious content than religious content is to overcome trivial style, hardly resolves the issue. It is not a simple matter of the artist's intention or of the work's subject matter. The believer who has encountered God in both the Bible and the sacraments interprets art with two eyes trained to test the spirit shining through and discern whether it is of God. Lutheran teaching about the real presence of Christ in the Eucharist suggests an approach to art that appreciates its beauty (when it is beautiful), acknowledges its ability to let light shine through, recognizes that the artwork is not itself what it reveals, and also knows that what shines through is not the whole.

Sometimes such an encounter with the Holy comes as pure gift, as a moment of sudden enlightenment. Jane Hirshfield's poem "Inspiration" includes these lines: "'Enlightenment,' writes one master, 'is an accident, but certain efforts make you more accident prone.'"[11] Carol Gilbertson draws upon her experience as a teacher to suggest ways that learning can make us accident-prone. She notes that because both religion and art are devalued in American public education her students need permission, instruction, and practice if they are to recognize either religious content or religious style in literature. If they are to gain the personal benefits she desires for them, including developing their religious imagination, they must be equipped to give literature the close attention that Duffy advises paying to music. In Gilbertson's examples, learning and faithful imagination move together in a sort of meditative thinking that recalls Luther's approach described by Thompson. Although the students do not follow Luther's steps, they are "stirred in their inmost parts." They come to understand more richly both what they have read and also themselves; some are moved to action. Gilbertson points to the importance of context—human community and physical location—for such interpretive work. Her students' reading is encouraged by participation in a literature class at Luther College, with specific classmates and Gilbertson herself as their instructor. This opens

---

self-transcendence"; (2) "a religious dimension of life, to a capacity for self-transcendence that is actualized by the holy, however that may be understood"; and (3) "a specific type of religious experience such as Jewish, Christian, Muslim, or Buddhist."

11. Jane Hirshfield, *The October Palace: Poems* (New York: HarperPerennial, 1994), 47.

possibilities not available in a theology course and excludes some opportunities appropriate to a chapel talk.

Karen Black also indicates the importance of context—physical and social—in her chapter on the use and benefits of music, particularly in Christian worship. Herself an accomplished organist and teacher, Black recognizes the necessity of a musician's knowing the particulars Duffy examines and of practicing the technical aspects of the craft. Here, however, her concern is less with preparing to make music and more with being made by music. In the context of the marketplace or the school, music may be judged by its commercial value or its capacity to make children smarter—the Mozart effect. Beginning with the premise that music is a gift from God, Black emphasizes instead music's transformative potential for individuals and communities. With George Steiner she argues that music's temporality contributes to its power to stop time and transport the performer and auditor into eternity. Similarly music can forge social bonds and take us beyond ourselves. She quotes Steiner's assertion that music brings us into the *real presence* of meaning. Here the term lacks its specific Lutheran meaning but still carries the suggestion that such an encounter is transformative. Along with its use for instruction, entertainment, or expression, music produces knowledge that is other than mere rational cognition and is not reducible to utility. Awed apprehension of glory, for example, may not serve a practical social function, but it is a true response to the creation. While music's temporal existence and use of sound are different from the materials of film or sculpture, this sort of knowledge is evoked by other arts as well as by metaphor.

As Black evokes her experience as a performer of Bach's *St. Matthew Passion* and Hanson recalls his enlivened response to the Gospel of Mark performed, Paul Beidler provides an autobiographical example of participation in art's translucence. Tutored by Jacques Derrida, his meditation on the time-specific particularity of his own life suggests that recollection of experience may itself be an artistic impulse. Emphasizing the instant and its repetition as a re-membering that also destroys, he intensifies the claim that art conceals or distorts the spiritual. His concern with iterability highlights the matter of temporality and eternity introduced by Thompson. Can any single moment—the time spent watching a ballet or reading a novel—provide access to any other? Although Beidler doubts that it can, he asserts that his deconstruction is a prayer. What sort of prayer, he does not specify. In the liturgy of the central Christian act of remembering, the Eucharist, Lutherans commonly pray by singing, "give us a foretaste of the feast to come." Recalling a specific moment, we participate in this instant, and we taste another glorious meal shining through the crumb of bread and the drop of wine.

Neither the conversation of art and religion speaking with one another nor the conversation about religion and art is finished by this volume. Other aspects of Lutheran tradition, of Christianity, and of religious studies could fruitfully engage with these and other arts, including photography, architecture, or dance.[12] Connected by the notion of art's translucence, these authors suggest that the conversation between art and religion is less an argument and more of a dance. When faith lives with art, its imagination is nourished; when art turns with faith, its glory shines. Through art the Christian interpreter, whether the maker of the work or its audience, may glimpse the divine Word. If so, the seeing will be "in a mirror dimly"—not yet face to face. Nonetheless, such an encounter provides essential, transforming knowledge not only for eternity but also for living faithfully in this time and place.

---

12. For an exploration of the interaction of theology and architecture in the work of Lutheran Edward Søvik, see Mark A. Torgerson, "An Architect's Response to Liturgical Reform: Edward A. Søvik and His 'Non-Church' Design," *Worship* 71/1 (May 1997): 19–41. See also Tom Christenson, "Is There a Lutheran Aesthetic?" and Steven Schroeder, "Nothing Lutheran Is Our Subject Matter," papers presented at the annual meeting of the Midwest American Academy of Religion, Chicago, April 2004. Christenson lists "favors metaphor (tense conjunction)" among his characteristic principles of a Lutheran aesthetic. A provocative commonality in these papers is both authors' identification of affinities between Lutheran sensibilities and Buddhism. An earlier version of Heggen's contribution to this volume was presented in the same session.

Part One
Philosophical Assumptions

1

Interpreting
God's Translucent World

Imagination, Possibility, and Eternity

CURTIS L. THOMPSON

The world we live in is glorious, both because it is God's excellent creation and because it is a translucent medium through which shines the divine reality that is the world's ground and goal. These related notions of translucence and glory suggest the dialectical relationship between God and the world. The world conveys God, and God is present "in, with, and under" particular realities of the world. *Translucence* suggests a "shining through," from the Latin verb *translucere;* it suggests the capability of the natural and human worlds to allow God's light to shine through, while that which shines through can be called *glory.* In mediating glory the world itself also becomes glorious; glory refers to the penetrating light and to the medium itself, which takes on glory as that light shines through. God is both the origin and the content of the world's translucence: the world is translucent because of how God has created it, and the world is translucent to God's very reality.

Interpreting God's translucent world is only possible for the imagination. Whether we are talking about translucence manifested in meaning, passion, glory, freedom, or love, the referent can only be grasped by the imagination. Sometimes dubbed *fancy* or *fantasy,* the imagination brings home to us the color of human experience. Through the imagination, life's drabness is punctuated with vivid hues, those bright and vibrant shades that stand out in our memories and make our expectations more evocative. Our imagining makes possible those powerful translucent life experiences that enrich and ennoble us, that give us chills, that make us deeply sense we are undergoing something extraordinary. Imagination makes possible those moments when we experience the light shining through reality in an unforgettable way. Without the imagination such translucence would not take place.

The province of imagination is the future, and the domain of the future is possibility. In the Western world possibility has been set against actuality, and the latter has typically been granted the higher position. But possibility needs to regain our attention: in opening the door to possibility, we avail ourselves of *the impossible;* we unleash a power, what Kierkegaard called the power of the absurd, which makes possible the impossible. With this power we are close to the old, half-forgotten concept of eternity, which needs another look.

The essay that follows is informed by a theology of freedom. Influenced by the theological view developed by the line of thinkers beginning with F. W. J. Schelling (1775–1854) and running through Søren Kierkegaard (1813–1855) and Paul Tillich (1886–1965), I understand the Christian God as eternal freedom.[1] Other words that Schelling uses for eternal freedom are the absolute, absolute freedom, the unconditioned, pure subjectivity, the pure Godhead, pure love, being itself, and God's highest self. This eternal God is the fullness of actuality. But this God is dipolar. The fully actual God is also the God who creates the world and is active within it. In relation to the world, the actual God is possibility: eternal freedom is not yet at home in the world. God, eternal freedom, lovingly desires to communicate its freedom to the world of time and space. God does this through possibilities. As eternity touches time in the moment, freedom begets freedom.[2] Temporality that is free manifests itself in the world as power. Art is one place where freedom

---

1. See especially F. W. J. Schelling, *The Ages of the World: (Fragment) from the Handwritten Remains, Third Version (c. 1815),* trans. Jason M. Wirth (Albany: State University of New York Press, 2000). See also *Schelling: Of Human Freedom,* intro. and notes James Gutmann (Chicago: Open Court, 1936).

2. It is Kierkegaard who develops most fully the category of "the moment" as "an atom of eternity." See his *The Concept of Anxiety: A Simple Psychologically Orienting Deliberation on the Dogmatic Issue of Hereditary Sin,* ed. and trans. Reidar Thomte in collaboration with Albert B. Anderson (Princeton, N.J.: Princeton University Press, 1980), 82–91.

receives powerful expression. Works of art are translucent to the extent that they express freedom, for then eternal freedom is shining through them.

In his 1960 essay on "Art and Ultimate Reality," Paul Tillich offers interesting, clarifying thoughts on how the finite, temporal world gives expression to ultimacy or eternal freedom. According to him, "everything that has being is an expression, however preliminary and transitory it may be, of being itself, of ultimate reality." He comments on what the word *expression* means in this context:

> First, it is obvious that if something expresses something else—as, for instance, language expresses thought—they are not the same. There is a gap between that which expresses and that which is expressed. But there is also a point of identity between them. It is the riddle and depth of all expression that it both reveals and hides at the same time. And if we say that the universe is an expression of ultimate reality, we say that the universe and everything in it both reveals and hides ultimate reality. This should prevent us from a religious glorification of the world as well as from an antireligious profanization of the world. There is ultimate reality in this stone and this tree and this man. They are translucent toward ultimate reality, but they are also opaque. They prevent it from shining through them. They try to exclude it.

Tillich points out that expression is always intended for someone to receive, and he sees the human as the only creature able to distinguish between expression and that which is expressed. Only humans are capable of consciously differentiating between the medium and the message, between the manifest and the hidden, between surface and depth.[3]

Following G. W. F. Hegel, Tillich holds that there are three ways in which the human is able to experience and express ultimate or eternal reality in, with, and under the realities he or she encounters. These are in art, philosophy, and religion. The first two are indirect ways of experiencing and expressing ultimacy or eternal freedom, and the last, religion, is a direct way. Philosophy's immediate intention is to express the encountered reality in cognitive concepts; art's immediate intention is to express the encountered reality in aesthetic images. Philosophy, seeking truth about the universe, is driven to make assertions about ultimate reality. Art, striving to give aesthetic expression to reality, makes ultimate

---

3. Paul Tillich, *Main Works / Hauptwerke,* ed. Carl Heinz Ratschow (Berlin: De Gruyter, 1989), 2:317–32.

reality manifest through its images. Art uses the word *image* in the large sense of including "lingual and musical figures." Both philosophy and art, then, also express ultimacy or eternal freedom, although they do so indirectly, unlike religion, which intentionally expresses ultimacy by means of symbols and myths.

The essay that follows does not fall neatly into art, philosophy, or religion. As a theological essay, it might be best characterized as a religiously inspired philosophical interpretation of translucence, culminating in reflections on power and art. An *essay* means literally an "attempt" or an "effort." While this essay hopefully is not bereft of a deeper rational structure and coherence, it is intended to be more an attempt at meditation than an effort at argumentation: it endeavors to gently evoke through reflective ideas and comments rather than to forcefully defeat through logical propositions and assertions. The essay includes two sections, dealing respectively with the possibility of translucence and with its actuality. In the first section I attempt to make the case for two-eyed interpreting that attends to both the temporal and the eternal dimensions of life. Such interpreting is key for humans' appropriating life's meaning and growing as free creatures. By bringing into play the dialectical relation between part and whole, I include the two essential aspects of interpretation. I then draw on Luther for insights into interpreting. First, we learn from him how meditative thinking can help us to see life's eternal dimension in relation to particular realities of God's created world. Second, Luther's insistence upon viewing the Scriptures as "testimonies" to future actions and deeper disclosures of eternal freedom reminds us that our interpreting is never adequate and never done.

Having considered the form of interpreting required for translucence to be experienced and appreciated, I engage, in the essay's second section, in an interpretation of translucence as actually manifested. Here power and art become the focus. The art of power can teach us much about how freedom is best shaped. Eternal freedom's power, understood as the art of making free, elicits artful human power that makes free. Art's power emerges from the way a work draws people into its concrete reality, in which eternal and temporal freedom meet. Art, understood as the power of freely making, manifests both of freedom's dimensions. Freely making their art out of language, melody, bodily movements, clay, or paint, artists offer their work to the world. Powerful art is translucent to the eternal freedom that has become incarnate in time and space.

Interpreting Creation and Scripture:
The Possibility of Translucence

What is required for us to be able to experience and enjoy God's translucent world? One thing needed is a way of interpreting the world that will not preclude translucence from the outset but give it a chance. Needed for translucence to be a possibility is a two-eyed form of interpreting the world in which both life's eternal dimension and its temporal dimension are brought into play.

"*Do Mundo da Leitura para a Leitura do Mundo.*" Those Portuguese words were printed in red letters on a rather flattened blue image of the world, an eye-catching poster on a classroom blackboard in Carijás, an iron-ore mining company town carved out of the Amazon rain forest in northern Brazil. Reflecting on this caption, I had thought a very broad meaning might be "From the world of learning to learning about the world." One internet Portuguese translating service gave "written materials" for *Leitura*. That suggested "From the world of written materials or literature, to written materials or literature about the world." But another source pointed to *Leitura* as involving the act of reading. So the phrase might suggest the empowering that comes from gaining the capacity to read: "From the world of reading to the reading of the world." Later I came across a definition for *Leitura* that spoke of cognitively understanding written materials, suggesting that this statement was not simply about written materials or literature or the reading act, but rather about *interpretação*, "interpretation." That made good sense to me: "From the world of interpretation to interpretation of the world."

The struggle of experience and thought entails the back-and-forth movement depicted in the Portuguese phrase. The world in which we operate shapes how we create meaning, and in creating meaning we shape our world. Karl Marx, in number fourteen of his "Theses on Feuerbach," criticized Hegel for merely interpreting the world; he insisted that the point is not to interpret the world but to change it. Hegel would likely have agreed with Marx, for both were interested in transformation. But Hegel would contend that the act of interpreting is itself transforming, because interpreting cannot be separated from the actions that follow. The spirit of life is able to move the world closer to its goal through the act of interpreting and the actions that result.

When they create art, artists are interpreting, and a work of art elicits the interpretive act in those who experience the artwork. In both cases, our Portuguese dialectic comes into play. Artists and experiencers of art are always caught up in the movement from the world of interpretation to interpretation of the world: in interpreting a particular reality we at the same time arrive at a reinterpretation of reality's whole. We can consider the world of interpretation the "part" and our interpreting of the world the "whole." Interpreting the part influences the whole, and interpreting the whole then influences our next interpretation of the part. The act of interpreting, or the hermeneutical enterprise, as it is called, is a circle, wherein both artists and art experiencers are as caught up in the movement from part to whole as whole to part. Interpreting is never finished.

In the act of interpreting, we honor both part and whole by tending to both sides of the crucial distinction. If translucence is to regain within our lives the place it has held for religious persons in the past, we will need to operate with a two-eyed understanding of interpretation. The essential distinction to be made goes back at least as far as St. Augustine, who distinguished between the "eternal things" *(res aeternae)* and the "temporal things" *(temporalia)*.[4] The eternal things are to be enjoyed for what they are in and of themselves. The temporal things are to be used for the enjoyment of the eternal things. In other words, the temporal things mediate the eternal things. The road toward blessedness, according to Augustine, is "that by means of corporal and temporal things we may comprehend the eternal and spiritual."[5] As readers or viewers or listeners experience eternal things through temporal things, they experience what we are calling translucence: the temporal is translucent to the eternal. The competent interpreter keeps both eyes open,

4. Augustine, *On Christian Doctrine*, trans. D. W. Robertson Jr. (Indianapolis: Bobbs-Merrill, 1958), I:7–33. For a similar distinction, see Gerhard Ebeling, *Word and Faith*, trans. James W. Leitch (Philadelphia: Fortress Press, 1963), in which he distinguishes between the historical and the dogmatic interpretations of a biblical text. These two types of interpretation in Ebeling correspond to Augustine's temporal and eternal dimensions of interpretation. Eberhard Jüngel makes use of Ebeling's distinction in *God as the Mystery of the World: On the Foundation of the Theology of the Crucified One in the Dispute between Theism and Atheism*, trans. Darrell L. Guder (Grand Rapids: Eerdmans, 1983). In that work Jüngel also discusses Augustine's distinction (4). Robert Cummings Neville, *Religion in Late Modernity* (Albany: State University of New York Press, 2002), 49, makes a similar distinction between extensional and intentional interpretations.

5. Augustine, *On Christian Doctrine*, I:10.

gives due consideration to temporality and eternality alike, and includes these two aspects in interpretation.

Of course, the notion of eternity has fallen on hard times since the premodern world gave way to the modern and then postmodern worlds and what some are calling a newly emerging late modern world. Eternity lost currency because it was viewed as the opposite of time or temporality. It was thought that affirming eternity entailed denying our everyday, temporal life. But if we look at the concept of eternity with greater imagination, we will once again be able to appreciate its true meaning. Eternity provides the brackets for our existence,[6] enables us to understand the past, present, and future as coherently held together so that our temporal lives take on meaning. God's eternity, as the singular matrix encasing and ordering the modes of time, makes possible time itself as well as our temporal experience.

Two-eyed interpreting gives an eye to the temporal and an eye to the eternal. Kierkegaard contended that the human is a synthesis of the temporal and the eternal. We can suggest that this is no less true of sound, two-eyed interpreting. To construe is to show the meaning of something. What we might call a temporal construal tends simply to the temporal realities. And what we might call an eternal construal tends to the eternal realities that are being mediated through the temporal. A two-eyed interpretation makes sure that both temporal and eternal construals are allowed to have their place. Regardless of the artwork being interpreted, the universe in which the work is created and received consists of cultural signs and symbols operating within a network or system. A two-eyed interpretation of a work of art attends to the two different sorts of relations within the universe of meaning.

Interpreting a statue, for instance, involves on the one hand asking questions of a quantitative nature: What is the material out of which it is made? Whom is this a statue of and from which historical period

---

6. Compare the definition of eternity by Neville, *Religion in Late Modernity:* "Eternity is the act that creates everything determinate, everything variously determinate in all of their dates as past, present, and future, and as mutually conditioning one another in whatever ways they do" (20). Compare also the statement by Robert W. Jenson, *The Triune Identity: God according to the Gospel* (Philadelphia: Fortress Press, 1982): "Human life is possible—or in recent jargon 'meaningful'—only if past and future are somehow bracketed, only if their disconnection is somehow transcended, only if our lives somehow cohere to make a story. Life in time is possible only, that is, if there is 'eternity,' if no-more, still, and not-yet do not exhaust the structure of reality. Thus, in all we do we seek eternity" (1–2).

does she come? What techniques were used in making this work? What are the physical dimensions of this piece? We might also ask questions about the artist and the tradition out of which he or she is operating. We can sense that limiting our interpretation to these types of questions yields results that are one-dimensional or one-eyed. A one-eyed interpretation asking only quantitative questions is inadequate because it flattens the work to extraneous concerns and never gets to the heart of the matter. A temporal construal alone does not suffice. A construal from another eye is required to supplement the first. One needs, then, on the other hand, an inquiry that is more qualitative, personal, existential. The theological perspective calls for a consideration of the eternal, that is, of ultimate meaning, import, significance. One might ask oneself and others what effects this work has on one's person. How does it make me feel in my innermost being and what of substance does it bring to mind? What does it mean at the personal level? Can I sense something really important being communicated to me through this work? Does it move me to reflect more deeply on life? Does the artwork make me pause and reflect? Does it lead me to converse about it with others? Does it make me want to share it with others? Do I want to experience it again? These questions lead to experiencing the work with a different eye. They result in an "eternal construal" or one in which its relation to ultimate concerns is allowed to surface.

If one were to object, "I don't see how this second set of questions leads me to see God's reality translucently," the appropriate response would be, "Do not allow inappropriate anticipations to blur your vision and delimit your interpretation. Do not overlook the dim, hidden presence of the gentle, immanent God because you are anticipating the vivid, explicit presence of the transcendent God of all glory, power, and might." Eternal freedom's disclosures come veiled—in nuanced shades of meaning, troubling questions of doubt, sudden rushes of emotion, powerful feelings of compassion, remarkable transformations of the heart, or fleeting glimpses of insight. Human freedom can be deepened in many ways, and all of those ways allow an experience of the divine reality of eternal freedom. Interpreting God's translucent world calls for two-eyed interpreting in which temporal and eternal construals together disclose the fullness of meaning being experienced.

Our contemporary temptation is to limit our interpreting to the temporal. "Signs and symbols within the linguistic and cultural network merely point to other signs and symbols," we sometimes hear from deconstructionists who have misconstrued the early work of Jacques Derrida. The only reality to be experienced, according to this view, is created by the signs and symbols themselves; there is nothing beyond them, no reality exterior to the symbol system. However, this leads to a world of utter opacity, a world devoid of any transcendent signatures. The postmodern turn to language as reality brings important insights about ways in which words and their meanings are our "house of being," as Heidegger says, and we dismiss those insights at our peril.[7] But interpreting ought not to alienate us from the real, external world that exists independently of language. As Robert Neville reminds us, reality is not created by signs and symbols but is engaged by them.[8] Interpreting translucence remembers the temporal/eternal balance and recalls that our signs and symbols refer to an objective reality rather than merely mirroring other signs.

Martin Luther, the Reformer and biblical theologian who spent his life interpreting the Bible as the Word of God, can teach us much about interpreting. Luther was a gifted interpreter of the Jewish and Christian Scriptures, but his thoughts on interpretation are also relevant to other areas, including art. Luther's theology continually sets up dialectical distinctions. Law and gospel, faith and works, creation and redemption, kingdom on the left and kingdom on the right, heaven and earth, alien righteousness and proper righteousness—making such distinctions is what Luther considers doing theology. One could make the case that the distinction between eternity and temporality is as important as any for Luther. He holds both of these to be essential and believes that they are best understood as interpenetrating one another. Surely, for him, interpretation involves both temporal and eternal aspects of whatever is being interpreted. We will see that for Luther interpreting the Scriptures as testimonies entails meditative thinking no less than does interpreting the world of creation or nature.

Translucence can be experienced in relation to the created realities of the world, in relation to what the medieval scholastic theologians called the book of nature. Translucence can also be experienced in relation to the book of revelation. Luther can teach us about the interpreting

---

7. Martin Heidegger, *Basic Writings,* ed. David Farrell Krell, rev. ed. (New York: HarperCollins, 1993), 213.
8. Neville, *Religion in Late Modernity,* 45–65.

involved in both of these areas. As concerns interpreting creation or nature, Luther understands meditative thinking—in which the believer takes delight in the eternal shining through the temporal—to play a critical role. As concerns interpreting the Scriptures, Luther believes one needs to consider the Bible as "testimonies." The Bible tells the story of the promises of the eternal God whose activity in time continues into the future. The Scriptures are testimonies for Luther insofar as they bear witness to the future—both to the divine actions that will take place in history and to the divine inspirations that will unfold new understandings. These two types of interpreting require a closer investigation.

Between 1513 and 1515 Luther presented a lecture series on the Psalms.[9] Particularly instructive are his comments on two of these psalms, 77 and 119, from which we can learn, first, how to meditate on the world as a way of ensuring that the temporal/eternal distinction is honored in interpreting creation or nature, and, second, how viewing the Scriptures as testimonies can lead to some helpful insights on interpretation.

On the first point, in commenting on Psalm 1:2 ("And on His law he meditates day and night"), Luther distinguishes between thinking and meditating:

> Meditating is an exclusive trait of human beings, for even beasts appear to fancy and to think. Therefore the ability to meditate belongs to reason. There is a difference between meditating and thinking. To meditate is to think carefully, deeply, and diligently, and properly it means to muse in the heart. Hence to meditate is, as it were, to stir up in the inside, or to be moved in the innermost self. Therefore one who thinks inwardly and diligently asks, discusses, etc. Such a person meditates.[10]

Meditating is that deep thinking, that "musing in the heart," which moves our innermost being. Meditating, however, works in conjunction with delight. Luther continues:

---

9. Martin Luther, *Luther's Works,* ed. Jaroslav Pelikan and Helmut T. Lehmann, 55 vols. (St. Louis: Concordia; Philadelphia: Fortress Press, 1955–1986). References to Luther's writings are hereafter cited as *LW*, with volume and page number. This lecture series of Luther on the Psalms is in volumes 10 and 11.

10. Luther notes in the full passage that the ungodly do not meditate on God's law, "since as false plants they did not take root. Yet they meditate on other things, namely, on things in which their delight is rooted, things they themselves desire and love, such as gold, honor, and flesh" (*LW* 10:17).

But one does not meditate on the law of the Lord unless his delight was first fixed in it. For what we want and love, on that we reflect inwardly and diligently. But what we hate or despise we pass over lightly and do not desire deeply, diligently, or for long. Therefore let delight be first sent into the heart as the root, and then meditation will come of its own accord.[11]

According to Luther, the proper form of meditating—that form of thinking that leads to experiencing God's translucent world—operates in union with delight. But how does one learn to delight in the appropriate realities?

Delight emerges from translucence, which can only be perceived through the right meditative disposition toward the created world. In introductory comments on Psalm 77, Luther offers a four-step approach to relating to created works, which we can read as steps toward a full, two-eyed interpretation that expects to experience translucence. He states, "All things were created as an aid to the mind and the heart of men."[12] God's creatures can minister to us if we relate to these works properly, allowing God's wisdom or glory to "shine forth in them":

> Thus the great Creator has created all things in wisdom, so that they may minister in such countless functions and services not only to the body, which, nevertheless, cannot grasp the wisdom in which they were created and which *shines forth in them,* but also to the soul, which can grasp the wisdom, as far as the mind and the heart are concerned. Therefore the Holy Spirit exhorts us in Ps. 32:9 not to become like the horse and the mule, which have no understanding. For to make use of creatures only according to the body, and not through them to direct the heart and the mind toward God, is to perceive them only with the senses, like the horse and the mule. They can see them only as long as they are present. Thus these, too, forget the works of the Lord and do not remember them. To indicate this, the psalm does not say "I will see," "I will hear," or "I will feel" Thy works, which all irrational creatures do, but "I will remember and meditate." This is what the thinking and spiritual man does.[13]

The spiritual woman is capable of this as well, even if the language of Luther's time excludes her. Luther urges us to "note these four verbs, 'I remembered,' 'I will be mindful,' 'I will meditate,' 'I will be exercised.'" Luther underscores the important verbs of Psalm 77 and counsels

---

11. *LW* 10:17.
12. *LW* 11:15.
13. Ibid.; my italics.

us to "observe their order": "Again, 'the works of the Lord,' 'Thy wonders,' 'all Thy works,' 'Thy inventions,' whether there is not something more in them than what has appeared and was said."[14] He is convinced that a regimen—a systematic procedure of discernment for experiencing God's wisdom shining through the creation, or what we are calling the translucence of created things—can be teased out here: "Step by step devotion and instruction, understanding and love increase. Therefore these four parts can be applied one by one to any work of the Lord, whatever it might be."[15]

The fourfold process of discernment begins with the first step of remembering. In remembering, a person sees the Lord's works, recalling the way in which these works appeared vividly before the mind: "First, the heart remembers, acknowledges, and confesses His work to the Lord. And thus it appears that it is the work of the Lord, for the heart does not remember what the mind does not show. But when it does, the heart is touched and it remembers."[16] The second step is to be mindful, to see in the present that God's works are wonderful:

> Then the works will be regarded as amazing and wonderful, because their knowledge and clearer grasp increases. Indeed, the more profoundly a created thing is recognized, the more wonders are seen in it, namely, how full it is of God's wisdom. Hence the spiritual man sees in the same matter many things and the wonderful wisdom of God. The irrational, however, as the psalm points out, did not understand the works of the Lord; they only felt them. But from this knowledge there arises a greater flame of love, so that the person wishes always to remember in this way and says, "I will be mindful of Thy wonders from the beginning."[17]

Step three involves meditating, which "sees all things" and in this way experiences the full, two-eyed temporal and eternal meaning of creaturely realities:

> From there he now turns the word toward the Lord, while he at first speaks only of "the works of the Lord" as in the third person, and then "of Thy [wonders]." For from the works the mind is lifted to a higher level toward God, so that now it may see God more than the works, as on the first step it had seen the works more than God. Then, on the third step,

---

14. Ibid.
15. *LW* 11:15–16.
16. *LW* 11:16.
17. Ibid.

he has advanced still more and draws the conclusion that thus all works are wonderful, and he wishes to meditate on them in like manner, that is, remember them thoughtfully and wisely. But here the end has been achieved, since it is perfection. The first step begins, the second advances, and the third brings to perfection. For the first sees only the works of the Lord, the second sees that they are wonderful, and the third sees all things; for nothing remains beyond these. And to have been mindful is less, to be mindful is more, but to meditate is most.[18]

Luther's three steps of interpretation, remembering, being mindful, and meditating—though leading to perfection in that the discerning process is complete—are transcended by a fourth, for the person has yet to move outside himself or herself. Experiencing God's translucent world, then, necessitates the individual's four relational processes toward creaturely realities: remembering (seeing the work as God's), being mindful (wondering over God's presence in the work), meditating (musing in the heart so that the experience penetrates to the innermost self), and sharing (conversing with others about one's translucent experience).

In step four, therefore—interpreting the world—translucence experienced becomes translucence shared: "But the perfect man is like this: Behold, he wants to be of benefit also to others, not have the talent just for himself. He says, 'I will be employed in Thy inventions,' that is: 'I will relate, I will speak to others in word and deed about Thy wonders, so that they, too, may know the works of the Lord.'"[19] Having remembered that a particular reality is part of God's creation, then wondering over God's presence within it, and then seeing it in relation to the whole endeavor of eternal freedom that interpenetrates the world of temporal realities, one indeed experiences God's glory shining through creation and is moved to communicate the results of one's meditation to others.

It is interesting that the later Heidegger calls for a way of thinking similar to what Luther is suggesting. Heidegger distinguishes between calculative thinking and meditative thinking:

Calculative thinking computes. It computes ever new, ever more promising and at the same time more economical possibilities. Calculative thinking races from one prospect to the next. Calculative thinking never stops, never

---

18. Ibid.
19. Ibid.

collects itself. Calculative thinking is not meditative thinking, not thinking which contemplates the meaning which reigns in everything that is.[20]

Heidegger sees contemporary men and women as being in flight from meditative thinking. Luther, who saw the same in his time, labeled the phenomenon "sin." Heidegger warns "that the approaching tide of technological revolution in the atomic age could so captivate, bewitch, dazzle, and beguile man that calculative thinking may someday come to be accepted and practiced *as the only* way of thinking." Should that happen, Heidegger avers, then the human "would have denied and thrown away his own special nature—that he is a meditative being." In Heidegger's view, the issue is that of saving the human's "essential nature" by "keeping meditative thinking alive."[21] The sixteenth-century Martin would wholeheartedly agree with this perspective of the twentieth-century Martin. Luther, like Heidegger, believes that meditative thinking is essential for interpreting the world as translucent to God.

We can learn more from Luther about interpreting, this time in relation to the book of Scriptures rather than the book of nature, from his trenchant comments on Psalm 119.[22] Luther maintains that meditating on Scripture "gushes forth abundant streams and flowing waters of knowledge and wisdom"; to meditate "means to have many meanings and an abundance of understanding burst forth."[23] Serving as the basis for understanding the Scripture's essential character, the Reformer contends, is the notion of "testimonies." Psalm 119:24 reads, "For Thy testimonies are my meditation, and Thy statutes my counsel." "Testimonies," Luther writes, "testify concerning future goods"; "they are not exhibitions of things present, but testimonies of things to come."[24] Testimonies are to be believed; they are not certain knowledge that can be fully understood. Luther points out that the person who wants to understand before believing thinks he or she has sure knowledge rather

---

20. Martin Heidegger, *Discourse on Thinking*, trans. John M. Anderson and E. Hans Freund (New York: Harper & Row, 1966), 46.

21. Ibid., 56.

22. Unless otherwise noted, the following quotations are from Luther's comments on Psalm 119 included in *LW* 11:414–534 and especially 431–35. For a contemporary development of the notion of testimony in relation to interpretation, see Paul Ricoeur's essay "The Hermeneutics of Testimony" in his *Essays on Biblical Interpretation*, ed. Lewis S. Mudge (Philadelphia: Fortress Press, 1980), 119–54.

23. *LW* 10:20.

24. *LW* 11:421.

than testimonies. He sternly insists: "But now let us learn this, that Holy Scripture is 'testimonies.'" Therefore, Luther counsels, "wherever it may be, you never understand a passage of Scripture to the end, and you do not comprehend all the truth it conceals."[25] The Scriptures have a translucent quality: they reveal, but some of their truth remains hidden. Luther writes that "though you may perhaps understand some things, perhaps many things there, know that it is always there for you as a testimony of truth still to be revealed to you, or at least of truth that can be revealed." That is why "it is called a 'testimony,' because it testifies and prophesies concerning future things."[26]

Luther regards the act of interpretation as "spirit" and the meaning that is arrived at as "letter." Here we see that St. Paul's distinction between "the spirit and the letter" (2 Cor. 3:6) plays a key role in Luther's interpretation of Psalm 119, as well as in his interpretation of interpreting itself. He states that this "whole psalm is nothing but a petition that the spiritual law be revealed and the letter be removed."[27] Grasping the text's spiritual meaning, of course, requires the appropriate level of spirituality on the interpreter's part: "For no one understands another in spiritual writings unless he savors and possesses the same spirit."[28] The interpretation of the world one offers in interpreting a particular biblical passage or artwork is not going to be very rich if the interpreter has no connection with the interpretive world from which the passage or work originates. Each scriptural passage contains infinite richness, so it possesses great propensity for the interpreter's ever deeper plumbing.[29] The Scriptures' fecundity demands that we recognize the limits of our interpreting. A statute, a passage whose meaning has taken a finalized form, is associated with the letter. Since the interpretive act arrives at

---

25. *LW* 11:433.
26. Ibid.
27. *LW* 11:422.
28. *LW* 11:414.
29. See Luther's comments on this infinite meaning of a passage: "But every Scripture passage is of infinite understanding. Therefore, no matter how much you understand, do not be proud, do not fight against another, do not withstand, because they are testimonies, and perhaps he will see what you do not see, and what is to him statute or utterance is still testimony to you. Therefore it is always a matter of making progress in the understanding of Scripture. And always the first step is like the spirit, the latter step, until it is revealed, like the closed letter, which the former did not see. Hence also the apostle says: 'But we all, beholding the glow of the Lord with open face, are transformed from glory to glory as by the Spirit of the Lord' (2 Cor. 3:18)" (*LW* 11:433).

meaning, this can be glorious indeed. The glorious meaning that is arrived at tempts the interpreter to stop the interpretive process, to declare that he or she has grasped the final truth or full transparency of a particular passage.

However, Luther urges the interpreter to continue growing into deeper truth, transforming the letter or arrived-at-meaning into an occasion for another interpretive act in a never-ending process. This process points toward an authentic theological affirmation of glory, which does not stop short with the first experience of glorious meaning but is always being "transformed from glory to glory." When the psalmist pleads with God to "enliven me," Luther interprets it as a plea to "make me have merit for the vivification of the glory to come." Then in a marginal gloss, he adds, "So it is necessary for everyone to perfect in the spirit, not in the letter, whatever he does." Perfecting takes place as one refuses to settle for the letter but continues the act of spiritual interpreting. This ongoing process of interpretation leads to ever richer experiences of meaning (or glory) as one continues to be open to what the future brings. These expanding rings of meaning are one important piece of what might be called Luther's "theology of glory."

Just as this ongoing process of interpreting applies to human knowing in contemplative or speculative life, so too it applies to human action.[30] Whether leading to knowledge or to action, interpretation ought not to become too invested in its putatively "conclusive" results but ought always to be moving into a deeper grasp of the passage's translucence by remaining open to the future and to others' interpretations. The interpreter's appropriate posture is humility; the interpreter wants to continue to seek meaning—not to pause but to be continually making progress. Otherwise sloth and/or superstition will set in, and the

---

30. Luther writes: "So it happens also in the active life: It is always a progressing from act to act, from virtue to virtue, as here it is from understanding to understanding, from faith to faith, from glory to glory, from knowledge to knowledge. This is the true contemplative life. And thus the first step is always the spirit, and the later step is the letter. Therefore, as the end is not to be obtained speculatively, so it is not actively either. Therefore do not be proud but forget the letter and follow [that is, stretch out] the spirit, that is, do not rest on the second or third step, but take also this one for yourself, from the letter to the spirit. And so the preceding lack of knowledge is always the letter of the following knowledge, which becomes spirit. And this again is the letter for what follows, etc. This is what being 'testimonies' means" (*LW* 11:433–34).

interpreter will become a "righteous and holy literalist" who is filled with "spiritual pride."[31]

If the Scriptures are testimonies, what then does the Psalmist mean by "Thy testimonies are my meditation"? In this context Luther writes: "For to meditate means to think deeply and to explore the inner parts and always to follow the spirit within and not to construct a wall for yourself and set up a boundary, as if you had already achieved the end of understanding or acting." That is why "the testimonies rightly require faith above all": "so that in what you do not yet understand you believe one who understands and you do not by your own authority set up the meaning for yourself or fight against another in what you do not know or about which you have doubts."[32] Since there is no biblical passage that we understand fully, interpretation necessarily includes doubt: self-doubt about any interpretation's adequacy as a final account of the passage's meaning. Relativity, then, characterizes our interpretations, according to Luther: "He who does not understand the Scripture in a relative way or does not work toward the future, namely, that he always knows that there is something left over for him to understand and do and faithfully to await and desire finally to understand and do, he certainly does not let the Scripture be the testimonies of the Lord."[33] Luther precludes absolutism in scriptural interpretation. Interpretation is a spiritual process that has no end.

Luther wants to understand freedom in relation to this spiritual process of interpreting, which dissolves absolute rules. He writes:

> Therefore you must never be proud, as if you were already full, rich, and well provided. Always they are to you testimonies of what you have not yet understood or done. And yet you ought to wish and expect to do and understand them, as above: "My soul has coveted too long for Thy ordinances at all times" (v. 20). Not that it is necessary for us to understand

---

31. Luther in typical form has no trouble lambasting the absolutists: "Therefore those who have been placed on any step of understanding or acting and either neglect in a lukewarm and slothful way the step beyond which is still hidden, or in pride and superstition understand and act in their own way, as the heretics and hypocrites and those zealous of peculiarities do [they are the ones who do not understand the Scriptures to be testimonies], they do not accept them all as testimonies, but as the truth already finished and resolved, which the testimonies might judge" (*LW* 11:434).

32. Ibid.

33. Ibid.

and do everything in this life, but that the mind should be prepared never to want to stop doing and understanding more fully to eternity, to know no boundary, no end, no restriction. This is what it means to be in the spirit of freedom, for which no law and statute has been set, because it does more than is commanded, so that if one could live eternally, one would strive eternally to know and do, and never move backward. He is the one whose meditation is the testimonies of the Lord and who keeps His testimonies.[34]

Applying to both knowing and doing, the spiritual interpretive process is situated at life's heart. We are capable of growing in understanding life and in actualizing life's virtues. The Scriptures as testimonies call us into lives of continual becoming.

We saw above that meditative thinking on the world culminates in sharing with the community. Here we find that the Scriptures also call us into community: the interpretation process is a communal one. One does not rest content with a private meaning: "For even if the truth were with us, if it becomes a private and personal matter, it is no longer truth, which is, wants to be, and should be altogether common to all." If one's interpretation is purely private and personal, then, according to Luther, "it is not truth, but a lie"; then truth "has been vitiated by this private ownership."[35] The translucence that is interpretation's goal is an experienced reality arrived at and shared in community.

Luther's hermeneutical discussion suggests some principles of interpretation that are applicable not only to biblical but also to art interpretation. In no sense the "Ten Commandments of Aesthetics," these ideas from Luther are better viewed as "Ten Suggestions for Interpreting Translucence." First, the interpretive process applies to knowledge and action alike (art is relevant to the intellectual and moral world of humans). Second, the interpretive process is spiritual and relative, so interpretation's conclusions (the letter) are provisional rather than final. Third, doubt plays a positive role in the interpretive process by helping to relativize its results (recognizing conclusions as merely letter). Fourth, the interpretive process is communal, since the truth—the understanding of translucence—arrived at finally unfolds in relation to others engaging in interpretation. Fifth, other interpreters with differ-

---

34. *LW* 11:434–35.
35. *LW* 11:431.

ing "readings" ought not be viewed as antagonists to one's private grasping of translucence but as partners in moving more deeply into a communally experienced and expressed translucence. Sixth, as the locus of the self's cognition and volition—self-consciousness's knowing and self-determination's doing—the spiritual interpretive process is freedom ("Where the Spirit is, there is freedom." [2 Cor. 3:17]). Seventh, one's final allegiance is to be given not to particular results of the interpretive process (the created goods) but rather to the spiritual process itself (the creative good, Spirit, eternal freedom, the power of creative transformation, or the power of the impossible). From our earlier discussion of Luther on Psalm 77 we can draw three further hermeneutical principles to add to Luther's list. Eighth, meditative thinking, as opposed to immediate thinking, can enable one to experience a work of creation or artwork in an appropriately "thick" or translucent manner, which includes both temporal and eternal construals. Ninth, the meditative regimen of a work of creation or art involves the fourfold process of remembering, being mindful, meditating, and sharing. Tenth, following the fourfold process facilitates potent results in interpreting God's translucent world.

Creating Power and Art: The Actuality of Translucence

Interpreting is an activity we are engaged in all our waking moments. With the right form of interpreting, translucence becomes a real possibility. Theological interpreting from the Christian perspective, as well as from the viewpoint of many other world religions, confesses that the entire universe caught up in the flow of time has its alpha and omega, its origin and fulfillment, in eternity. The whole set of finite, temporal realities owe their origin to the creativity of eternal freedom and will find their ultimate consummation in relation to that divine freedom that loves. Theological interpreting seeks to declare a coherent word about eternal freedom but knows that "eternity is engaged through the temporal."[36] It desires to discern those places where eternity touches time and does so most deeply. In one sense, as we have seen, the whole creation is sacramental, in that eternal freedom can be experienced in

---

36. Neville, *Religion in Late Modernity*, 98–102.

relation to any particular temporal reality. Yes, freedom begets freedom, and God's eternal freedom can be experienced in, with, and under any of the temporal realities that have been created by God. When God's eternal freedom meets humans in temporality, freedom results and power is experienced. But within human culture, some cultural creations come to possess special status because freedom's power expressed in them is especially great.

In this section we turn from the possibility of translucence to its actual manifestations. Interpreting God's translucent world directs one to those places where the power of freedom manifests itself with great intensity. Two places evidencing freedom's power are in the works of human lives and in the works of human arts. In the first of these, the works of human lives, the art of power or artful power becomes manifest in the freedom that gives to and lives for the other in love. Considering the art of power, then, brings us into the moral arena of self-constitution. The second area of the works of human arts allows us to consider directly the power of art as cultural creating. The artist, who has engaged in interpreting the world and meditating on its translucent quality, gives expression to her freedom in creating a work of art, which others will experience as more or less powerful. In what follows, after some introductory comments, we will first examine the art of power and then the power of art.

We can take from Kierkegaard a clue for how to proceed. The Danish Socrates notes "that the art of power is precisely to make free."[37] Divine power is the art of making free. To be able to use this clue, we need to distinguish two theological types of making free. These types have to do respectively with freedom's ground and freedom's goal.

There is, first, "making free" in the sense of establishing freedom. Here making free refers to creating autonomy or self-determination, apart from which there is no freedom. Such autonomy or self-legislation is freedom's very foundation. It institutes a power capable of making decisions and thus giving concrete life to the center of freedom, which is doing the actualizing. Making free in this first sense, then, leads to the power of self-actualization. It creates a creature with the wherewithal to

---

37. *Søren Kierkegaard's Papirer*, ed. P. A. Heiberg and V. Khuh; 2d ed. Niels Thulstrup (Copenhagen: Gyldendal, 1968–79), VII[1] A, 181; *Søren Kierkegaard's Journals and Papers*, 7 vols., ed. and trans. Howard V. Hong and Edna H. Hong (Bloomington: Indiana University Press, 1967–1978), 2:#1251.

create itself by exercising its autonomy. If the gift of self-determination has not been bestowed, the creature is not made free. This first sense of making free has to do with the *ground* of freedom.

Secondly, there is "making free" in the sense of liberating freedom. The free creature with the power to actualize itself predictably becomes enslaved by its own power. It tends to give its ultimate allegiance to it-self and its power to create itself. However, enclosed within itself, it is not able to become all that it might. The autonomous creature, enamored of its tremendous power to actualize itself, becomes bound by its own dazzling propensities as it gets caught in the web of self-concern that it has spun. The result is a creature that is not free. The free creature has become servile, having lost the transcendence that is essential for true freedom. It needs to be recreated. The second sense of making free, then, is liberating freedom so that it might grow and become. Here making free takes the form of empowering the creature to love. Love is freedom's proper destination and names the outcome of freedom's liberation. The transcendence of eternal freedom makes free the creature whose freedom has become bound, which it does by reorienting the creature to its proper destination, healing it, so that it can move toward "genuine freedom." This second sense of making free, namely, the redeeming of freedom or the liberating of liberty, is the *goal* of freedom.

Creation and redemption are the two traditional doctrines of Christianity dealing respectively with freedom's ground (making free as bestowing the power of self-consciousness and self-determination upon the human in the context of a world that sustains it) and freedom's goal (making free as emancipating the human from being sinfully turned in on itself, opening it again to the world of future possibilities, and empowering or potentiating it to full and healthy life in the world). Both of these doctrines involve affirmations about time. The same God of eternal freedom is lovingly at work in the world in both cases, so these two doctrines, creation and redemption, ought not to be divided. Divine power as the art of making free operates under the singular intention to love. Creation is the basis of redemption, and redemption is the culmination of creation.

In the eternal act of creating, God creates time with its three modes and creates the conditions for reality. With time and these conditions created, the process of creativity can advance. All creatures emerging within this process of creative advance are dependent upon the created conditions for their existence. Since creatures are contingent, that is,

they might not have been apart from these certain conditions charac-
terizing the temporal process, these creatures, we can say, are "temporally dependent." They are dependent upon the temporal conditions
providing the appropriate structure and determinants for existence. I
would not exist as I am if it were not for all the causal forces at work
upon and within me, from the particular genetic inheritance that shapes
my genetic code, to the environmental features of the natural world
that nurture my development, to the social and cultural forces that cultivate my personality. All creatures are also dependent in a second
sense. The temporal conditioning factors are themselves dependent
upon the eternal divine act that makes them possible. In that sense
creatures are dependent upon eternity. Since they are dependent upon
the eternal act that creates the whole universe of creative advance and
sustains it in each new moment, we can say that these creatures are
"eternally dependent." I would not be at all if God had not created and
was not now continuing to create me and the universe I am in through
the eternal decision to lovingly create. The doctrine of creation affirms
the Creator God whose eternal act of creation results in the universe as
we know it and in the fact that we are both temporally and eternally
dependent creatures. The Creator God makes free by grounding our
lives as free creatures.[38]

In redemption the eternal God is at work in a different way, though
expressing the same divine love. Lutheran Christians lift up the Reformation principle of justification by grace through faith as the central
Christian theme and the principle of redemption on which the church
stands or falls. We cannot grasp the full significance of the Christian
claim of divine justification apart from the notion of time. The justification principle is crucial because it affirms that the God who in eternity creates time in its three modes and holds those modes together is
also the God who, as the source of time, possesses the power to redemp-
tively recreate time. For us in our temporal experience, time is irre-
versible. We have learned of the future as home of possibilities. Future
time passes away into the present and then into the past. All reality,
then, comes from the future. However, the future, as a temporal mode,

---

38. In this paragraph I am temporally dependent upon Neville's *Religion in Late
Modernity.* See especially his discussions of "cosmological contingency" and "ontological contingency" that lead respectively to cosmological and ontological dependence
(comparable to my temporal and eternal dependence), 13–24.

cannot be the source of time, since it passes away into present and then past. We need to distinguish, then, with Jürgen Moltmann, "between the future as a mode of time and the future as source of the times."[39] Future time, therefore, is not the future of time. Future time is a *mode* of time and the future *of* time is the *source* of time. The future *of* time is not locked within the temporal flow but "is present to every time, future, present, and past." The God of eternal freedom is this future *of* time. The eternal God is a nontemporal event constituted by the divine decision to love. The eternal God, as the future *of* time, is the condition making possible temporal experience as we know it. This God functions for the world as "a reservoir of inexhaustible energy."[40]

The eternal God, by means of promise, bridges the gap between our historical present and the future to come. As the future *of* time the eternal God makes the impossible possible. Forgiveness of sins can be a reality for God because God can recreate the past out of love. Divine forgiveness is God redoing the past by reassessing its place within the whole, larger scheme of things. Justification by grace through faith is a central principle or doctrine because it expresses the experience of eternity in time, the depth-dimension of the present, in which God brings home to the human, by means of faith, the divine promise to "deal with the past." The eternal God, lovingly receiving us as we are, heals us by forgiving and thus recreating our past. This is divine art at work as the power of making free in the sense of liberating; it is why we sing praises to the God who will not let us go. Through faith in God's promise to forgive, we are healed: as eternity touches temporality in the moment, our future is freed from the anxiety of worrying about past guilt. The Redeemer God makes free by empowering us to move toward the goal of being fulfilled, free creatures by liberating us from the past and giving us an ever new future.

Divine power, then, is the art of making free. The eternal God of freedom makes free by establishing freedom. As Creator, God is freedom's ground: the God of eternal freedom creates the whole process of reality that is the creative advance, and then through that process

---

39. See Jürgen Moltmann, *Science and Wisdom,* trans. Margaret Kohl (Minneapolis: Fortress Press, 2003), 91. See in addition Eberhard Jüngel's essay "The World as Possibility and Actuality. The Ontology of the Doctrine of Justification," in *Theological Essays,* ed. and trans. J. B. Webster (Edinburgh: T & T Clark, 1989), 95–123.

40. Moltmann, *Science and Wisdom,* 91.

creates particular creatures. In this sense human beings are both eternally dependent and temporally dependent. God also makes free by liberating freedom. As Redeemer, God is freedom's goal: the God of eternal freedom redeems the whole process of reality by accepting it into God's eternal life and judging it in a spirit of gracious, forgiving, healing love. In this way humans are empowered toward fullness of life, which is life marked by eternal freedom. Not the love of power but the power of love stands behind God's art of making free.

Being made free by the art of God's divine power, the individual now needs to consider how to use that gift responsibly and charitably; the individual must learn the *art of power.* Religion, contends G. van der Leeuw in *Religion in Essence and Manifestation,* finds its center in Power.[41] At the heart of religion one identifies that which is unusual or great, effective or successful; but whatever its form, the essence manifested is Power. Van der Leeuw's whole phenomenological project is a typology of the different manifestations of Power. In religious history, manifestations of power have not always been interpreted as the art of making free, as Kierkegaard wants to interpret them. But Kierkegaard defines divine power while reflecting on divine omnipotence, seen in God's creation of the free human being. Kierkegaard is in awe of God's incredible power, which is supposed to make dependent but manages to do precisely the opposite. In divine omnipotence Kierkegaard sees "the determination to be able to take oneself back again in the expression of omnipotence in such a way that precisely therefore that which has come into existence by omnipotence can be independent."[42] God bestows freedom but in the bestowing is able to take Godself away: the creature does not sense a trace of being dependent upon God. Kierkegaard argues that "only omnipotence can take itself back while it gives away, and this relation is indeed precisely the independence of the recipient."[43] Just as this real autonomy is God's creative work, making free

---

41. G. van der Leeuw, *Religion in Essence and Manifestation,* 2 vols., trans. J. E. Turner, incorporating the additions of the second German edition by Hans H. Penner (Gloucester, Mass.: Peter Smith, 1967), 1:23–28.

42. *Søren Kierkegaard's Papirer,* VII[1] A 181; *Søren Kierkegaard's Journals and Papers,* 1251. Compare Schelling's comment in *The Ages of the World:* "Actual power lies more in delimitation than expansion and that to withdraw oneself has more to do with might than to give oneself" (14).

43. Ibid.

in this sense of establishing freedom's ground is the initial intention of divine creative power. Without it, the divine project of creation would not have the same depth. God's purpose in moving the creature from real independence to genuine dependence upon God would lose its full significance without the stable starting point of a thoroughly autonomous creature.

Hegel had understood power as *Geist* or spirit, which is the becoming that unites being and non-being. Paul Tillich rendered Hegel's thoughts more intelligible. He developed the notion of self-actualizing power as a process that involves uniting being and non-being, centered in decision-making. Non-being is the realm of possibilities that the self has access to for its actualizing. Non-being is best understood as not-yet-being. Non-being is nothing, yet; but non-being can be transformed into being if the free human decides to actualize these possibilities that are not-yet. We could say that in touching temporal freedom, we experience eternal freedom as possibilities, as non-being. To decide is literally "to cut off," to cut off possibilities from the realm of non-being and to bring them into actuality. The free human being can incorporate more or less non-being into its being. Its power is measured by the extent to which it is able to integrate non-being into its existence. Incorporating minimal non-being or little novelty into itself, the human runs the risk of dying from stultifying sameness. On the other hand, incorporating too much non-being into itself runs the risk of self-disintegration. The powerful human being is ever expanding by incorporating non-being into being in the process of becoming. This human, then, continually relates to the possibilities of eternal freedom.

The art of power can be viewed as walking the fine line of how one lives life in relation to non-being or possibility. The self is ever involved in the project of self-constitution. This is the never-ending, ongoing task of morality: to constitute oneself through one's freedom. Power is self-constitution, and the art of power is constituting oneself in such a way that one is continuously made free. The free human who is always being made free is the human whose commitments to past being, or what might be called the created goods of life, are in service to a deeper commitment to the present process of becoming, or what might be called the transformative, creative good of life. The God of eternal freedom calls the human beyond law-dominated morality into a transmoral arena. This call is somewhat similar to Nietzsche's call for moving "Beyond Good and Evil," understood as the stifling system of morality that heteronomously legislates life in disrespecting freedom. But it is also a call "Beyond Imperial Self-Constitution," understood as the self's inevitably failing stoic effort to autonomously legislate life by elevating human freedom to absolute status. Eternal freedom's calling of human freedom into the transmoral world of religious relationship negates both an oppressive squelching heteronomy and an imperial autonomy in favor of a liberating theonomy, or an autonomous freedom that nevertheless uses its freedom to acknowledge its need for empowerment by eternal freedom as its ground and goal.

Humans who recognize eternal freedom as the source of their freedom also readily acknowledge both the infinite distance between eternal freedom and their temporal freedom, and that eternal freedom desires that other centers of temporal freedom continue to be made free. Allegiance to the creative transformation of eternal freedom relativizes the value of the individual creature's being made free by acknowledging the value of the other's need to be made free. Lutheran theology, traditionally placing a premium on sin, might be tempted to scoff at the possibility of serving the other in love, judging such other-regard as impossible. But Christian faith digs deeper by really trusting in the promise, by relying on the power of the absurd, the power of the God of eternal freedom to make possible the impossible. When faith remembers that with the eternal God all things are possible, then it discovers that faith can truly be active in love. The person of faith learns that commitment to actualizing oneself and commitment to participating in community need not run counter to each other, but can rather function as a polar relation in which individuation contributes to better participation in community and community participation strengthens one's individuality.

The art of power is guided by the art of making free. This makes for a peculiar form of power. Dominating power does not make free; it rather makes dependent. Power enlightened by the art of making free strives not to dominate the other but to sustain relationship with the other. Artful power is relational while unilateral power is dominating or hurtful. Artful power empowers by affirming the other—accepting, encouraging, motivating, judging, and thus bestowing power on the other. It is "a communication of efficacy," as Kyle Pasewark puts it.[44]

---

44. Kyle A. Pasewark, *A Theology of Power: Being beyond Domination* (Minneapolis: Fortress Press, 1993).

Artful power is an event, not a possession. The event of power is a relational happening: the free creature shares its resources as a gift to the other and in the process receives. Artful power, then, occurs when two centers of power are united. Plato designates such an event, in which separated beings are brought into unity, as "love." Love, the reunion of the separated, results when one's power is guided by the art of making free. Such love is the proper destination of power as the process of self-actualization that makes free. Power's inner desire is moved by anticipating love that reunites.

The world in which we live suffers from a dearth of artful power and an excess of hurtful power. As Alfred North Whitehead has written, the "glorification of power has broken more hearts than it has healed."[45] Only power that artfully makes free is worthy of glorification. The Christian church in which many of us operate falls short as well. Sometimes one encounters hurtful power in the church, but more often we find anemic or pallid power. Pallid power, due to lack of imagination and expectation in relation to the activity of the divine reality, legitimates Nietzsche's criticism of Christianity as leading the masses away from powerful self-actualization into the resentment-filled lives of feeble acquiescence and empty resignation. Lutheran Christians' understanding of grace has sometimes contributed to the omnipresence of pallid power. Van der Leeuw notes how, in the New Testament, *pneuma* or spiritual power is transmitted like some sort of fluid, as are the other psychological powers such as *charis* (grace), *dynamis* (power), and *doxa* (glory).[46] They flow from God to the human, with God imparting divine grace or *charis* by formulas of benediction. We translate this term *charis* as "the grace of God," although it should not be understood as a friendly divine disposition or mercy but as power that is poured out and absorbed. This *charis* effects *charismata*, the gifts of grace. These gifts, however, are no mere gifts of divine generosity, as we might rationally interpret them; they are rather the consequences of divine power, communications of divine power. Divine grace is divine power; and the gifts of grace given us are not just expressions of acceptance and forgiveness but manifestations of God's eternal freedom whose presence is artfully intended to empower us to be made free so that we in turn

---

45. Alfred North Whitehead, *Religion in the Making* (New York: Free Press, 1926), 55.

46. Van der Leeuw, *Religion in Essence and Manifestation*, 2:35.

can empower others to be made free. Dietrich Bonhoeffer's notion of "cheap grace" takes on new meaning as one thinks about the tendency to reduce grace to a dispositional attitude and to diminish the sense of grace as an incarnational empowering.

The late modern view of Richard Kearney, in *The God Who May Be: A Hermeneutics of Religion,* is helpful for understanding the art of power.[47] Kearney argues that it is not that "God is" nor that "God is not" but that "God may be." Traditional or premodern theism understood God in terms of act or actuality, that is, Aquinas's *purus actus* (pure act). The understanding of God as eternal freedom informing this essay also affirms God as pure actuality, but that is only one side of the dipolar God. The eternal God is also fully engaged in the life of temporality, presenting and empowering possibilities to be actualized. This second pole of God's reality means that God is in a process of becoming. Kearney, reacting against the monopolar, traditional God of pure actuality, wants instead to understand God in terms of possibility. Kearney walks the tightrope between traditional theology's interpreting of divinity as "pure being" and negative theology's view of God as "pure non-being," in favor of construing God as "possibility to be."[48]

The God-who-may-be does not impose a kingdom on humans but rather offers humans the possibility of realizing the promised kingdom by opening themselves to God's transfiguring power. Each person possesses the possibility to be transfigured and in the process to transfigure God. Kearney's God promises to bring new life and bring it abundantly, and promises a kingdom of justice and love.[49] This God of promise empties the deity of power and presence so that God may be the promised kingdom. Kearney's God is, then, the God of possibility to come, the God of *posse* who calls us beyond the present to a promised future.[50] At the *eschaton,* or the end, this God will be God.[51] At this point, however, the *eschaton* has not arrived, so there is a free space, a space of the possible, a gap, within God's core. God is not yet. The divine gap makes possible all that would otherwise be impossible for us. God as *posse* rather than *esse* means that the possibility of being prevails, rather than the

---

47. Richard Kearney, *The God Who May Be: A Hermeneutics of Religion* (Bloomington: Indiana University Press, 2001).
48. Ibid., 4.
49. Ibid., 2, 38.
50. Ibid., 3.
51. Ibid., 4.

actuality of being as accomplished fact, and that the promise is impotent unless and until we respond to it. When possibility is transfigured into actuality, God is doing something for us and we are doing something for God; God's coming is thus enabled to come into being. As Kearney says, God depends on us to be: "We are free to make the world a more just and loving place, or not to."[52] Foreknowledge in the traditional sense is given up, for the future can be known only in terms of possibilities. This God reminds us that what seems impossible to us is only apparently so. As transfigured by God, all things are possible. Hope is enlivened within us as we are confident that possibility will become more incarnate in life. The philosophical story of the eschatological God that Kearney narrates is a winsome, late modern story from which theologians can learn. His story can help us better tell our story about eternal freedom as the God who may be—the God who emblematizes power of the artful form and who creates the world for us so that we may artfully recreate it for God.

Understanding the art of power, we can attempt to understand how the artist uses that power to create *the power of art.* By reversing Kierkegaard's assertion about power, we can arrive at a definition of art. If power is the art of making free, we can say that art is "the power of freely making." The artist as the possessor of the power to freely make has functioned as an ideal image in both modern and late modern cultures and to a much lesser extent in postmodern culture. The artist who freely makes serves to symbolize the creative constructor. Modernity stressed the rational and systematic features of the creatively constructing artist. Postmodernity has emphasized the irrational and piecemeal qualities of the artist's novel productions and has seen the "freely making" as more complex and problematic than the modern vision of artistic freedom. Late moderns affirm the modern vision, with greater limits placed on subjectivity and creativity. All three cultures, however, have presumed that humans hold or express the power to freely make. Modernity and late modernity share the view of the human, in important senses, as autonomous, independent, self-reliant, and self-legislating. The modern vision does not understand the artist's creative construction as owing anything to a higher power, eternal freedom, who is the genuine Divine Artisan empowering the artist's creativity; postmodern sentiment depersonalizes the creative process but is

---

52. Ibid., 5.

equally reluctant to allow divine transcendence a place. Moderns, post-moderns, and late moderns alike, if forced to choose between regarding the artist's work as human constructivity or divine disclosure, would all declare in favor of the former. The late modern would protest, though, that it need not be an either/or, because the divine disclosure can be seen as taking place precisely through human constructivity.

If we can agree, with some quibbles, that art is the power of freely making, then we can note the rather broad array of forms that art assumes: arts of freely making, whether music (a favorite within the Lutheran tradition), architecture, sculpture, painting, poetry, novels, or dramas. Within each of these art forms a given work of art can be more or less translucent. In short, not all works of art are created equal. Some possess more power than others. But what makes one work more powerful than another? What are the criteria for judging the truly great work of art?

Hegel believed the greatness of art was due to three factors that are dialectically related, and Kierkegaard followed him on this.[53] The method advances from the side of objective spirit to the side of subjective spirit to the reconciliation and unity of these two. There is, first, the objective content of the artwork. In this first stage of Hegel's three-fold dialectic, the focus is on the concrete, existing object. We might call this the art's subject matter. Here we have the work's content. If I create a sculpture of an ant that I have seen on the sidewalk during a walk downtown on the sunny morning of June 12, it is not likely to be very significant. First, it is going to be very small physically, so small that people will need to be very close even to see it. Second, my creative construction is not going to be able to indicate how this ant differs from the millions of other ants that people have encountered over the years; so there will be no distinctive significance in this object or subject matter of the work. Third, if the ant sculpture is constructed out of mud, it is insignificant also because of its material. We can think of other ways in which the object of my work establishes itself as weak rather than powerful. Were I, on the other hand, to give shape to a huge, beautiful

---

53. See Hegel's discussion of "The Idea of the Beautiful" in *Hegel's Aesthetics: Lectures on Fine Art,* 2 vols., trans. T. M. Knox (Oxford: Clarendon, 1975), 1:111–15. See also Søren Kierkegaard, *Either/Or,* 2 vols., trans. Howard V. Hong and Edna H. Hong (Princeton, N.J.: Princeton University Press, 1987), 1:47–58, and Jon Stewart's discussion of "The Work of Art and Its Dialectic" in *Kierkegaard's Relations to Hegel Reconsidered* (Cambridge: Cambridge University Press, 2003), 209–18.

sculpture of Søren Kierkegaard, that would be a different story, especially if this object could be formed from marble, in large proportions, in an interesting pose. Then it would have a good chance of being more powerful that my statue of the tiny ant.

There is, of course, says Hegel, the other side of the matter to consider. It is not enough to make the judgment simply in terms of the object or subject matter. One must also look to the subjective side, to the subject or artist who is doing the creating. The formative activity of the individual artist gives the work its essential form. If I am a pathetic artist trying to pull off the Kierkegaard statue and a truly gifted sculptor is laboring on the statue of the tiny ant, my botched work of art might actually be less compelling and powerful than the master's magical, diminutive art form that glistens in the sunlight and displays the delicate bodily form of the industrious little creature. The subjective side of the work of art should not be underestimated. The artist's skills and spirit can do wonders for creating a translucent work.

The really powerful work of art in Hegel's view, of course, is the work in which the objective and subjective sides come together in an effective union. Here the dissonance between content and form is sublated in the artwork itself. When the appropriate subject matter, on the one hand, and the gifted subjective artist with the requisite conception and execution skills, on the other, come together to creatively construct a work so that each side offsets and overcomes the limitations of the other side, that union achieves the "idea of the beautiful." A universal idea has been given concrete expression in an existing work. Every classic work of art enjoys intimate mutuality of content and form in its unification into a unique ensemble of objectivity and subjectivity.

In his lectures on aesthetics, Hegel sees art as communicating images of excellence or freedom. Art's subject matter, then, is different understandings of freedom. For Hegel, the more complex, adequate, and complete the form of freedom given expression by art, the higher and more adequate the form of art. Since realizing freedom within history constitutes the highest work of Absolute Spirit or God, art is a cultural form, along with religion and philosophy, which translucently reveals life's absolute or ultimate reality. Hegel believes, then, that the more abstract the idea given concrete expression in the work, the more powerful and great the work of art. Abstraction becomes the measuring rod. The greatest work of art is the one whose idea possesses the greatest degree of abstraction. Since freedom is the highest expression of the

Idea in Hegel's systematic understanding and, in that sense, the most abstract concept, those works of art giving powerful expression to freedom are great. Realizing the Idea of freedom in history is the work of the Absolute Spirit.

When works of art bring the abstract Idea of eternal freedom home to people in a concretely existing way, they are translucent. In this translucence, the Spirit of Life is at work, enriching creation by imaginatively evoking and artfully empowering the world to let God's glorious light and love shine through. To connect art's power to our consideration of the art of power, we can make an observation about one particular form of the art of making free, namely, that of the poet, a representative artist. An apt example can be drawn from the poetry of the great English poet Gerard Manley Hopkins, in the poem "God's Grandeur" (1877):

> The world is charged with the grandeur of God.
>   It will flame out, like shining from shook foil;
>   It gathers to a greatness, like the ooze of oil
> Crushed. Why do men then now not reck his rod?
> Generations have trod, have trod, have trod;
>   And all is seared with trade; bleared, smeared with toil;
>   And wears man's smudge and shares man's smell: the soil
> Is bare now, nor can foot feel, being shod.
>
> And for all this, nature is never spent;
>   There lives the dearest freshness deep down things;
> And though the last lights off the black West went
>   Oh, morning, at the brown brink eastward, springs—
>   Because the Holy Ghost over the bent
> World broods with warm breast and with ah! bright wings.[54]

Art is powerful because its symbolic splendor enchants us. Through imagination the poet goes out to the world of the Idea—that is, the world of non-being, or the array of possibilities present in language—in order to give expression to "God's Grandeur," which has been experienced by playing with possibilities in giving a poem shape. Like other artists, the poet creates another world in the imaginative work of art, an imagined place that expands the world of those entrenched in the

---

54. Gerard Manley Hopkins, *Poetry and Prose*, ed. Walford Davies (London: J. M. Dent, 1998), 44, 269–270.

everyday of hurtful and pallid power. In this poem Hopkins can give expression to the brute materialism of industrial human beings because art makes non-being palatable by presenting the possibilities within a plausible structure, often narrative. Hopkins's poem articulates the dynamic presence of God's eternal freedom at work in and behind God's created universe. A great artwork expands our lives by ushering us into a world of the not-yet that enables us to see our actual world with both critical eyes and hopeful eyes. Against the devastating effect of fallen humans on the natural world, "God's Grandeur" juxtaposes the resilient novelty at the heart of nature itself. By introducing us into its own world, art captivates us and reconstructs our world, revealing gleams of a more brilliant reality. Translucence characterizes powerful art, for shining through it is God's grandeur, splendor, glory.

Translucence is a shining through, so it cannot be opaque, but it also cannot be transparent. Translucence refers to the dialectical relationship between the ultimate reality of eternal freedom and the particular temporal creature or creation mediating that reality. Art is one effective way in which mediating eternal freedom becomes possible or we are enabled to experience ultimacy in the world. The revelation of eternal freedom takes place in and through the world's particular, translucent reality. But one of the prime features revealed is precisely the mysterious nature of this freedom: God's mysterious hiddenness is disclosed as itself an important part of the revelation. Translucence respects the mystery of God. *Transparency,* unlike translucence, suggests a disclosure of the ultimate too complete, clear, and unambiguous. Opaqueness or opacity, unlike translucence, conveys too much murkiness, too much materialism, and thus too little disclosure. Translucence, standing between transparency and opacity, is the light shining through a medium that qualifies its disclosure through partial opacity. Ultimate reality—the underlying, eternal freedom that grounds finite reality and provides its goal becomes comprehensible and perceptible, visible and palpable, in the temporal, material world. If we take the word "God" to be the personal manifestation of this ultimate mystery of eternal freedom, then we can also understand the world of finite realities to be translucent to God.

St. Paul writes that now we see as in a mirror dimly, but then we will see face to face. The *eschaton* may be marked by transparent eternal reality, but the present possesses merely the possibility of translucence. And yet the glorious filter of translucence is a gift to be celebrated. The artistic celebration has its focus in the ultimate, infinite reality of eternal freedom that radiates through the finite, but the celebration also embraces the finite. The penultimate reality of the medium is clearly distinguishable from the ultimate or the eternal (and to confuse the two is the classic theological miscue), but this world of penultimate, temporal realities gains dignity because of its sacramental, mediating quality—its translucence.

Translucence and Freedom

We have considered how translucence can become a possibility when humans encounter the temporal world with a two-eyed form of interpreting. The Christian tradition has called such interpreting "faith." Two-eyed interpreting operates with a tensive relating of part to whole and through a meditative disposition that is able to discern deeper layers of meaning that point to eternal freedom shining through the temporal reality, whether in the book of nature or in the book of revelation. We have noted how the finite, created, temporal world we experience is itself glorious insofar as eternity interpenetrates it and incarnates within it the glorious fullness of eternal freedom's possibilities, even though that fullness remains hidden even in the most translucent moments. From this interpretive framework the artist's created work of art, like Scripture, is best seen as a testimony, to be understood in relation to the future (the incognito of the eternal) that holds its yet undisclosed meanings.

We have considered the actual manifesting of translucence under the notions of power and art. Whether consciously realized or not, the individual interprets and creates through the divine power of eternal freedom, which artfully makes humans free, both in the sense of establishing freedom's creative ground and empowering its redemptive goal. By incorporating non-being (those possibilities of life that have not yet been actualized) into one's being or self in the process of becoming and by using power artfully, as relational rather than dominating, we can relate to eternal freedom as the God who may be. Art results from our God-given power of freely making, and in art we freely give others our translucent vision as embodied in the particular art form. The power of a particular work of art depends on its content, its form, and the way these two have been united to give expression to freedom.

We have maintained that the reality of the imagination delivers us to the realm of possibility, which in turn is the gateway to the eternal. When the imagination is flattened, possibilities are squelched, eternity is silenced, and freedom and life are leveled. Among life's possibilities we find the possibilities of the relative future that are totally in our control. But in relating to possibilities, we also encounter the impossibilities of the absolute future that are completely out of our control. It is here that we can experience the God of eternal freedom who empowers the impossible to become possible. In the God of the impossible we encounter eternity: the God of eternal freedom gives us a basis for tying past, present, and future together in a meaningful way, making possible our very narrative identities as human selves, making possible a narrative identity for world history, and even making possible a theological narrative for God's translucent world. This God empowers us to freely create ourselves and our world in artworks that translucently balance the world's possible opacity and God's ultimate transparency. This God of eternal freedom, whose fullness of freedom is eternally identical with the fullness of love, is the creative ground and redemptive goal of our freedom. This God empowers us to be potent co-creators, both in our interpreting of translucence and in our creating of it: God inspires two-eyed, tip-toed interpreting to be ever straining to enlarge our vision of the world as interpenetrated with eternity's possibilities. And God stirs powerful, free creating of lives and artworks that extend freedom's reign in the actual world of time and space.

2

In Praise of Subtle Thinking

GREGG MUILENBURG

The dreams were something like this: the same dream often came to me in the past, now in one shape now in another, but saying the same thing: "Socrates," it said, "practice and cultivate the arts." In the past I imagined that it was instructing and advising me to do what I was doing, . . . namely to practice the art of philosophy, this being the highest kind of art, and I was doing that.

But now after my trial took place, and after the festival of the god was preventing my execution, I thought that, in case my dream was bidding me to practice this popular art, I should not disobey it but compose poetry. I thought it safer not to leave here until I had satisfied my conscience by writing poems in obedience to the dream. So first I wrote in honor of the god of the present festival. After that I realized that a poet, if he is to be a poet, must compose fables, not arguments.[1]

Philosophers have always wanted to be of use to society. Even in the midst of our most abstruse metaphysical speculations, we feel compelled to demonstrate that abstraction is more necessity than luxury.

---

1. Plato, *Phaedo*, trans. G. M. A. Grube, in *Five Dialogues* (Indianapolis: Hackett, 1981), 60e–61a.

Philosophers may not be unique in this self-consciousness, but no profession is better practiced at it. Socrates is a ready example. When asked by Plato's brother Adeimantus, in the sixth book of the *Republic,* why philosophers should rule cities when cities, and for that matter philosophers themselves, proclaimed their uselessness, Socrates replies that a proper defense of the philosopher requires fantasy. The result is the famous parable of the ship and the mutinous crew. The worthy pilot, a student of navigation, is derided by the mutineers as a prater and stargazer. The control of the ship is taken over by those who, although possessing no talent for the task, are able to convince the gullible seamen that they are leaders. One of the morals of the parable, you will recall, is that a person can be useless in more than one way: one can be useless by being of no use but one can also be useless by not being put to use. Socrates' lesson is that philosophers fall into the latter category.

Plato's story is wonderful, if less than convincing. For as long as anyone can remember, philosophers have compared themselves to physicians. Since this has been the case both when the medical profession was held in high esteem and when it was the object of deep suspicion, it does not appear to have been a strategy of self-aggrandizement. The reasons for this comparison are not difficult to find. Philosophy ministers to the mind, just as medicine ministers to the body. Medicine palliates or cures physical afflictions. Philosophy does the same for mental maladies. This division of labor, it would seem, is as cogent as mind/body dualism. Each of the oldest disciplines has a role to play in the maintenance of the total human being. The two might interact, they might occasionally conflict, but each has a domain to govern and a job to do. That only seems right. The symmetry is pleasing, even if the analogy is not completely compelling.

Philosophers have always had a love/hate relationship with the real world. On the one hand, we believe that we have something valuable and useful to offer, yet on the other, we are keenly aware of the disastrous history philosophy has had in the making of such offers. From Plato and Syracuse to Bishop Berkeley and the Bahamas, the results have been nearly uniformly abysmal. That did not, however, dissuade the philosophers of the past from accepting their perceived obligation to serve a larger constituency than their own. The philosopher king Plato envisaged may have never existed, but there have been a good many princes and even more advisors. Twentieth-century philosophers largely abandoned the role. Very few of them felt the need to preach to anyone but the choir.

The rapid rise of the Analytic school of philosophy coincided exactly with this abandoned obligation. This is no coincidence. That school valued precision of thought and certainty of knowledge above all else. Those who would be physicians of the soul were seen as selling their birthright and abandoning "true philosophy." So, not only were philosophers generally inept in their forays into the public arena, they were also ostracized by their guild members. The situation was demoralizing, and the philosophical community was fractured.

However, we have reason to believe that all this is changing. Perhaps we are finally dreaming Socrates' dream after so many years. In this chapter I would like to argue that philosophy can return to this genuine obligation by looking to the example of the arts, specifically by looking to metaphor. Undoubtedly, many other elements are involved in this return to public service, but I will concentrate on a pattern of thinking that I call *subtle thinking,* which is central to it.

Goals and Methods

Philosophers, no matter how contentious about theoretical detail, are almost universally agreed on the purpose and goal of the enterprise. Philosophy is dedicated to the attainment of the good life. The ancients taught us to pursue this goal and gave us the tools to rediscover or redefine it as needed in subsequent generations. Its essence, however, has never changed. Aristotle described it best as *eudaimonia* or human well-being. Always the biologist, his definitions are typically functional. Human welfare is determined by the character of human beings. Since human beings are thinking agents, their ultimate well-being must be understood as composed of both a contemplative and an active side. On the contemplative side, we must be able to know the good and appreciate it as the underlying principle of all that makes life meaningful. It is the axiom from which all theorems are derived. On the active side, we must pursue the good by reasoning clearly, desiring appropriately, and choosing well. Aristotle's *Nichomachean Ethics* is a vivid description of knowing and doing coming together in the pursuit of the good life. His message has not been forgotten.

Recently, Martha Nussbaum has argued eloquently for a return to the Hellenistic understanding of philosophy as therapy for the soul:

> Philosophy heals human diseases, diseases produced by false beliefs. Its arguments are to the soul as a doctor's remedies are to the body. They can

heal, and they are to be evaluated in terms of their power to heal. . . . In short, there is in this period broad and deep agreement that the central motivation for philosophizing is the urgency of human suffering, and that the goal of philosophy is human flourishing, or *eudaimonia*. Philosophy never ceases to be understood as an art whose tools are arguments, an art in which precise reasoning, logical rigor, and definitional precision have an important role to play.[2]

Nussbaum develops this conception of philosophy with care and precision. There can be little doubt that it represents a coherent account of both philosophy's goal and its method. It describes a type of thinking that has characterized philosophy from its inception: *precise thinking*. But disciplines as old as philosophy typically pursue their goals by more than one method and develop a facility with more than one set of intellectual tools. I suggest that there is another method by which philosophy can attain its goal. The analogue for this method is not the physician but the artist. The method is not rooted in precision but in subtlety. Its tools are not arguments but tropes. This method is not antithetical to the precise therapeutic approach of Aristotle and the Hellenistics, but complementary to it. It emphasizes the active aspect of philosophy's goal but depends upon the contemplative as well. There are many progenitors for this method of subtle thinking in the history of philosophy, and Aristotle himself is one of them.

Among the more endearing qualities of Aristotle's approach to the practical sciences is his keen observation of human nature. He knew as well as anyone the truth of the Platonic contention that knowing the good is tantamount to doing the good—that all moral failure is attributable to ignorance. Yet, that theoretical dictum did not fit well with his observations. Good people, well aware intellectually of the right thing to do, often failed to do it. Interestingly, these people were surprised by their failure. They obviously were unable, somehow, to translate their knowledge into proper action. Aristotle concluded that there was a much more complicated structure to the practical syllogism governing the sphere of knowledge and action than the relatively straightforward demonstrative syllogism that governed theory.

The demonstrative syllogism is about the certification of knowledge. As its name indicates, it is designed to demonstrate that something we

---

2. Martha Nussbaum, *The Therapy of Desire: Theory and Practice in Hellenistic Ethics* (Princeton, N.J.: Princeton University Press, 1994), 14–15.

already know in a provisional way can be deduced from a set of premises that we know with certainty. There is little, if any, value afforded novelty. Surprises and flashes of insight are not part of the plan. Generally, this pattern of scientific demonstration concerns itself with causes of scientifically observable effects. The causes are known. What is demonstrated is the connection between the body of established knowledge and the causal relation. The demonstrative syllogism proves things are the way we think them to be.

As its name indicates, the practical syllogism is about action.[3] It is concerned with the production of what might be termed understanding, that is, knowledge given life through action. The goal is production. The point is efficacy. The practical syllogism is designed to show how practical knowledge of the good *(phronesis)*, educated desire for the good, and rational decision come together to produce right action. If right action does not result, the practical syllogism has aborted, and the pattern must be repeated with appropriate changes. The logical difficulty with this form of argument comes with the realization that the argument's conclusion is not a decision to act, nor a moral resolve to act, nor any sort of statement at all. It is an action. The practical syllogism bridges the gap between knowledge and action. In so doing, it performs something of an epistemological miracle. Modern action theory has been trying to understand that miracle for nearly a hundred years.

It seems to me that there is more than an accidental correspondence between the two syllogisms of Aristotle and the two types of thinking described above. Demonstrative syllogistic logic has been incorporated into modern symbolic logic and scientific methodology. Both of these are components of precise thinking—thinking that informs us. It describes the world carefully with predominantly literal language. Its therapy is the correction of error and the reduction of ignorance. Precise thinking enables us to evaluate our theory structure and unify our knowledge. It rigorously adheres to the standards and protocols of rational discourse, testing its truth claims in the logical crucibles of consistency, coherence, and completeness. It requires explanations and knowledge of objective reality, which are certified, and it re-hones its definitions and assumptions when it fails to achieve that certainty. The

---

3. A fine and fascinating interpretation of Aristotle's practical syllogism can be found in Anthony Kenny, *Aristotle's Theory of the Will* (New Haven, Conn.: Yale University Press, 1979).

precise thinking of science and demonstration epitomizes it. Not only does it have an enormous reputation for success, but its standards have been canonized as definitional. Yet the demonstrative syllogism never motivates us to act. Its precise thinking is not designed for that task.

The practical syllogism has fared differently. There has been no sustained incorporation of its "miraculous" pattern of thought into either philosophical psychology or ethics. Many have attempted to reduce the practical syllogism to the demonstrative and so to precise thinking, but all have failed. So subtle thinking persists. It stimulates us to live what we know. It portrays the world impressionistically with the aid of figurative language. It is primarily concerned not with truth claims, but rather with equipping one for the performance of tasks, the meeting of needs. The therapy of subtle thinking is the activation of a proper desire.[4] It seeks an understanding that weds knowledge to action. It alters its images and metaphors looking for a more intimate fit if it fails to produce such understanding. It is to be found in the arts as the expression of human experience.

A great deal needs to be said (or perhaps better, shown) about the difference between these two types of thinking. But it needs to be done in stages. Subtle thinking is not sloppy or failed precise thinking. It is not a method designed to address issues that elude precise investigations. It is not those things, and it is. It is a profoundly different way to see and think about the world. It is a way of educating our desires to the most important values and commitments we have, or hope to have. That makes the task of describing this sort of thinking both more urgent and more difficult. But that is to be expected.

Our understanding of subtle thinking will be partial for at least three reasons. First, the goal of this type of thinking, desire activated for living the good life, is, at best, an elusive notion. We recognize it in the lives lived by the best of us, but we are at a loss to describe it precisely or to reason our way to its possession. Second, the method found in this sort of thinking is most often exemplified subjectively and idiosyncratically. It is very difficult to separate this method of thought from the thinker. In fact, it is so difficult to do so that one accustomed to precise thinking is easily seduced into concluding that there can be no such method. Finally, the object of subtle thinking is translucent, not

---

4. See Gregg Muilenburg, "An Aristotelian Twist to Faith and Learning," *Intersections* (Summer 1997).

something that is clearly discernible. It is the referent of much of our most honored names and descriptions, but it is ultimately ineffable. Little wonder that an idiosyncratic method, directed at an ineffable object, in pursuit of an elusive goal, resists explanation.

Some things we do know. Subtle thinking is obviously not deductive reasoning, as it presents no universal premises, employs no inviolate logical laws, and claims no certainty of inferential result. Yet subtle thinking is in no way antithetical to deductive reasoning; they are just different tools. Inductive reasoning, rooted as it is in particularity and the uncertainty of probability, seems closer. But it too aspires to conformity with inviolate laws, albeit statistical ones. This is too restrictive for subtle thinking's goals. Inductive reasoning, too, is not antithetical to subtle thinking, as its probabilities are often the best guides to effective action. Abductive thinking, championed by Charles Sanders Peirce and others, appears to be the closest to this subtle form of thinking in that abduction is touted as the only way to introduce new ideas. It does so by generating hypotheses. However, the newly formed hypotheses are only abduced *as* hypotheses. Their truth must be judged by more conventional inductive and deductive means—means that do not seem to be an integral part of subtle thinking. Thus, we must conclude that the thinking we are trying to understand is not closely related to any of its more illustrious cousins.

Difficult philosophical issues are involved in understanding subtle thinking, but perhaps an image and some insights from the Cretan novelist Nikos Kazantzakis can guide us in this early stage of the investigation. Precise thinking and knowledge certification are the work of even numbers. "Even numbers," Kazantzakis once said, "run contrary to my heart; I want nothing to do with them. Their lives are too comfortably arranged, they stand on their feet much too solidly and have not the slightest desire to change their location."[5] The odd numbers better describe subtle thinking. Odd numbers conform more nearly to the rhythm of Kazantzakis's heart. "The life of the odd number is not at all comfortably arranged. . . . It stands on one foot, holds the other ready in the air, and wants to depart."[6] Subtle thinking is the vehicle for change, the change that is the result of our motivation for the good life. Kazantzakis's tradition taught him the value of subtle thinking.

---

5. Nikos Kazantzakis, *Report to Greco* (London: Faber and Faber, 1973), 136–37.
6. Ibid., 137.

The great artist looks beneath the flux of everyday reality and sees eternal, unchanging symbols. Behind the spasmodic frequently inconsistent activities of living men, he plainly distinguishes the great currents which sweep away the human soul. He takes ephemeral events and relocates them in an undying atmosphere. . . . This is why . . . all the artists of classical Greece relocated history in the elevated and symbolic atmosphere of myth.[7]

He also understood the power of embodying abstractions in metaphors and myths.

Every one of my emotions, moreover, and every one of my ideas, even the most abstract, is made up of these four primary ingredients [earth, sea, woman, and the star-filled sky]. . . . Even now, in the most profound moments of my life, I experience these terrifying elements with exactly the same ardor as in my infancy. . . . The four joined indissolubly inside me and became one. . . . Within me, even the most metaphysical problem takes on a warm physical body which smells of sea, soil and human sweat. . . . Only then do I understand—when I can smell, see, and touch.[8]

Kazantzakis believed all of life to be the struggle to transform matter into spirit, to animate it, and to thereby imbue it with value for human beings. The Greek term he chose for this process was *metousiosis*, that is, transubstantiation. The evidence of this struggle appears everywhere in his writings but always as images and stories. The rich attempt to free themselves from comfort; believers attempt to free themselves from doubt and contradiction; the pious attempt to free themselves from smugness; and the righteous attempt to free themselves from temptation. All are struggles to spiritualize matter—to accomplish what God accomplished. They are all attempts to save God. No description can capture this process—no argument can establish its existence. But it exists everywhere about us. It can be seen in the flying fish, which breaks free of the confines of its nature and for an instant becomes what it cannot be. It exists in the flower that blossoms from the mud; in the laughter that explodes from a child's full belly. Only art, Kazantzakis contended, could point to the struggle and inspire people to continue the fight. Only art can allude to the struggle's reality and the reality of our involvement in it. Only art can put flesh on the bones of theory and motivate us to spiritualize that flesh.

---

7. Ibid., 173.
8. Ibid., 43.

> I swaggered as I wrote. Was I not God, doing as I pleased, transubstanti-
> ating reality, fashioning it as I should have liked it to be—as it should have
> been? I was joining truth and falsehood indissolubly together. No there
> were no longer any such things as truth and falsehood; everything was soft
> dough which I kneaded and rolled according to the dictates of whim,
> without securing the permission from anyone.[9]

Later, in describing the transforming power of myth, he wrote:

> I traveled through Greece, and gradually I began to see with my eyes and
> touch with my hands something that abstract thought cannot touch or
> see: the means by which strength and grace combine. I doubt that these
> two ingredients of perfection, Ares and Aphrodite, have ever joined to-
> gether so organically in any other part of the world, have ever joined to-
> gether so organically as in the austere ever-smiling land of Greece....In
> Greece one confirms the fact that the spirit is the continuation and flower
> of matter, and myth the simple, composite expression of the most positive
> reality.[10]

The transformation of matter into spirit or, in other words, knowledge
into understanding and action, is not the result of abstract thought.
Kazantzakis knew that a different kind of thought was required—a more
subtle kind of thinking. His tools were images, myths, and dreams, but
above all metaphors—rich, vibrant, unforgettable metaphors. In fact
the notion of spiritualizing matter is itself a metaphor for the cyclical
process of transforming experience into one's own meaning and moral
action. Since such things are very difficult to describe, metaphors are the
only sufficient option. Kazantzakis constructed metaphors that lived
and could be lived.

Appreciating the power of living metaphors and their role in subtle
thinking requires a new view of metaphor. Metaphor is here understood to be more than a technical category of trope. I would like to use
the term *metaphor* to refer to any device (linguistic, musical, visual, or
tactile) designed to facilitate subtle thinking by, in Kazantzakian words,
putting flesh on the bones of abstraction. It would be gratifying to call
this "philosophical metaphor," but that would not be accurate. While
philosophy is only recently returning to this project, the arts have always conducted it. This sense of metaphor is both a more restrictive

---

9. Ibid., 145.
10. Ibid., 157.

and a more expansive use of the term. It is more restrictive in that it ignores many types of metaphors that do not facilitate subtle thinking but serve other purposes, such as illustrative metaphors, weapon metaphors, and aesthetic metaphors. It is more expansive in that it is not restricted to linguistic metaphors. Although this examination will concentrate on the linguistic, one must remember the image of Kazantzakis traveling the world with an actual lump of Cretan red clay in his pocket, which he viewed as a powerful, embodying metaphor for his love of Crete. He could not write without kneading it. The following comments concerning the general character of metaphor should be applicable *mutatis mutandis* to nonlinguistic metaphors as well.

A Basic Theory of Metaphor

Any systematic theory of metaphor must accomplish at least two tasks. It must supply criteria for determining the presence of metaphor, that is to say, recognitional criteria. It must also offer a theory of metaphor's workings. Because these two tasks are not unrelated, a genuinely systematic theory will reflect their relationship. This somewhat abstract discussion will be helped by a sustained example. Since our present concern is metaphor, why not a metaphor about metaphors? With apologies to Jacques Derrida and Anatole France, we might say that metaphors are white mythology written in white ink. If one pauses for a moment to collect initial intuitions, the raw data of philosophical theory, three predominate.

First of all, one is startled by the radically different language use the metaphor involves. This paper was going along using language in something like the received fashion, making truth claims that may or may not have struck you as true, using words with their customary references, and putting concepts together in relatively predictable ways. But metaphor's language startles us: it seems to perform few if any of these normal linguistic tasks. In fact, it cannot be doing those things; why, otherwise, would we be startled? At this pre-analytic stage, it is tempting to say that a different sort of language is being used, a metaphorical language in contrast to the literal language that preceded the metaphor. Similarly, it is tempting to say that the metaphorical language is designed to capture something like metaphorical meaning and truth, as literal language captures literal meaning and truth. All this, as I say, is tempting, but it is also wrong.

A second, equally powerful intuition is more difficult to describe, but no less familiar for that difficulty. When we hear a metaphor, as when we hear a joke, we feel the immediate need to "get it." It is not clear what this "getting it" involves, but it is palpable and accounts for the close relationship between metaphor and one of its linguistic neighbors, jokes. Correspondingly, when we do get it, a bond of sorts is shared between the metaphor maker and receiver. This bond varies in scope and intensity depending on audience and context, but it is always there marking the occurrence of a metaphor, albeit not uniquely.

The third immediate intuition is perhaps the strongest of all. When we hear a metaphor, we are invariably inclined to paraphrase or to fill out the metaphor. That metaphors are white mythology written in white ink inclines us to think that metaphors are invisible, that they are hidden from us somehow, that they are covert in their working, that they are constructed in such a way as to do their work without drawing attention to themselves, that they are maps or blueprints for life's meaning. Very often, as the last phrase indicates, we resort to other metaphors in our attempt to paraphrase. Acknowledging that virtually all paraphrases are unsuccessful in their attempt to say what the metaphor says does not dissuade us. We need to paraphrase anyway. But if success in paraphrase is not the point, what is? Why do we feel this need so strongly? A good theory of metaphor recognition must accommodate these intuitions and answer these questions.

It is by no means clear how these immediate intuitions can be made consistent with one another, let alone incorporated into theory. It seems to me the key to accomplishing this task and the foundation of a comprehensive theory of metaphor recognition is an additional observation about metaphors, but not an immediate one. If one thinks about it, metaphors are false. They make false truth claims. When one says that metaphors are white mythology written in white ink, one is saying something that is not the case. Metaphors share that trait with some close linguistic neighbors, lies and jokes. Lies differ from metaphors in that they are false statements disguised as true statements. They depend upon the good graces and expectations of a truth-telling community. Jokes, on the other hand, while also making false statements, do not disguise them as true. They depend on plausibility but also openly announce that they are false. They are designed not to challenge the hearer by their falseness. Not so metaphors. They are preposterously and ridiculously false and do not hide it. They disdain plausibility and often shock us with their novelty. They do not, however, depend on a different language to do this. Metaphors are literal language put to an aberrant use. Allow me to suggest how this singular observation of metaphor's preposterous falseness can serve as a foundation for a theory of metaphor recognition—a theory capable of accommodating the aforementioned immediate intuitions.

The work of literal language is the making of truth claims. When we say, "The sky is blue" or "The river is higher than it was at this time last year" or even "The moderate life is the good life," we are making truth claims and we are, semantically speaking, making them the same way. The members of the subject class are said to be included in the members of the predicate class. The claims will be true if the inclusion can be verified in some way, false if it cannot. The subject terms refer to classes of existing things in the customary fashion, as do the predicate terms. The concepts or categories that are invoked in the statements are often juxtaposed and are familiar to us in that juxtaposition. When, however, we make a Chicago metaphor and claim that "The Big Lake Razor is kissing us today," something else is going on. We are making a truth claim, with customary referents in place (given the context), but the categories are juxtaposed in a startling way—startlingly enough to give us pause and occasion paraphrase. What the native Chicagoan is saying is roughly that the wind off Lake Michigan is more benign than expected this winter day. The paraphrase is inadequate, to be sure, but that is not the present point. The point is that only one element in the semantic analysis of the metaphor is different from the analysis of the literal statements. The metaphor puts two concepts together that startle us: razors and kissing. Razors do not kiss; the claim that they do is preposterously false. This, then, is the hallmark of metaphor: metaphors violently juxtapose categories, concepts, or images, depending on the medium. This irrational juxtaposition alerts us to the fact that a metaphor is being offered. Notice that all of this is done without recourse to any new or metaphorical language. Literal language is enough. In fact, literal language is essential to the recognition of metaphor. Without it, the preposterous falseness that earmarks metaphor would be lost.

This is not the whole of the story. Metaphor is not the only linguistic phenomenon that startles us with its preposterous falseness. Malapropisms, for example, do the same thing. When I say, "The purpose of sex is the publication of the species," I am not making a metaphor, only making a mistake. The mistake is readily ascertainable through attempts at paraphrase. The paraphrases are recognized not only as inadequate, but as silly.

Paraphrases play a further role in the theory I am advocating. They promote the intimacy that we noticed accompanied metaphors and jokes. Interestingly, jokes do not need paraphrases, only retellings.[11] Their intimacy is automatic, so to speak. But metaphors need paraphrase to reassure us that aberrant literal language is being used to do something very different from its normal work. They serve to reassure us that it was not just a mistake or a trick that the language was so used: it was intended. Once assured, we enter into a bond with the metaphor-maker—a bond that promises us we will see something differently, understand something anew, if we follow the metaphor through its workings. "White mythology written in white ink" will somehow enlighten us. To recapitulate: we are alerted to the presence of metaphors by their preposterous falseness, which is the result of the metaphor-maker's juxtaposition of clashing categories. Paraphrase enables us to separate metaphor from its neighbors, deepens the intimacy so characteristic of metaphor, and alerts us to some benefit from this aberrant language use. Thus, all the initial intuitions we have concerning metaphor are captured without recourse to a shadow metaphorical language.

Many students of metaphor object that a mere confirmatory role for paraphrase is too restrictive. They suggest that paraphrase is an attempt to capture the metaphor's meaning, which escapes from the collision of categories presented in metaphor to become "metaphorical meaning." I think this is wrong for several reasons. First of all, we have already seen how inadequate and disappointing paraphrase is. No one paraphrase is the measure of the metaphor. Undaunted, the paraphrastic position suggests that it is a combination of paraphrases that captures the metaphor's meaning. That too seems unlikely due to the lack of a suitable logical connective for the combinations. Conjunction is too strong, for it requires that each conjunct be a good paraphrase in its own right. Disjunction is too weak, for it requires that only one paraphrase need be a good one, but which member of the combination suffices? That is exactly what eluded the single paraphrase view. Introducing some weighing factor to index the paraphrases is possible but hopelessly arbitrary in the subjective domain of good paraphrase. So

---

11. See Ted Cohen, *Jokes: Philosophical Thoughts on Joking Matters* (Chicago: University of Chicago Press, 1999).

paraphrastic theory is in trouble for internal reasons. We just cannot get it to work, if by "working" we mean the capturing of the metaphor's meaning. That damning indictment necessitates a new approach, yet gives little indication of where to look.

There is another possibility. Perhaps the overwhelming inclination to paraphrase is not misguided. Perhaps the failure of paraphrase to capture the meaning of metaphor is due to metaphor's having no meaning to capture. Metaphors do not *mean;* they *show.* They show to "all who have eyes to see with and minds to think with," as Kazantzakis says. This is a revolutionary notion. When Donald Davidson first suggested this possibility in a larger discussion about the superfluity of semantic meanings, it was met with great opposition. That opposition has subsided as semanticists have grown accustomed to the distinction between meaning and meaningfulness. A metaphor may be meaningful (have import) without having a meaning (a paraphrase).

There may be yet another, more integral role for paraphrase in a viable theory of metaphor. There is an almost irresistible urge to paraphrase immediately following the experience of a metaphor. It is also important to offer the paraphrase even when all agree that the paraphrase will fail. In fact, it seems as if the failure is a part of the process of paraphrase. Thus, when one hears the claim that metaphor is white mythology written in white ink, the initial response is paraphrase. Suggestions of invisibility, inconspicuousness, and stealth immediately come to mind as potential for constructing such paraphrases. Yet as soon as they are formed, they are rejected or denied as inadequate to the task. Yes, metaphors are white. No, they are not. Positive paraphrases are followed by denials as quickly as they are replaced by alternate paraphrases.

This rather bizarre situation is reminiscent of the very old Christian tradition of apophaticism—the dialectic of saying and unsaying. In a recent and important book on mystical language, Michael Sills characterizes *apophasis* as the necessary correction of any saying about the divinity by a corresponding assertion that the divinity cannot be so described. The referent of the supposed assertion thus remains undefined. This language's aim is to displace the referent of such statements as a way of maintaining or reflecting the divinity's ineffability.[12] The ineffability of

---

12. Michael Sills, *The Mystical Languages of Unsaying* (Chicago: University of Chicago Press, 1994), 207.

the referent is, of course, not a phenomenon restricted to the divinity. The theological claim that all ineffability is ultimately traced to the divinity is not the issue here. We use metaphor to say that which cannot be said. With metaphor we speak the unspeakable. This seemingly paradoxical task is better understood in a context of apophaticism. In "philosophical" metaphors, we embody abstraction for the purpose of activating our desire for right action. Paraphrase is used to encourage and sustain us in the task. We cannot define metaphors as white mythology written in white ink, but we can paraphrase the notion freely so long as we know we can submit a subsequent retraction. In so doing, we do not violate the "whiteness" of metaphor, nor do we condemn ourselves to the silence of consistency. Paraphrase, understood "apophrastically," is empowering and encourages subtle thinking.

The study of language is conveniently, but not necessarily accurately, divided into three parts: syntax, semantics, and pragmatics. On the theory I am advocating, it is evident that the work of metaphor resides solely in the pragmatic realm.[13] Metaphors make truth claims but only vestigial, patently false ones that enable us to recognize them as metaphors. Claiming metaphors are white mythology written in white ink involves standard predication, standard reference, and standard referential truth claims. But it is not about truth. We are shocked by the metaphor because it is so preposterously false. The literal devices of truth-claiming are necessary only to establish this preposterousness. That is all there is of the truth-related semantic involvement of metaphors. The work they do is pragmatic: they perform tasks. So long as they perform those tasks, they live. When they no longer perform them, they slip back into the semantic realm, and they acquire meaning or truth conditions. In that way, dead metaphors help to expand the scope of literal language. When some computer nerd initially dubbed the systematic malfunction of a computer's operating system through outside intervention a "virus," or some MBA called an advantageous severance package "a golden parachute," they were making powerful metaphors with all of the characteristics just described. Quite quickly, undoubtedly through overuse, they lost their original function as aberrant literal language and slipped into normal literal language, expanding it in the

---

13. This view is rooted in the pioneering papers on issues of meaning and metaphor written by Donald Davidson and collected in *Inquiries into Truth and Interpretation* (Oxford: Oxford University Press, 1984).

process. Now they fail to startle us and are rather easily paraphrased. Most importantly, they are no longer preposterously false, or even false at all. They are tantamount to definitions. All this serves to bolster the claim that metaphor's work is pragmatic.

Clearly, it is one thing to insist upon metaphor's pragmatic character and quite another to elucidate the details of that character. Perhaps not surprisingly, such an elucidation must resort—perhaps retreat—to metaphor. Metaphors are like finger-pointings. They direct, even redirect, our attention to something that has gone unseen. They allude to connections hitherto disconnected. They intimate and invite us to importance or significance we have ignored. They hint, provide clues, and prod us to pay heed to a new quality, a hidden facet. They do all of these things in response to the context and the need. This last point cannot be overemphasized: metaphors are sophisticated and subtle responses to need.

If metaphors are really like finger-pointings, then we can understand why they are white but not invisible. When I point out an interesting aspect of the Greek countryside, no one notices my finger—no one is supposed to do so. If they do, the finger-pointing has not served its purpose well. It is designed to draw attention to itself only so long as is necessary for identification and then direct attention away from itself toward something promising to fulfill a need. Though words and language do not have fingers, they do have colliding categories that function in the same way. Such collisions redirect us; they help us to solve problems. Notice that metaphorical meaning plays no role in this fundamental process.

But why should metaphor resort to pointing when literal language can describe perfectly well? What purpose does metaphor serve? Metaphors are responses to the need to understand something. This something is less well served by description and its definitions than by metaphor and its allusions. Very often this is the case with our need to understand the most important things in our lives: human purpose, death, faithful reasoning, human suffering, the life of faith, war's atrocities, the need for love. As important as it is to acknowledge metaphor's role in these portentous circumstances, it does not explain how metaphors aid by alluding. It seems to me that the answer is found in the nature of *understanding* as I am presently employing the term. A homely example might be more perspicuous at this point. The Christmas Eve ritual of toy assembly is always better served by using the assembly diagram than by using the assembly instructions. The understanding needed in the situation requires that belief or knowledge be wedded to action in the most effective way, and a diagram used well results in productive action. So too metaphor is designed to bring about understanding, the merger of knowledge and action. Thinking subtly through lively, vibrant metaphors helps us to live our lives well.

Some Apparent Advantages of Subtle Thinking

If the theory presented here is plausible, the immediate advantages of living metaphors in subtle thinking are obvious. They perform the task of Aristotle's practical syllogism, bringing knowledge and belief together in action. The intimacy required in the recognition and the participation in the metaphor provides mutual identity and binds individuals into communities of effective agents, much the way that charter myths functioned in ancient cultures. "Getting" a metaphor, following its lead to some insight, participating in some problem's solution—all serve to solidify a group in a course of action. This intimacy can easily be overlooked in the furor for meaning, but it plays a greater role than meaning could ever play. Moreover, paraphrasing a metaphor apophrastically by allowing saying and unsaying commits us to the profundity and ineffability of the object of our subtle thinking. Knowing a claim's truth, a contention's cogency, or a position's consistency does not bring these benefits. Those who "get" a metaphor are empowered to act out the understanding the metaphor provides. The community of individuals similarly motivated by the metaphor encourages them. The metaphorical image of the Cretan *pallikari*, the freedom fighters and heroes of Turkish occupation, lives on to motivate generations of Cretans long after that occupation ceased: they still aspire to be *pallikari*. Perpetuating the metaphor provides them with the occasion and the support needed to be something and do something they find very difficult to describe. It puts flesh on the bones of abstraction. It helps them to be Cretans. Such is the power of subtle thinking.

Moreover, since the purpose of metaphor is no longer tied to truth and meaning but to action and thinking, we are free to see metaphors differently. Truth and meaning are universal notions: they speak to the general human condition and as such inform, but rarely motivate. Metaphors operate regionally, in personal, context-dependent ways. They bring understanding but do so in ways designed to motivate us to action. When Kazantzakis refers to the life of faith as a steep ascent following the bloody trail of Christ, he is not informing us of anything that we did not already know. When he speaks of life's struggle as a chrysalis's attempt to transform itself from mud-encrusted worm into a free-floating butterfly, he is not teaching but inspiring. When he speaks of the silkworm as the image of transformation, he refers to its gut becoming glistening strands of web—matter becoming ethereal. Those metaphors are not put together to elicit our assent or entertain our imaginations. Kazantzakis is rallying us to the task, calling us to fight under the banner of Christ and so also the banner of Crete. The images give us the courage and direction. They give us the desire to literally live the metaphor. As I see it, these are the marks of subtle thinking.

Subtle thinking motivates us to action. We need to temper it with precision and fact, but we need to recognize the powerful force that it is in our lives. Living well will never be the result of mere knowing. It will result from the power of subtle thinking. We do not need to trust this or believe this to be the case; we can smell, see, and touch it. When Kazantzakis felt the need to communicate something of the nature of the struggle to transubstantiate, to live well, he resorted to metaphors. His doctrine of Bergsonian transubstantiation is frightfully abstract and marginally consistent. He believed humans were created to be like God in that they had to make themselves wholly flesh in order to cast off the flesh through transubstantiation. This is the emulation of Christ's bloody ascent that he thought to be Christianity's heart. This act takes place every day all around us. All the images mentioned above testify to it, but occasionally Kazantzakis produced a special metaphor to reinforce the view.

In *Report to Greco* he recalls his lengthy estrangement from things Greek. Most of his dissatisfaction centered on the church and its teachings, but there were political issues as well, especially during his Communist years. He also felt a profound sense of guilt for not defending Greece in the traditional manner of the *pallikari*. His grandfather and his father were heroes. They expected him to be one as well. But his sword was a pen, and even though his father acknowledged that he could fight for Crete with a pen, Kazantzakis never quite accepted this role as sufficient. His solution was to abandon his ancestors and his country for the life of the exiled intellectual. Ultimately, he found that

Crete would never leave him. The red clay had stained his soul, and he could never be other than Cretan. That message is not one presented in precise language but in subtle images. Greece had been an abstraction, but now it became flesh again—his flesh.

> After each of my wanderings through the Attic countryside, at first without knowing why, I climbed the Acropolis to view and review the Parthenon. This temple is a mystery to me. . . . But when, after longing to see it for so many years, I confronted it for the very first time, it appeared immobile to me, the skeleton of a primordial beast, and my heart did not bound like a young calf. . . . The building seemed a feat of the intellect—of numbers, geometry—a faultless thought enmarbled, a sublime achievement of the mind, possessing every virtue—every virtue except one, the most precious and beloved: it failed to touch the human heart. . . . But after each new return from Attica's olive groves and the Saronic Gulf, the hidden harmony, casting aside its veils one by one, slowly, gradually revealed itself to my mind. Each time I climbed the Acropolis again, the Parthenon seemed to be swaying slightly, as in a motionless dance—swaying and breathing. . . . Never have numbers and music coupled with such understanding, such love.[14]

Once flesh, the Parthenon was spiritualized; its matter was transformed into spirit in the only way possible—metaphorically. The change took place; it was real. It was a change in Kazantzakis and in us.

---

14. Kazantzakis, *Report to Greco,* 136–38.

Part Two
Art as Translucence

3

Discerning the Composer's Voice

KATHRYN POHLMANN DUFFY

When Handel was complimented on how entertaining *Messiah* was, he responded, "I did not wish to entertain them. I wished to make them better." While we cannot say that every composer intends to make the listener or performer better, we can surely allow that composers intend to say something. The musical conventions of an era afford a glimpse into the composer's own musical world. Conversely, when we see a composer writing beyond the conventions of the time and employing unique features, we focus more on that particular composer than on the musical milieu. If we do more than simply consume music, perhaps we can allow music to engage us and thereby listen to what it can teach us.

A historical understanding of music is of considerable help in allowing music to teach us. Every composer lives and works in a specific historical context. The listener likewise exists in a temporal context. While the sheer beauty—the power, passion, or purity—of a musical piece may speak to us even when we neglect music's historical framework, this emotional content may not necessarily be what the composer intended to communicate. In fact, under such circumstances, the musical conversation is framed largely by the listener. When a listener expects to be emotionally charged by music, that becomes the standard by which the music will be judged. On the other hand, if a listener expects to ponder the music's meaning, that becomes the standard. The task for the careful listener, one who wishes to be engaged by music on its own terms, is to determine which standard is appropriate. When we inform our listening with a historical perspective, we allow the music to set its own parameters, and we can better hear what the composer wishes to communicate.

The emotional quality of music has been the dominant criterion of its quality only since the early nineteenth century. Earlier, when composers were generally employed at court, in the church, or by the civic community, the compositional genres were generally oriented toward the needs of the patron and the available performing forces. This patronage system, however, began to disintegrate in the eighteenth century with what we know as the Age of Enlightenment. Just as Enlightenment thinking irreversibly affected the political realm with ideas about democratic rule, so it also affected the arts. Although the church continued in its role as a patron of the arts, the court was often unable to do so. Without this form of patronage, composers were, admittedly, no longer viewed as servants, but they were also often left without employment. Composers had more freedom to select genres for composition, but they lacked ready access to performing ensembles and concert opportunities. Often they needed to assemble ad hoc ensembles for concerts with subscription ticket sales to supplement their living. In time, civic-minded groups were formed to sponsor public concerts, maintain orchestras, build concert halls, and eventually establish schools to train musicians. But the musical landscape had been irreversibly altered.

Emphasis on the emotional quality of music emerged in the nineteenth century, as Romanticism placed emphasis upon individuality and the expression of personal ideas and emotions. Romantic composers strove to communicate their own subjective thoughts and feelings in music, with the result that each composer developed and expressed a unique musical language. This characteristic style provided the listener an immediate window into the composer's own internal world. Because of this nineteenth-century elevation of the individual, the listener's reaction to the composer's work also gained in significance, especially since the public had become the composers' most important patron.

Most music heard today in our concert halls and elsewhere dates from the Enlightenment onward. Consequently, it is not surprising that we are accustomed to expect a direct connection between the music and the composer's ideas and emotions. For earlier music, however, we need to suspend these modern ways of listening—remove, as it were, our Enlightenment and Romantic filters—in order to discern more clearly the composer's own voice. In listening ahistorically to early music, we impose modern judgments on it and thus cloud its meaning and lose its deeper dimension. But if we listen historically, with an understanding and appreciation of the composer's own time, the music becomes more translucent. We are able not only to hear the beauty of the music itself, but also to hear beneath the music's surface to a deeper level, having a richer conversation with the composer and thus a better sense of the composer's intent.

In order to listen to the composer's voice, we must also guard against a tendency to view music teleologically. Specifically, we must avoid the temptation to think that music improves over time. Music changes, but change is not equivalent to improvement. Nineteenth-century music is not in itself better than sixteenth-century music. It is different, certainly, in terms of its harmonic and formal vocabulary and its aims, but it is not necessarily better.

Calling some thing better than another always implies a criterion. A comparison can be made about whether or not something is better only when the things compared pursue the same aim. In this regard, some music may indeed be better for specific purposes. But when the aims are different, we cannot simply say one work is better than another. For instance, in comparing Schumann's songs *(Lieder)*, piano pieces, and symphonies, one immediately recognizes that these compositions are performed in different ways, requiring different performance media as well as different performance space. One genre is better suited to the orchestra and the large concert hall, while the others are better suited to the piano, or voice and piano, in a smaller recital hall. More significantly, they vary in their potential to convey or evoke particular ideas. Within the language of symphonic writing, Schumann has both intimate and grand moments, and similarly so within the language of *Lieder*. His *Lieder*, however, will always be able to communicate a greater sense of the intimate than will his symphonies, while the symphonies will always better communicate a sense of the grand. Thus, one genre is not inherently better than the other, although it may be better suited to some end than another.

Similarly, across time, some music may be better suited to accomplish a particular end. Whatever the mood Schumann may be trying to evoke in his music, he will always be more successful at it than will a sixteenth-century composer. Evocation of a mood was characteristic of Schumann's era, but the sixteenth-century aim, as we will see, was to convey the structure and meaning of a text. Although the two are indeed different, neither approach is superior.

Through musical analysis and examination of historical context, this essay explores how early composers dealt with the relationship between music and text. The relationship between text and music changes over time as composers arrive at various solutions for setting the text. For some composers the connection between word and music is simply not a consideration; others are drawn to clarify the text's grammatical and rhetorical emphases; still others project the meanings of the individual words in their music. Drawing on examples taken from plainchant, early polyphony, and motets of the fourteenth, sixteenth, and seventeenth centuries, we will examine stylistic features and compositional practices employed in the music in order to discover this connection. In this way we may better discern the composer's voice and thus see beyond the music to hear the content to which the composer points.

Plainchant

In order to lay a foundation for examining the work of later composers and to see how music can teach us even when we do not know the details of a composer's life, we turn first to plainchant, where the composer is completely unknown. The following six pieces of plainchant represent two different categories of chants from three different occasions within the church year. One category of chant is the introit, the first chant in the Mass; the other is the alleluia, sung to introduce the Gospel. The three occasions—Easter Sunday, All Saints Day, and the Third Sunday after Epiphany—range from the most solemn feast of the year to a simple Sunday in ordinary time.

Because the three feasts differ in rank, one might expect the music to reflect this difference. The pieces, however, show more similarities than differences. In fact, chant displays virtually none of the expressive characteristics so valued in nineteenth-century music. One may well wonder why plainchant existed at all. In Christianity, as in most religions, the sacred is communicated in ceremonial actions employing not simple speech, but rather a heightened form of speech, namely, chant. Since the holy is beyond the human, speaking of it requires an elevation of conventional speech. In medieval worship, all portions of the Mass and Offices—including prayers, Scripture lessons, and the choir's portions of the services—were chanted.

Each of these liturgical portions has a clarity of form and function that is echoed in the music. The introit, as the first chant in the liturgy, is a processional piece during which the clergy enter the sanctuary to take their places at the front of the assembly. In early Christian worship, this entrance piece consisted of an entire psalm with a *Gloria Patri,* framed by an antiphon (a psalm verse or another text serving as a sort of refrain). At times the antiphon was also repeated between verses of the psalm, which was chanted to a simple psalm tone formula. This pattern may be familiar to modern worshippers, who are accustomed to singing the psalm with its antiphon between Scripture lessons. Gradually, within the first few centuries of Christianity, the introit was shortened until it took on its customary shape—antiphon, psalm verse, *Gloria Patri,* antiphon—which is reflected in the music. The psalm verse and the *Gloria Patri* are both sung to a basic psalm tone formula. The music for the antiphon, however, while not particularly elaborate, is more florid.[1]

Our post-Enlightenment sensibilities lead us to expect that, in sung pieces, the composer is attempting to express the text melodically. If this were the case, we would expect the music for Easter, All Saints Day, and the third Sunday after the Epiphany to differ greatly in complexity, with more elaborate music for the great festival and simpler music for a non-festival Sunday. Even if the composers did not differentiate their music in this way, we might expect to see clear textual declamation, with attention paid to the natural word accents or the sentence syntax.

This expectation, however, is not borne out in the music. At times the text is set so that the word accent is retained, but more often the setting works either against the natural word accent or without any particular stress. When we observe how often a syllable normally accented in speech is not stressed in the music, it becomes clear that the objective

---

1. For basic descriptions of the categories of plainchant and their liturgical contexts, see Richard H. Hoppin, *Medieval Music* (New York: Norton, 1978). Consult also the article on plainchant in the *New Grove Dictionary of Music and Musicians,* 29 vols., 2nd ed., ed. Stanley Sadie and John Tyrrell (London: Macmillan, 2001) [*New Grove II*]. The *New Grove II* is the standard reference work for music and can be consulted for further information on any of these musical issues.

is not the correct declamation of the text. Example 1 provides the antiphon portions of the three introit texts. The accented syllables are underlined, and the words with contrary or equal stresses are shown in small capitals.

Example 1: Word accent in sample introit chants

Easter Introit—Resurrexi

Resur̲rexi, et a̲dhuc te̲cum sum, alleluia: posui̲sti su̲per me ma̲num tu̲am, alle̲luia: mir̲abilis fac̲ta est sci̲entia tu̲a, alle̲luia, alle̲luia.

All Saints—Gaudeamus omnes

Gaudeamus o̲mnes in Do̲mino, di̲em fes̲tum cele̲bran̲tes sub ho̲nore Sanc̲torum o̲mnium: de quo̲rum solem̲ni̲te gau̲dent An̲geli, et coll̲audant Fi̲lium De̲i.

3 Epiphany—Adorate deum

Ador̲ate De̲um o̲mnes An̲geli e̲jus: au̲divit, et lae̲tata est Si̲on: et exsulta̲verunt fi̲liae Ju̲dae.

This lack of emphasis on word accent does not mean that plainchant is stiff or unmusical. Rather, its lack of fixed rhythmic values or meter gives it a distinct flexibility that requires that both listener and singer be actively engaged. The sensitive singer takes advantage of this flexibility to shape the musical phrases in order to communicate the text gracefully.

In comparing the complexity of these three chants, we find that none has a more complex melody than another. They are all equally *neumatic* (that is, a few notes for one syllable of text) and equal in length. Nor can interpretation rely on a major/minor distinction, for these pieces were written before the major-minor harmonic system had developed.

Some modern listeners associate major melodies with happiness and minor melodies with somberness, but this dichotomy also proves unhelpful. These pieces are all modal, using a combination of half-steps and whole-steps different from today's major-minor scale systems. Singers altered pitches in certain contexts according to the complex rules of *musica ficta*. As a result, certain modes, with enough accidentals added through *musica ficta,* did gravitate toward what later became *major* sounding melodies, while others moved toward *minor* ones. The Easter and All Saints introits both use modes that later gravitated toward the minor system (modes 4 and 1, respectively) while the introit for 3 Epiphany is written in mode 7, which gravitated toward major.[2]

Turning to the alleluias, we again find similarities between the chants. Although the alleluia emerged as a standard part of the liturgy somewhat later than the introit, it is found consistently by the early seventh century. Sung immediately before the Gospel to herald its reading, the alleluia was not a processional piece, as was the introit. It was of fixed length and, given its position and its relationship to the Gospel (the high point of the liturgy's first half), it commanded attention.

Like the introit, the alleluia also has a defined form, namely, that of a threefold alleluia with verse. After the word "alleluia" is sung twice, a short text from Scripture related to the day's focus follows. The alleluia is then repeated once more, with an extension, known as the *jubilus*. The result yields a threefold alleluia with its verse. Often the music at the end of the verse duplicates the *jubilus* and thus unifies the alleluia with its verse.

The music of the alleluias is noticeably more florid than that of the introits. Each of the three alleluias contains significant *melismas* (many notes for one syllable of text). Although it might be tempting to assume that the higher the feast the more melismatic its alleluia, the evidence does not bear this out. The alleluia's form and melismatic nature had practical ramifications. In general, neumatic and syllabic chants, such as the introits, were sung by the entire choir, while the melismatic alleluias were divided between a soloist (or perhaps a small group) and the choir. In the case of the alleluia, the soloist sang the opening alleluia once and the choir repeated it. The soloist then sang the verse section and the choir joined at its conclusion, after which they sang the alleluia section a final time.

Clearly what is being communicated in these alleluias and introits is not the specific meaning of a specific text. Nor do we have a composer's personal communication to the listener about the texts or their particular feast days. Aurally communicating the rank of the feast day is not

---

2. Much has been written on the issues of *musica ficta* and modal theory; two of the more recent and comprehensive studies are Margaret Bent, *Counterpoint, Composition and Musica Ficta* (New York: Garland, 2002), and Cristle Collins Judd, *Tonal Structures in Early Music* (New York: Garland, 1998).

the objective either, for none is more audibly paschal or ordinary than another. And declamation is also not decisive here, for there is no effort, in either the introits or the alleluias, to stress word accents or particular syllables within a larger textual phrase. Rather, each chant had its own specific form, which the music supported. Consequently, the chant's form was audibly discernible to the listener through the music, and, once the form was identified, the function of the liturgical item was clear. In plainchant, then, the music's aim is merely to transmit, rather than to express or interpret, the text.

Understanding plainchant's intent to communicate form and function rather than emotion or content does not diminish this music's power to move us. Whatever its crafters' purpose, many people today find plainchant soothing, timeless, or calming. Christians and non-Christians alike use chant in relaxation exercises. There is a distinction, however, between use and intent. To lose sight of this distinction diminishes our ability to understand music on its own terms: we render the music opaque rather than translucent. The plainchant creators saw their work as part of a cohesive whole within which the chant's form and function, rather than its emotional effect on the listener, were its primary concerns. Keeping these aims in sight, we perceive more fully the chant's translucence and hear both its beauty and its underlying truth.

Notre Dame Polyphony (Twelfth and Thirteenth Centuries)

Leonin and Perotin: *Viderunt*

While plainchant basically consisted of a single line of pure melody, a single voice part with neither harmony nor fixed rhythm, polyphony added new linear musical aspects. By the early tenth century, composers were seeking to write more elaborately by creating additional voice parts. Even as they explored new sonorous possibilities, however, they never lost sight of plainchant's original design and function. The new parts were conceived as melody, not harmony. It would be several centuries, in fact, before composers began to think in harmonic terms. Whether the additional voice parts were designed to be sung in parallel with the primary melody, as was the case in the earliest polyphony, or to move more freely against it, as was the practice later, the music was conceived linearly, not harmonically.

The first institution for which a large body of polyphony was created was the Cathedral of Notre Dame in Paris, which played a pivotal role, particularly in the period 1160–1250.[3] The new polyphony complemented the new Gothic architectural style rising around it. Even as its cornerstone was laid in 1163, the cathedral fostered music that was as breathtaking as its storied architecture. The architecture stood as a harbinger of the many great cathedrals yet to come, but it did not lose sight of its primary purpose as a worship center: a heaven on earth. Similarly, the new polyphonic music exceeded any sound yet heard, but retained its connection to the form and function of the chants that were being transformed.

The first two composers whose names we do know—Leonin and Perotin—appeared in Paris in connection with this compositional type. Leonin is credited with writing a large number of such pieces, which were collected into a volume known as the *Magnus liber organi* or the *Great Book of Organum*. His successor, Perotin, revised and expanded the repertory. As students came from all parts of Europe to study at the University of Paris, they heard the wondrous polyphony reverberating within the great cathedral's walls. Typically, they copied some of the music and took it with them when they returned home, thus disseminating the practice of polyphonic writing throughout Europe.

A new feature of early polyphony is the presence of rhythmic patterns. In plainchant, there had been no need to notate rhythm, but as musicians began to experiment with this element of music they needed to develop means to communicate their intentions. At Notre Dame such a system was developed. The accurate notation of rhythm was to undergo many further developments and refinements before reaching current practice, but Notre Dame witnessed its first infant steps.

One chant that both Leonin and Perotin set in polyphony was "Viderunt omnes," the gradual for Christmas Day. In practice, graduals followed a pattern similar to that of the alleluias already examined. Since singing in polyphony was much more difficult than singing the

---

3. For a detailed study of Notre Dame polyphony and its context, see Craig Wright, *Music and Ceremony at Notre Dame of Paris: 500–1550* (Cambridge: Cambridge University Press, 1989).

monophonic plainchant, early polyphony was intended for soloists, and only the chant's solo portions were set in polyphony. The soloist sang the opening words ("*Viderunt omnes*"), and then the choir joined for the remainder of the opening section (the "respond"). The verse section was sung by the soloist with the choir joining toward the end, as in the alleluias.

Leonin uses polyphony to transform the chant's solo sections. His lower voice, the tenor (derived from the Latin word *tenere,* meaning "to hold"), consists of the original plainchant (nearly note for note) in long notes, above which his newly composed top voice part energetically gallops. At particular points, the chant voice turns to shorter notes, corresponding to the original chant's melismatic portions. It then returns to its extended notes in the sections corresponding to the original chant's more syllabic portions. Example 2 compares the original plainchant with the portions of it set in polyphony. The shaded areas mark the solo sections of the chant, which are the sections set in polyphony by both Leonin and Perotin.

Perotin's reworking of "Viderunt omnes" witnesses to another layer of musical evolution: he reworked and expanded the polyphonic repertoire. "Viderunt omnes" is one of only two pieces that Perotin wrote for four voices. It is, therefore, remarkable not only among his own works but also among musical pieces in general, since four-part texture did not become standard until the second half of the fifteenth century—some 250 years later. Nearly three times the length of Leonin's piece, it stands as monumental.

Despite this piece's significance, Perotin shows continuity with Leonin in remaining faithful to the original chant melody and structure. He achieves a radical new sound through new melodic techniques and new sonorous capabilities derived from his expansion to four polyphonic voices. By exchanging voice parts, Perotin relates the voices to each other, at times interchanging figures in the upper voice between two voices or even rotating them through all three upper voices. Further, as he approaches a cadence, he increases the activity of the upper voices. At the cadence points, Perotin uses the consonant intervals of unisons, fifths, and octaves, but within phrases he uses a rich variety of dissonant intervals, producing a regular and audible ebb and flow in the music.

In writing these pieces, Leonin and Perotin evinced a new *Weltanschauung* that revealed a search for a new sound in keeping with the

Example 2: Solo and choir portions of "Viderunt omnes"[4]

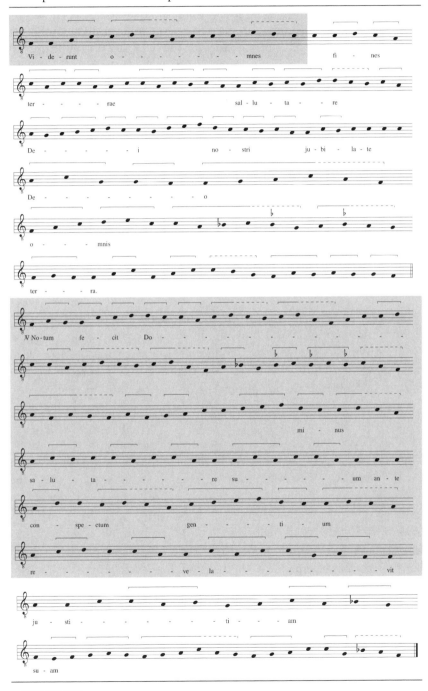

4. My thanks to Charles Davis for preparing the musical examples in this chapter.

new architectural style. The soaring layers of the architectural elements were echoed in the layering of the new melodic voices. This new sound, however, was also grounded in plainchant, retaining its form and function. "Viderunt omnes" retained its customary place in the liturgy as the gradual for Christmas Day, complete with the chant's solo and choir sections. Neither composer attempted to transmit a sense of the text's meaning or to declaim it, nor did they seek to express a personal interpretation of the text or of the Christmas festival. When we are aware of the chant basis, the alternation between solo and choir, the state of rhythmic notation, the innovative nature of the four-voice "Viderunt," the place of the Notre Dame polyphony within the larger history of music, and, for that matter, the place of the Cathedral of Notre Dame and the University of Paris within the history of civilization, we hear much more than the sheer beauty and power of the sound.

Isorhythmic Motet (Fourteenth Century)

Machaut: *S'il estoit nulz*

The motet was a natural outgrowth of polyphony. During the fourteenth century, monophonic and polyphonic writing coexisted side by side. Some attention was given to creating polyphonic settings of Mass Ordinary movements, but even more creative energy was devoted to secular music. In Notre Dame polyphony the discant section was that portion of the piece where the tenor moved in relatively quick note values compared with the tenor's typically extended note values. Certain chants, such as "Viderunt omnes," took on a sectional quality, with choir sections and solo sections, the latter in turn composed of organal sections (with the tenor in extended note values) and discant sections (with the tenor moving more quickly). Gradually composers began to conceive of excising one discant section and replacing it with a newly composed one. As new composers tried their hand at writing substitute discant sections, they created a sort of library of such sections, which could be inserted into a pre-existing organum. These discant inserts, called *clausulae*, contained minimal texts since they were composed for the chant's melismatic portions. The chant to which they belonged could be identified from the tenor melody, and from whatever syllables might be included.

Substitute clausulae served another function and unwittingly spawned a new genre. Although they were discrete units intended for use with their parent chant, they began to be viewed as autonomous units. All that was needed to transform them into a new, independent piece was to add text to the upper voices—something easily accomplished. The earliest motets were thus created by texting substitute clausulae. Although at first the new texts were in Latin and complemented the sense of the parent chant, composers were soon creating new motets by retaining a chant-based tenor but writing entirely new upper voices in French or Latin with sacred or secular texts.

"S'il estoit nulz" by Guillaume de Machaut (1300–1377) is just such a motet. The era's emphases are reflected in its music. The University of Paris was then the celebrated center of scholasticism, which prized rational, methodical philosophy. In its curriculum, music was classified as a science, not an art. As an educated man of his day, Machaut was familiar with the scholastic emphasis on logic. The isorhythmic motet, with the same sense of the logical and systematic, emerged as scholasticism's musical equivalent.[5]

Among Machaut's works are one large four-voice piece, his *Missa de Notre Dame,* a great many monophonic French secular songs *(chansons),* and several three-voice motets. Machaut did not invent the isorhythmic motet, but he used it extensively. An isorhythmic motet has a tenor that, although untexted, actually governs the piece's organization. The tenor melody is a small portion of plainchant—just as in the substitute clausulae and the earliest motets. Although the plainchant had no definite rhythmic values, here a repeated rhythmic pattern is imposed upon the pitches of the tenor line. This rhythmic pattern could be varied through the use of proportions, resulting in either diminished or augmented note values, but the overall relationship of the note values remained unchanged. Occasionally a composer would adopt a new rhythmic pattern at some pivotal point, or repeat the tenor to create a longer work. Over this the composer placed two free upper voices, sometimes also incorporating in them repeating rhythmic patterns.

In "S'il estoit nulz" Machaut created a unique combination of simplicity and complexity. He used two isorhythmic patterns in the tenor, each five measures long, repeated three times, and concluding with one incomplete statement. The tenor melody is also repeated, but only once. The point at which this repetition occurs is the work's turning

---

5. For a detailed presentation of Machaut, his music, and its context, see Anne Walters Robertson, *Guillaume de Machaut and Reims: Context and Meaning in His Musical Works* (Cambridge: Cambridge University Press, 2002).

point—the point where Machaut shifts to his second isorhythmic pattern. This isorhythmic tenor is quite simple, for Machaut employs no statements using proportion. He does, however, create further complexities by making the upper voices nearly isorhythmic as well, with very slight variations in the upper voices. The regular pattern of rests stands out very clearly. While at times a musical phrase corresponds to a textual phrase, often this correspondence is negated, for rests frequently interrupt the text phrase.

In this piece we see that although Machaut was a major literary figure of his time, the text's integrity was not his primary concern in writing the motet. Instead, he emphasized the motet's methodical, scientific, and isorhythmic foundation. The most complex of the fourteenth-century musical forms, the isorhythmic motet afforded a worldview: it was the epitome of the era's scientific and scholastic emphases.

The Motet around 1500

Josquin: *In principio erat verbum*

While the connection between word and music was not a primary consideration for composers of fourteenth-century isorhythmic motets, it gained in significance throughout the Renaissance. Josquin des Prez (1440–1521), acknowledged by his peers as the generation's greatest composer, played a pivotal role in promoting this connection. Martin Luther placed great value on Josquin's work, ranking him above all other composers. In examining one of his motets, "In principio erat verbum," we can sense why Josquin was so revered. Although we know nothing about its dating or compositional circumstances, this motet is undoubtedly by Josquin. The primary historical context we bring to this piece is a general understanding of Renaissance humanism, with its interest in language—both ancient and modern—and its aesthetic of balance and symmetry.

Josquin's sensitivity to the subtleties of both language and balance is manifest in his motet writing. During the fifteenth century the motet had recovered its nature as a sacred genre. By Josquin's time the motet was an a cappella work with a scriptural text in four (or sometimes more) voices. Motets commonly were written in two *partes* although "In principio" is in three *partes*. The text is the Gospel for Christmas Day—the first fourteen verses of the Gospel of John, shown in example 3 below. Immediately, Josquin displays his sensitivity both to balance and to word, giving equal emphasis to all voice parts and balancing them against each other. Through his musical design, Josquin very clearly communicates the text's structure. The music's cadence points correspond directly to the textual cadences. Furthermore, each new text phrase receives a new melodic phrase. To be sure, these traits are not uncommon for the High Renaissance, and other composers of the era used the same techniques. But in Josquin's hand these techniques are much more masterfully worked out.

Josquin begins his motet with one of the hallmarks of his style—paired duets. The opening sentence consists of three phrases of text, each of which Josquin places in a paired duet. Each duet, beginning in the tenor and soprano and echoed in the bass and alto, is unified by the fact that both duet voices employ the same motivic material. Moreover, Josquin unifies each phrase in this sentence by repeating the rhythm of the opening fanfare-like motive in the subsequent phrases, although in diminution. Josquin drives to the conclusion of this opening sentence through the insertion of a third voice, the tenor, into the bass/alto duet. This variation adds interest for the thought's conclusion, but it also assists him in forming a hierarchy of cadences leading to the final punctuation. The first phrase's final cadence is avoided and overlapped: the two duet voices cadence at different times, with a new voice beginning before the previous phrase concludes. In the second phrase both sets of duets cadence together, moving out to the octave. The first duet in the third set uses the octave cadence again, but in the final statement the added voice allows for a cadence using the octave and the fifth, yielding a stronger and richer cadence.

Josquin uses the music to clarify and heighten the text's meaning. The next sentence, "He was in the beginning with God," is very short—actually only a single phrase. Josquin uses only a single duet here and, as if to show the unity of God about which the text speaks, cadences on a single note. Since Josquin used one duet (tenor and soprano) here, he begins the next sentence with the other voices; however, this statement is not a paired duet. The new thought, "All things were made through him," has a new musical phrase, even though Josquin is balancing one duet with another. Josquin continues the text, "and without him was nothing made that was made," with a new technique that departs from the duet procedure: he sets this text with a short motive sung imitatively in all four voices, although only three voices are singing simultaneously until nearly its conclusion.

Example 3: Text of Josquin's "In principio erat verbum"

Prima pars:

In principio erat verbum,
  et verbum erat apud deum,
  et deum erat verbum.

In the beginning was the word,
  And the word was with God,
  And the word was God.

Hoc erat in principio apud deum.

He was in the beginning with God.

Omnia per ipsum facta sunt,
  et sine ipso factum est nihil quod
  factum est.

All things were made through him
  and without him was not anything
  made that was made.

In ipso vita erat et vita erat lux
  hominum, et lux in tenebris lucet,
  et tenebre eam non
  comprehenderunt.

In him was life and that life was the
  light of man and the light shines
  in the darkness and the darkness
  did not comprehend it.

Secunda pars:

Fuit homo missus a deo cui nomen
  erat Iohannes.

There was a man sent from God
  whose name was John.

Hic venit in testimonium ut
  testimonium perhiberet de lumine
  ut omnes crederent per illum.

He came for testimony, to bear
  witness to the light so that all
  might believe.

Non erat ille lux sed ut testimonium
  perhiberet de lumine.

He was not the light, but he came to
  bear witness to the light.

Erat lux vera que illuminat omnem
  hominem venientem in hunc
  mundum.

The true light that enlightens all
  humanity was coming into
  the world.

In mundo erat et mundus per ipsum
  factus est, et mundus eum non
  cognovit.

He was in the world, and the world
  was made through him, yet the
  world knew him not.

In propria venit, et sui eum
  non receperunt.

He came to his own home and his
  own people received him not.

Quotquot autem receperunt eum,
  dededit eis potestatem filios dei
  fieri his qui credunt in nomine eius.

But to all who received him, who
  believed in his name, he gave
  power to become children of God,

Qui non ex sanguinibus, neque ex
  voluntate carnis, neque ex
  voluntate viri sed ex deo nati sunt.

Who were born not of blood nor of
  the will of the flesh, nor of the will
  of men, but are born of God.

Tertia pars:

Et verbum caro factum est, et
  habitavit in nobis.

And the word was made flesh and
  dwelt among us.

Et vidimus gloriam eius, gloriam
  quasi unigeniti a patre, plenum
  gratie et veritatis.

And we have beheld his glory, glory
  as of the only son of the father,
  full of grace and truth.

Just as Josquin had previously built the sentence conclusion through an increase in voice parts from two to three, so here he increases from three to four. The four-voice cadence, then, should be splendid. However, just at the cadence point, Josquin drops the tenor and uses the same pitch in the three remaining voices, yielding a curiously hollow sound. The tenor and bass have a tag ending before beginning the next sentence. Here Josquin appears to be making a musical statement about the nature of God's creation of all things (through the pervasive motive tossed among all four voices), and the emptiness of anything brought into existence without God (by the hollow, incomplete cadence points).

Not only does Josquin use musical complexity to correlate with the text, but he also restrains the music to allow the text primacy. For the final sentence in the *prima pars* Josquin begins with his customary duet for the text's first phrase. He does not repeat the text (nor, of course, the melodic idea), but in a heightened state of urgency moves on through the text. He adds the two upper voices for the second phrase, thereby creating a solid four-voice texture for the first time in this piece, highlighting the importance of the phrase "and that life was the light of humanity." The significance of this textual phrase is further underscored by the passage's fairly static melody. It is as though Josquin wants to place this text as direct, proclamatory speech. Throughout this piece Josquin's attention to the accented text syllables is impeccable, but here his simple treatment of the text is particularly noteworthy. The limited melodic activity heightens the simple rise at "hominum," shown in example 4. It appears that for Josquin, in this text, God's connection to humankind is crucial.

Josquin continues his treatment of the text by setting the next phrase, "and the light shines in the darkness," with pervading imitation that cascades through all four voices, each one dropping out as it completes the phrase so as to thin the texture after the central, previous phrase. He concludes this section by returning to the full, four-part texture for the final phrase, "and the darkness did not comprehend it," with the two upper and lower pairs of voices in imitation of one another. To effectively conclude this section, he repeats the text phrase and moves the beginning of the previous soprano/tenor motive to the alto and bass, finally repeating it one more time in the tenor and bass voices. In both phrases the lower three parts cadence together, while the soprano voice carries through the cadence. This carrying over at the final cadence provides an opportunity for the tenor and the bass to

Example 4: Josquin, "In principio erat verbum" (mm. 50–54)

[musical notation]

et vi - ta e - rat lux ho - mi - num, et lux

et vi - ta e - rat lux ho - - - mi - num, et

et vi - ta e - rat lux ho - mi - num, ho - mi - num,

et vi - ta e - rat lux ho - mi - num,

join with a restatement of the closing words. Together with the gently curving, descending melodic shape in the soprano, this restatement gracefully rounds out the *prima pars*.

In the motet's remaining *partes* Josquin carries on his meticulous presentation of the scriptural text. The *secunda pars* begins as did the *prima pars*, namely with paired duets, and culminates with the revelation of "the man sent from God," named as John (again with full four-voice texture). The next phrase includes the curious repetition of the word "testimonium." In English two different words are generally used here in order to avoid the repetition, but Josquin uses the repetition to his advantage. Although a new text phrase normally warrants a new melodic phrase, here—although the two words are taken from different text phrases—Josquin links them by musical repetition, not of the entire phrase, but only of "in testimonium."

Sometimes Josquin seems insistent on making a musical-textual point. A particularly significant moment occurs beginning in m. 118. Here Josquin's text is in mid-sentence in this passage: "He was not the light, but he came to bear testimony to the light. The true light that enlightens all humanity was coming into the world." For the next eighteen measures Josquin repeats the simplest of figures—a three-note rise in the soprano and alto over a repeating bass line.[6] Through the changing tenor line, Josquin maintains forward progression. With the repeated

---

6. I am grateful to Herbert Kellman for his generosity in sharing his helpful insights into Josquin's musical rhetoric.

figure, Josquin grabs our ear and will not let go until he has made his point. What point is that? We remember that in the *prima pars* Josquin focused on the passage about the relationship between God and humankind ("and that life was the light of all"). Similarly, here he has singled out this passage about the true light that is coming into the world. By combining these points of emphasis, Josquin creates a musical exegesis of the opening of the Gospel of John in order to theologically underline that God's purpose in coming into the world is to enlighten humankind.

The third passage to which Josquin gives special attention is the text "And the word became flesh." Since these are the opening words of the *tertia pars,* Josquin does not need to draw additional attention to the phrase. Yet he uses the special technique of setting the text in long notes of equal rhythm in all four voices, as had become customary in the fifteenth century, to allow the words "Jesus Christ" or other very holy words to stand out for the listener's contemplation. In this case Josquin holds up for our meditation the word becoming flesh as the most holy mystery.

Looking back over Josquin's setting of the beginning of the Gospel of John, we see much more than a choral work of exquisite beauty. In his rhythmic patterns, the composer is attentive to the nuanced patterns of the spoken language. He weaves all four voices equally in and out in a grand design, creating musical windows as voices drop out and emphasizing climactic moments by thickening the texture. Beyond this, moreover, Josquin wants to drive home a theological point. All three emphasized passages are directly connected to the fact and purpose of the incarnation. Josquin is not satisfied with merely conveying text; if we have ears to hear, he clarifies the text with the music, transcending the simple notes and syllables on the page. The piece epitomizes the Renaissance ideals of balance and restraint, and magnificently attends to the text's linguistic structure. Above all, the motet helps us to understand, through music, the marvelous message of God's taking on our human nature in order to enlighten the world.

Senfl: *Non moriar sed vivam*

The historical times in which Swiss-born Ludwig Senfl (ca. 1486–ca. 1542/3) worked are crucial to understanding his musical contributions. Senfl was a younger contemporary of Josquin and a protégé of Heinrich Isaac, court composer to the Holy Roman Emperor, Maximilian I.

Isaac and Josquin are often compared to one another (both in their own time and now) as the two greatest lights of their age. Senfl continued his mentor's compositional art in his own age.

The circumstances surrounding the composition of "Non moriar sed vivam" are pertinent to our understanding of it. When the 1530 Diet of Augsburg began in great optimism, Senfl had composed for it one of his finest psalm motets, "Ecce quam bonum," a setting of Psalm 133, which begins, "Behold how good and pleasant it is when brothers live together in unity." When the reformers presented an account of their beliefs to the emperor *(The Augsburg Confession)*, the hoped-for reconciliation between the reformers and Rome did not materialize, and the reformers were labeled Protestants and outlaws. When Luther, prohibited from attending by imperial ban, learned of the outcome, he wrote despondently to Senfl requesting a setting of "*In pace in idipsum, dormiam et requiescam*" ("In peace I will both lay down and sleep," Ps. 4:8). He inquired whether Senfl (or someone else) might already have written such a piece and, if so, whether Senfl would be willing to transcribe it and send it to him. Senfl did compose the requested motet, but he also responded by sending Luther a new composition with the text "*Non moriar, sed vivam, et narrabo opera domini*" ("I shall not die, but live, and declare the works of the Lord," Ps. 118:17). Like the previous text, this one also is taken from the body of liturgical chants, which both Senfl and Luther knew well, for Luther even mentions that "In pace" is an antiphon and refers to its chant melody.[7]

In the motet "Non moriar sed vivam" Senfl encodes a word of encouragement to Luther. With hope of reconciliation within the church waning, Luther had begun to question his own efforts. The text Luther had requested expressed this weariness—to lie down and sleep; in other words, to cease from his labors, even to die. Recognizing Luther's despair, Senfl responded not with an entire psalm, but concisely, with a single psalm verse: "I shall not die, but live, and declare the works of the Lord." Since Senfl served Catholic employers in the imperial and Bavarian courts, his open sympathy with the Protestant Reformation would have jeopardized his career. Yet Senfl's implicit word to Luther is not to cease from his efforts, not to lie down and sleep, not to long

---

7. For details on Ludwig Senfl, see Martin Bente, *Neue Wege der Quellenkritik und die Biographie Ludwig Senfls* (Wiesbaden: Breitkopf und Härtel, 1968).

for death, but to live—to get up and return to work—to declare the Lord's works.

The pointedness of Senfl's answer to Luther's request is brought into sharp focus through the single-minded way in which he set the text. Understanding his compositional approach to a text, very different from Josquin's, allows us to hear a truth far deeper than its sheer musical beauty. In liturgical contexts, psalms were typically chanted to simple formulas. Senfl makes his bow in that direction by creating a *cantus firmus* (a melody upon which the piece is based) of a decorated version of the eighth psalm-tone melody. Senfl then organizes the music so that this *cantus firmus* is stated once in each of the four voices consecutively, moving from the highest voice to the lowest. The other three voices are freely composed around it, with the melody set apart by moving slightly more slowly than the surrounding voices. Since motet composition customarily called for a correspondence of one musical phrase to one textual phrase, the result would be great redundancy, since the entire text is limited to only eight words.

Instead, Senfl uses pervading imitation sparingly. He begins the piece imitatively, with the lower three voices introducing an opening motive. When the last voice enters (the topmost voice), this motive is revealed in its fullness as the opening of the psalm-tone *cantus firmus*. Even in the imitative measures between the third and fourth statements of the *cantus firmus,* he is sparing in his use of imitation, which is derived from the second half and takes place only between two voices.

Throughout the remainder of the piece, the composer keeps it moving forward in a single large gesture. The free voices (that is, the voices that do not bear the *cantus firmus* at the moment) support and surround the *cantus firmus* with a delicate contrapuntal fabric, often employing parallel thirds. Senfl avoids strong cadential points until he reaches the end of the piece. The cadence points concluding each statement of the *cantus firmus* are obscured because the free voices, rather than cadencing with it, spin their accompanying counterpoint further, overlapping with the beginning of the next *cantus firmus* statement.

This brief examination of two motets by Josquin and Senfl reveals differences in the composers' styles or tendencies, summarized below in example 5. Both composers used their respective compositional techniques to communicate more strongly their understanding of the text. Josquin selected a relatively lengthy text, with a complex theological

Example 5: Summary of compositional differences between
Josquin, "In principio" and Senfl, "Non moriar"

Josquin: In principio	*Senfl: Non moriar*
4-voice motet	4-voice motet
historical context = unknown	historical context = known
14 verses (John 1:1-14)	1 verse (Ps. 118:17)
no *cantus firmus*	*cantus firmus* (psalm tone formula)—placed consecutively in all four voices
division into three *partes*	no division into *partes*
extensive use of imitation	limited use of imitation
open texture (1 or more voices frequently resting)	thicker texture (typically all four voices are singing simultaneously—short rests in voices)
careful hierarchy of cadences	cadence points obscured until final cadence
meticulous attention to word accent	word accent in free voices less important

point that could easily have been lost in a lengthy motet in three *partes*. By using particular compositional features, however, he was able to stress certain textual phrases and thus speak to attentive ears. On the other hand, Senfl, intending to communicate a single, straightforward point, used certain compositional techniques to retain sharp focus without redundancy. The characteristics are consistent with each composer's overall compositional preferences, which are quite different. Yet we see an important, fundamental similarity: both composers show their intention to communicate a truth deeper than their own compositional preferences. Both are communicating ideas that they have drawn from the texts.

The concern for communication of the text is a Renaissance rather than a medieval characteristic. Consequently, although Josquin and Senfl differ greatly in their compositional language, both reveal themselves to be composers influenced by their concern for the word—a characteristic of Renaissance humanism—and for their proclamation of the Word. Josquin and Senfl give voice to a musical exegesis of their texts. The degree to which we understand the historical context and the compositional devices of these motets, however, affects the degree to which we can discern the composer's voice proclaiming the Word in our midst.

Seventeenth-Century Motet

Schütz: *Sicut Moses*

While Josquin and Senfl perfected different ways for their music to communicate the text, Heinrich Schütz (1585–1672) sought to communicate musically beyond the text. Throughout the sixteenth century the humanist interest in language had inspired composers to seek additional musical ways of expressing text. One of the new techniques composers developed was text painting, where the meaning of a particular word (or small group of words) was expressed in musical onomatopoeia. For instance, the word "fly" might be set in quick, running notes or "sorrow" in strong dissonance. While this technique was limited to expressing individual words or short phrases, it was sometimes combined with other techniques—including ones we have already seen in the music of Josquin and Senfl—to effectively convey the textual sense. This technique of text painting is one of the important elements in Heinrich Schütz's motet "Sicut Moses."

A second development was a textural change with the addition of a basso continuo—a supporting accompaniment. The addition of a continuo part affected solo and duet sections perhaps most strongly. In Josquin's writing, where duets have the open, airy sound of two voice parts without additional harmonic support, the composer must carefully handle the counterpoint between the linear, interweaving voice parts. Seventeenth-century composers, however, had adopted a vertical aspect of music, namely harmony, to be background support to melodic writing: here, duet or solo writing was less exposed. Composers experimented with the new textural and harmonic sonorities possible through these new compositional techniques.

Schütz was perhaps the first German composer to gain international fame. In Italy, he mastered new compositional techniques under the champion of polychoral writing, Giovanni Gabrieli, at St. Mark's in Venice, and then brought these new sounds back to Germany. After being named *Kapellmeister* in Dresden, Schütz issued his first collection of music published in Germany, his 1619 collection of psalm settings, *Psalms of David (Psalmen Davids),* for double choir and instruments. With this collection Schütz showed his mastery of the new compositional techniques he had learned from his Venetian mentor. But he did not return again to the grand, polychoral scale until the end of his remarkably long life—with the publication of a second volume of the *Psalms of David* in 1671. While the Thirty Years War raged across Germany from 1618 to 1648, decimating communities and draining finances, including those of the Saxon government, Schütz turned to composing for smaller ensembles. The pieces composed in these intervening years—which include four- or five-voice pieces or works for a smaller number of voices together with one or two instruments—witness to the reduced, and sometimes meager, musical forces available to him during the war years.[8]

"Sicut Moses" is one of twenty-two Latin motets appearing in Schütz's 1625 *Cantiones sacrae*. This motet's text is from the Gospel of John: "As Moses lifted up the serpent in the wilderness, so must the Son of Man be lifted up, that all who believe in him shall not die, but may have eternal life" (John 3:14-15). Although some of the pieces in the *Cantiones sacrae* are set in multiple *partes,* this piece consists of only a single sentence. Since Schütz did not use a *cantus firmus,* he was able to freely create his own melodic material. Throughout the motet the composer displays his mastery of counterpoint. In keeping with the conventions of motet writing, which had developed through the fifteenth and sixteenth centuries, Schütz used the practice of one musical phrase corresponding to one textual phrase, with most of these phrases treated imitatively. By doing this, he reinforced the text's grammatical structure so that the text could be more clearly understood. This overall polyphonic fabric allows the homophonic moments to stand out in stark and effective contrast.

Schütz's effort to communicate musically beyond the words is clear in his text painting. Each phrase of "Sicut Moses" is given in italics in example 6 with a brief description of its compositional technique and its English translation.

Schütz begins the motet with an imitative duet between the soprano and tenor voices. The bass and alto voices join the same musical idea two measures later. Grammatically, the text's opening phrase contains the sentence's dependent clause, and Schütz differentiates between its subject and verb. The subject portion (*"sicut moses"*) is shaped solely by word accent, with accented syllables on higher pitches and longer note values. Curiously, Schütz often places a rest between the two halves of the text phrase. A grammatical separation would be incorrect, but hav-

---

8. For biographical information on Heinrich Schütz, see Hans Joachim Moser, *Heinrich Schütz,* trans. C. F. Pfatteicher (St. Louis: Concordia, 1959).

Example 6: Text phrases and techniques in Schütz, "Sicut Moses"

Phrase	Text	Description	Translation
Phrase 1	*Sicut Moses*	word accent	As Moses
	Serpentem in deserto exaltavit,	direct, rising line	lifted up the serpent in the wilderness
Phrase 2	*ita filium hominis*	word accent	so the son of man
	oportet exaltari	quick, circular rising motive	must be lifted up
Phrase 3	*ut omnis, qui credit in eum*	homophonic texture	that all who believe in him
Phrase 4	*non pereat,*	short motive followed by rest constructed according to word accent	shall not die
	sed habeat	homophonic texture	but have
	vitam aeternam	short descending motive coupled with rising long-note motive	eternal life

ing the rest between the final "s" of Moses and the initial "s" of *sicut* or *serpentem* makes the sung motive much clearer. The action of the clause ("*serpentem in deserto exaltavit*") provides Schütz with his first opportunity for text painting. He first skips down the interval of a fifth and then creates an upward sweep, driving to the accented syllable of "*exaltavit*," where he turns back to shape the phrase and end gracefully. In doing so he has used the music, in effect, to raise up the serpent from the ground. Through the use of steady quarter-note values (shorter values than encountered at "*sicut moses*"), Schütz presents Moses' action as determined and unhesitating. The culminating effort to raise the serpent is provided in mm. 12–15 (example 7), where the upward sweep begins in overlapping statements in the bass and rises through the entire choir to the soprano, which here does not turn back to end the phrase but continues the upward direction through to the very last note and syllable, where all four voices cadence together.

The text's second phrase contains the main clause of the sentence and consequently is the grammatical balance of the opening dependent

Example 7: Schütz, "Sicut Moses"

clause. As in the opening phrase, Schütz differentiates between the clause's subject and verb. His decision for setting the subject section is again governed by the text's word accent, as it had been in the first phrase. The rising motive in the verb section here is somewhat circular in that it doubles back on itself. Schütz interlaces these two motives toward a cadence where, as in the first phrase, the soprano rises in a direct ascending line. After this cadence Schütz reinforces the lifting up of the Son of Man with one more repetition of the motives and the same direct ascent in the soprano.

The next musical phrase becomes the theological lens for viewing the text. At this point, the evangelist John tells us the purpose for the Son of Man being lifted up: so that all who believe in him shall not die, but have eternal life. Schütz marks this textual event with the single effective use of text painting in strict homophonic texture. Instead of imitation, Schütz paints the universality of Christ's crucifixion by placing the same text and rhythm in all four voices. Although Schütz could easily have given weight to this text portion by lengthening this phrase, he chose not to do so. In fact, this moment's brevity suggests that the crucifixion was a one-time event for the sake of all. This crux occurs at the midpoint of the motet, marking the purpose of Christ's sacrifice and introducing the result of belief in Christ. Although this section is non-imitative and very short, it musically highlights the theological point: salvation by grace through faith.

The remainder of the motet is devoted to the result of Christ's sacrifice—that we not die, but have eternal life (*"non pereat, sed habeat vitam aeternam"*). Although the motive for *"non pereat"* is constructed according to its word accent, Schütz is nonetheless successful at incorporating text painting here. He does so by stating the motive followed by rests in imitation from the top to the bottom of the choir. The result is a dying down of the melodic idea. When the bass finishes the motive, the entire choir has a momentary rest of death before being resurrected in a defiant and homophonic "*non pereat, sed habeat.*"

Schütz reveals the gift of eternal life ("*vitam aeternam*") with two melodic ideas. "*Vitam aeternam*" is set in quick note values to signify life. Over this motive in the lower three voices, he creates a slow ascent spanning the interval of a ninth (the same interval he used at the motet's beginning for "*serpentem in deserto exaltavit*") to portray the unending nature of eternal life. To drive home this text's certainty, Schütz repeats the last phrase with the same motives and techniques. For this last statement, however, he rearranges the voices to offer an ever richer view of eternal life in heaven. He places the long-note ascent in the alto, with the bass foundation in imitation. Meanwhile, the tenor and soprano answer one another with five statements each of the faster "*vitam aeternam*" motive, each successive statement beginning on a higher pitch.

By the time Schütz reaches the final cadence, he has not only musically depicted Moses lifting up the serpent, but also Christ's being lifted up on the cross, with its consequent glimpse of the promise of eternal life, available to all who believe in him. He has done so through carefully applying his era's compositional techniques to the text's grammatical structure and content. Here again is a composer who most assuredly strove to create a thing of beauty according to the highest artistic standards of his time, but who also worked to lead us deeper into a truth expressed through the music.

Translucence and the Historical Fabric

This exploration of a sampling of music from a range of early composers, using a variety of compositional techniques and written during different periods, demonstrates that although we can certainly respond to a piece on the basis of its sheer beauty, each composer translucently communicates a truth that lies beyond beauty. Each approaches his task with a particular *Weltanschauung*, which shapes the music. For the composers' intentions, and thus the music, to become more translucent, we must engage our intellect in order to understand the appropriate historical fabric.

In order to understand this music, we need to meet the music on its own historical terms—to allow the music to retain its qualities of otherness as we are engaged by it. In this approach, we encounter the music in its appropriate historical framework, which allows us to understand not only its musical power, but also its intentional interrelationship of music, text, and worldview. The deeper benefit of careful musical analysis allows us to be engaged by music on its own terms, so that the notes, conventions, and surface beauty become translucent to the work's deeper meaning, allowing us a more substantive conversation with the composer and a more powerful spiritual experience. In the sampling of examples discussed here, an understanding of historical contexts, their musical conventions, and their innovations enables us to understand more fully plainchant's diversity, design, and purpose, as well as the Notre Dame composers' expansion of that repertoire in ways that are the musical equivalent of the cathedral's soaring architecture. Machaut's complex isorhythmic structures take their place alongside the intellectual developments of his day. Josquin and Senfl's efforts at musical exegesis bring a text into focus, and Schütz's musical onomatopoeia projects the meaning of specific words, but also gives a more holistic sense of the text. When we consider music only on the basis of how it affects us emotionally, we become our own conversation partner, failing to hear the other's voice. As in any conversation, we cannot hear the voice of the other when we fill the space with our own. Similarly, if we burden the music with our own ahistorical expectations, we cloud the composer's efforts and thus obscure the translucence of the music. As a result, by our own hand we not only fail to discern the composer's voice but also fail to discern the deeper truth of God's voice, which the composer would have us hear.

4

To Tell the Truth but Tell It Slant

Martin Luther's Theology and Poetry

BRUCE ALLEN HEGGEN

I must lie down where all the ladders start
In the foul rag and bone shop of the heart.

William Butler Yeats
"The Circus Animals' Desertion"

God hath given to some men wisdom and understanding, and to
others, the art of playing the fiddle.

Robert Sarton

Italian novelist Roberto Pazzi makes a passing comment on the "anti-Renaissance moral fervor" of Martin Luther, "who couldn't understand the typically Latin cult of beauty."[1] Pazzi does not offer a basis for his judgment. Perhaps it is Luther's memories of the city of Rome, which the young monk visited on Augustinian business in 1510. But when Luther discussed the journey later in life, the disdain he expressed was not for the art and architecture of the High Renaissance but for a decadence and corruption so pronounced that his contemporary Ignatius of Loyola had been advised not to make the trip. Eyewitness

---

1. Roberto Pazzi, "Why the Next Pope Needs to Be Italian," *The New York Times,* 11 January 2004.

accounts of Luther at the Heidelberg disputation in 1518 offer a different vision of him than that suggested by Pazzi: Luther was young, lean, wore a ring, and held a freshly cut rose which he occasionally looked at, and even sometimes lifted to his nose to smell.[2]

Martin Luther the reformer was never an ascetic after the manner of, for instance, the Florentine Savonarola. Luther valued beauty and things of beauty, both in nature and in culture. As Karen Black points out elsewhere in this volume, he especially considered music a "fair and glorious gift of God." Richard Marius suggests that Luther had "little sense of painting or sculpture," but he so esteemed the friendship of Lucas Cranach the elder that the Wittenberg artist was one of the few friends invited to Luther's wedding.[3] Luther also knew the literature both of the Latin and Greek classical writers and of contemporary poets.

It is beyond dispute that Luther's first concern is theological rather than aesthetic. He may even seem, as in his confrontation with the humanist Erasmus, *anti*-aesthetic. But Heiko Oberman observes that Luther's argument with the Dutch humanist serves to differentiate the cause of Erasmus's humanism from that of the Reformation. "The truth," Oberman quotes Luther as writing to Erasmus in 1522, "is mightier than eloquence, the Spirit greater than genius, faith more than education."[4] Luther's assertion does not dismiss Erasmus's concerns; it sets a priority so that faith and salvation are not equated with erudition. Neither does Luther's point dismiss musical, visual, or literary art, nor relegate art to a secondary function. Art is essential to Christian life. Like theology, art may express the truth, bear witness to the Spirit, and communicate and engender faith.

Luther himself might be surprised by this claim. At times he seems to ascribe a more utilitarian function to art, and to literary art in particular. That utilitarian attitude, coupled as it has sometimes been with a too narrow Christology, has tended to foster ideas like Pazzi's that Luther's Christianity does not value art. This position simply cannot be justified by Luther's theology.

---

2. Heiko Oberman, *Luther: Man between God and the Devil*, trans. Eileen Walliser-Schwartzbart (New York: Image, 1992), 326.
3. Richard Marius, *Martin Luther: The Christian between God and Death* (Cambridge: Belknap, 1999), 437.
4. Oberman, *Luther*, 300.

For Luther, art does not save any more than horses or trees—or even theology—can save. Luther's doctrines of sin and Christ forbid that. Yet Luther's Christocentricity is thoroughly grounded in a trinitarian theology of creation and yields a high eucharistic theology, all of which are comprehended in his theology of the cross. Furthermore, Luther's theology is not a system of abstract constructs but is profoundly experiential. Many artists and poets who discuss the creative impulse and disciplines of artistic creativity also speak of experience using a vocabulary strikingly comparable to Luther's description of the human encounter with the living God of judgment and grace. Granted, many modernist and contemporary artists do not identify their experience as an engagement with the God of Christian faith. Nonetheless, fundamental aspects of Luther's theology suggest that theological reflection and artistic creativity share a common root and that art engendered in the whole of human experience may be translucent to light behind darkness, to creative energy on the other side of tragedy and despair, and to the source of joy in the world. Art is not ancillary to theological discourse. It is an alternative medium of communicating the judgment and grace of human-divine encounter; it is revelatory, and it shapes Christian imagination and the Christian life.

The Place of "the Poets" in Luther's Writings and Conversation

In his record of Luther's *Table Talks,* Veit Dietrich reports that when young Luther entered the Augustinian monastery at Erfurt, he took with him only his copies of the Latin poets Plautus and Virgil.[5] (Some biographers add that he also brought with him his lute, making of Luther a worthy role model for every seminarian who ever began theological studies with a book of poems in one hand and a guitar in the other.) As the Reformer advanced in biblical and theological studies, he never left poetry behind. In the famous note written on his deathbed, he refers not only to Christ, John the Baptist, and the apostles, but also to Virgil and Cicero[6]—the literature that had been a part of his life since

---

5. Martin Luther, *Luther's Works,* ed. Jaroslav Pelikan and Helmut T. Lehmann, 55 vols. (St. Louis: Concordia; Philadelphia: Fortress Press, 1955–1986), 54:14 (cited hereafter as *LW*).

6. *LW* 54:476.

grammar school. As a scholar at the University of Erfurt in the first decade of the sixteenth century, Luther had been steeped in the classics. John Todd points out that after Luther completed his bachelor's degree he began a study of the quadrivium, which was an "academically rigorous study of all that was known," including music, astronomy, arithmetic, and geometry, as well as "classical authors, long sequences of whose work he had off by heart, due to his remarkable gifts of memory. Throughout his life he could quote easily from Virgil, Plautus, Ovid, and Livy; and he read at the time also Juvenal, Horace, and Terence."[7] Todd suggests that Virgil in particular became for Luther not simply the object of a classicist's scrutiny but a source of aesthetic pleasure, much as were "music and the love of ceremony," and that when as a monk he became familiar with the Psalms, he consistently measured them against the cadences of Latin poetry.[8]

Luther's lectures on the Bible are rich with allusion to the Greek and Roman poets.[9] By and large he judges them inferior to the holy Word of the God of Israel. According to his lectures on Psalm 111, the greatest poet is the Holy Spirit,[10] presumably not because the language of the Spirit of God the Creator is limited to Hebrew, but because in Hebrew the Spirit speaks more transparently. Nonetheless the Greek and Roman writers serve Luther in a variety of ways.

Luther uses the poets for exegesis, finding common themes in biblical and classical literature to compare and evaluate. He compares the spontaneity of Laban's guilt at the flight of Jacob with the guilt of Orestes tormented by the Furies for the murder of Clytemnestra.[11] Descriptions of the world of Greek and Latin classics illuminate his biblical descriptions of the ancient world: Cain's inadequate sacrifice to God is illustrated by the sacrifices found in Virgil and Homer.[12] Poetry illustrates compassionate evangelical claims: Luther refers to Virgil's Eighth Eclogue to demonstrate Lot's innocence in the matter of his incest with his daughters, "For people in love are really out of their mind and invent dreams."[13] Greek and Roman poetry also illustrates the world's

---

7. John Todd, *Luther: A Life* (New York: Crossroad, 1982), 18.
8. Ibid., 21, 35.
9. Ibid., 21.
10. *LW* 13:351.
11. *LW* 6:78.
12. *LW* 1:247.
13. *LW* 3:308.

condition apart from the gospel: Luther speculates that Abraham, in his godly greateartedness, must have learned of Lot's plight and taken him and his family in. Luther then suggests that those of "lascivious mind" who insist on judging Lot harshly should forget the Bible and "read Ovid, Martial and the like" instead.[14]

Luther found other aspects of the study of Graeco-Roman literature useful. Knowing classic prosody guided his rhetorical study of the texts: scanning Hebrew and Greek lines illuminated the Hebrew line's rhetorical particularity; the unity of Graeco-Roman poems of varying length led him to consider the literary integrity of Hebrew texts. He considered the study of metaphor significant, not only for recognizing metaphor in Hebrew poetry, but in theological reflection on the Eucharist. When referring to the poets Luther is sometimes inaccurate: he generally quotes his sources from memory and sometimes attributes to Ovid a line from a Horatian Ode or simply twists a line in order to make it serve his theological purpose. He is willing to manipulate the texts of Greek and Latin poets in other ways, too, such as borrowing epithets from Virgil and Horace to argue against Erasmus ad hominem.[15] But writing about educational reform in his "Instruction to the Visitors of Parish Pastors," he names Plautus, Terence, Virgil, and Ovid as essential for students.[16]

A cultured person of faith, Luther wrote hymn texts, sang, and performed music on the lute. He composed a respectable motet, admired the music of Josquin des Prez,[17] and, as Kathryn Pohlmann Duffy points out in her essay, exchanged correspondence with Ludwig Senfl, a contemporary Catholic composer whose music he admired. He was the friend and subject of the painters Lucas Cranach, senior and junior. This is not to praise Luther too highly in his love of literature, music, and art. What we know of Luther's lectures on the Bible is only the record of notes taken by his students, and modern editors are not always certain whether any specific reference to the poets was offered by Luther himself or by the note-taker who also knew the Greek or Latin source.[18] Because the whole educated culture was fluent in the classics,

---

14. *LW* 3:312.
15. For example, *LW* 33:17, 33.
16. *LW* 40:316–20.
17. *LW* 54:130.
18. Jaroslav Pelikan, "Introduction," *LW* 1:x.

phrases from classical texts had become buzzwords just as phrases from TV shows have become part of our popular parlance: Luther repeats certain phrases over and over with little more apparent significance than as a rhetorical flourish.

Luther's attitudes toward classical poetry are not typical of traditional Christian thinkers' views. Even among Italian Renaissance humanists, reading pagan literature was controversial. From Christianity's beginning, Christian thinkers had been ambivalent about the writers from antiquity. Jerome, for instance, admired Virgil's poetry but mistrusted the great poet's paganism.[19] Nonetheless a strong tradition had developed insisting that "only mischance prevented Virgil from dying a Christian."[20] From early on Virgil's fourth Eclogue was read as a prophecy of Christ's birth echoing that of Isaiah 9.[21] In the twelfth century an anonymous Parisian poet portrayed the apostle Paul weeping at Virgil's tomb in Naples: "What would I have made of you, greatest of poets, had I found you alive."[22] But at the dawn of the Italian Renaissance Petrarch was at the center of controversy about the use of Greek and Roman literature. Petrarch cited Augustine and Jerome in defense of his method of reading it.[23] In 1408 the Bishop of Ravenna countered to the late Petrarch's admirers that "a Christian would do better to till the land than to read pagan authors."[24] Ambivalence about the value of Greek and Latin pre-Christian literature continued well into the Reformation era among both Protestants and Catholics.[25]

Luther knew and valued Latin and Greek poets, and his influence over contemporary cultural currents included the promotion of literature. In Luther's time Petrarch's influence was apparent in the Netherlands and England, but no German was producing literature that modern

---

19. *The Oxford Companion to Classical Literature*, ed. M. C. Howatson, 2d ed. (Oxford: Oxford University Press, 1989), 305, 595 (cited hereafter as *OCCL*).

20. *OCCL*, 595.

21. T. S. Eliot, "Virgil and the Christian World," in *On Poetry and Poets* (New York: Farrar, Straus and Cudahy, 1957), 136.

22. *OCCL*, 595.

23. Anthony Levi, *Renaissance and Reformation: The Intellectual Genesis* (New Haven: Yale University Press, 2002), 86.

24. Ibid., 89.

25. Scott M. Manetsch, "Psalms before Sonnets: Theodore Beza and the *Studia Humanitatis*," in *Continuity and Change: The Harvest of Late-Medieval and Reformation History: Essays Presented to Heiko A. Oberman on His Seventieth Birthday*, ed. Robert J. Bast and Andrew C. Gow (Leiden: Brill, 2000), 400.

scholars would consider "recognizable as 'Renaissance Literature'":[26] one finds verses by the *Meistersinger,* Hans Sachs, and hymns by, among others, Ulrich von Hütten and Luther himself. The great poet of sixteenth-century Germany is the hymn writer and translator of the Bible, Martin Luther. In 1523 he wrote to a young humanistic poet, Eobanus Hessus, to congratulate him on a book of poems, the *Captiva,* which had praised Luther. Luther protested the accolades, praised Hessus for his artistry, disclaimed his own artistic merit, and then stressed the place of humanistic studies in Reformation theology:

> without the knowledge of the [Humanistic] studies, pure theology can by no means exist. . . . There has never been a great revelation of God's Word unless God has first prepared the way by the rise and flourishing of languages and learning, as though these were forerunners, a sort of [John] the Baptist. . . . Urge your young people at my request (should that have any weight) to study poetry and rhetoric diligently.[27]

"Instruction and Delight": The Craft of Poetry and the Problem of Christian Art

While Luther's estimation of classical Greek and Roman literary art, as well as that of his contemporaries, was positive, it also seems utilitarian. His subordination of literary art as instrumentally "in service of the gospel" partly reflects Luther's assertion of the supremacy of Scripture as God's self-revelation in written form, in light of which all created things, including philosophy and poetry, are recognized as fallen.[28] The ancient writers themselves also hinted at art as "utilitarian" and "merely entertaining." In the *Ars Poetica,* from which Luther quoted, Horace tells his readers that the purpose of poetry is "to instruct or else to delight."[29] Horace's guidelines for a poet's creation of good literature are classic, and still used by teachers of poetry. But Horace makes no claims for poetry like those made for Greek epic and dramatic poetry of the sixth and fifth centuries B.C.E., such as tragedy's cathartic power or comedy's ability to lighten the heart. Horace focuses almost entirely on

---

26. James Grantham Turner, "Literature," in *A Companion to the Worlds of the Renaissance,* ed. Guido Ruggiero (Oxford: Blackwell, 2002), 366.

27. *LW* 49:34.

28. Todd, *Luther,* 21.

29. *The Epistles of Horace,* trans. David Ferry (New York: Farrar, Straus and Giroux, 2001), 175.

craft as the formal aspects of poetic composition, so that *poiesis,* or "making," risks becoming little more than "carpentry," as W. H. Auden once put it. It is not surprising that Luther might value literature as entertainment and as preparation for the gospel, but would not claim more for it than do the poets themselves.

Auden, the brilliant twentieth-century poet, was a Christian who explained the relationship between Christian faith and literary art in a way that is, at best, overtly utilitarian. His position is the more interesting because he learned neo-orthodox Christianity from Paul Tillich and Reinhold Niebuhr, who in turn relied upon the early twentieth-century renaissance in Luther scholarship. One hears Lutheran accents in Auden's discussion of the relationship between Christianity and poetry. Yet his final position cannot be supported by Luther's theology. In his essay "Christianity and Art," Auden claims that the relationship is difficult because, on one hand, Christian faith is an obstacle to art, and on the other, art does not serve faith without compromising itself. He doesn't believe that there is a Christian art any more than there is a Christian science or a Christian diet, but only "a Christian spirit in which an artist or scientist works or does not work."[30] The latter point is helpfully suggestive, but he goes on to establish artificial categories and confuse them when he suggests that the artist for whom the sacred is self-evident would prefer to be a polytheist, a pagan, rather than a Christian:

> No artist or scientist, however, can feel comfortable as a Christian; every artist who happens also to be a Christian wishes he could be a polytheist; every scientist in the same position that he could be a philosophical materialist. And with good reason. In a polytheist society, the artists are its theologians; in a materialist society, its theologians are the scientists. To a Christian, unfortunately, both art and science are secular activities and therefore small beer.[31]

Here Auden seems to support Luther in giving Christian theology primacy over art. But it is a surprising statement from a poet who so compellingly carved some of the basic ideas of twentieth-century neo-orthodox Christianity in verse, as he did in his long poem, "For the Time Being." Several lines illustrate the theological issue:

---

30. W. H. Auden, "Postscript: Christianity and Art," in *The Dyer's Hand and Other Essays,* ed. Edward Mendelson (New York: Vintage, 1989), 458.
31. Ibid., 456.

> We who are about to die demand a miracle.
> How could the Eternal do a temporal act,
> The Infinite become a finite fact?
> Nothing can save us that is possible:
> We who are about to die demand a miracle.[32]

This fragment shows Auden's poetic skill, but the lines also indicate a religious need: a miracle. But in "Christianity and Art" the miracle is a constraint for the artist:

> The incarnation, the coming of Christ in the form of a servant who cannot be recognized by the eye of flesh and blood, but only by the eye of faith, puts an end to all claims of the imagination to be the faculty which decides what is truly sacred and profane.... The contradiction between the profane appearance [of the pagan god appearing on earth in disguise] and the sacred assertion is impossible to the imagination.[33]

Auden's distinction between the "eye of faith" and the "eye of flesh and blood" means that for the Christian artist that before which the imagination feels sacred awe and the way that the imagination may express it is rigidly, even painfully, delimited by orthodoxy.

The tension of artistic creativity and religious experience, and the theological presuppositions Auden uses to undergird that tension, surface in his 1940 sonnet "Luther." The poem begins ominously, "With conscience cocked to listen for the thunder, / He caught the Devil busy in the wind." Living in a God-forsaken world, Auden's Luther looks for a way to prevent the "disaster" that comes from sin and human "error" but is convinced that, as Luther himself would put it, neither "flesh" nor "the world" can help. Then comes the great *theological* insight:

> "...All Works, Great Men, Societies are bad.
> The Just shall live by Faith..." he cried in dread.
> And men and women of the world were glad,
> Who'd never cared or trembled in their lives.[34]

In a sense, Auden has gotten Luther right: the reformer was looking for God's grace to ease a dread not felt by every contemporary. Oberman

---

32. Auden, "For the Time Being," in *Collected Poems*, ed. Edward Mendelson (New York: Random House, 1991), 353.

33. Auden, "Postscript," 457.

34. Auden, "Luther," in *Collected Poems*, 301.

suggests that Erasmus, too, simply did not understand this aspect of Luther, nor did many of the emerging bourgeoisie of the new urban centers of Switzerland, the low countries, and England.[35] But Auden's lines, "Flesh is a silent dog that bites his master, / The world a still pond in which its children drown," present much the same caricature of Luther as does Pazzi's claim that Luther was an "anti-worldly moralist." It is true that Luther's writings can suggest such positions. Wilhelm Pauck quotes a passage from Luther in which a dry leaf rustling speaks the wrath of God:

> There is nothing more worthless and more despised than a dry leaf.... But there comes a time when its rustling will scare man and horse, spike and armor, kings and princes.... We do not fear God's anger.... But we can be scared and frightened by the anger of an impotent dry leaf, and the rustling of such a leaf can make the world too narrow for us and become a wrathful God to us.[36]

This, however, is not the full extent of Luther's thought on the world, and not the final point of a developed position. Auden, like many, has focused on Luther's theology of guilt and forgiveness at the expense of Luther's theology of creation. "All Works, Great Men, Societies" are not "bad" but fallen; riddled with sin, but not inherently evil. According to his Small Catechism explanation of the first article of the Apostles' Creed, Luther's dreaded world is God's creation and the arena of God's continuing providence. It is a place of danger, but also under God's protection, and the appropriate human response to God's love is thankfulness and praise.

For Luther, the world is a beloved place of conviviality and beauty. When he goes fishing, a good catch witnesses to God's grace in bountiful creation. Working in the garden, he dirties his hands mucking among the roses he loves. Luther is unabashed about the sexual pleasure he enjoys with his wife, Katherine. He commends music, dancing, and the company of women as antidotes for that dread that so plagues him and others. The world is not a bad place, nor are "all great men" bad, but they are fallen. If one is frightened by silent dogs, still ponds, and dry leaves rustling, it is not the fault of dog or pond or leaf: it is one's fail-

---

35. Oberman, *Luther*, 327.

36. Luther, cited in Wilhelm Pauck, *From Luther to Tillich: The Reformers and Their Heirs*, ed. Marion Pauck (San Francisco: Harper and Row, 1984), 8.

ure of faith to trust God's working in and through them. In Luther's world *all things* are the objects of God's creation and God's redemption, as well as the means by which that redemption is accomplished and the story of that redemption told. Luther refuses to conflate dogs and roses with God, but they are, he writes, the "masks" of God who in their very "dogness" and "roseness" live out their godly vocation of witnessing to—one might say they are translucent to—God's work of judgment and salvation.[37] As Oberman puts it, Luther is not a *moralist* whose imagination is constrained by faith: Luther does not ask, "what does God want *us* to do"; he asks, rather, "what is the *living God doing?*"[38] When this is the question, one is not tempted by the question of whether or not a particular poem, painting, or musical composition is Christian art; one asks instead, "How is the God of creation and redemption at work behind this particular created work of art?" Or one might ask, "How is this poem translucent to God's grace?"

Auden's judgment that for the Christian "art is small beer" suggests a limited understanding of Luther's theology of creation. It suffers as well from a limited Christology. For theological support of his position, Auden looks to the work of the German critic and philosopher Rudolf Kassner. According to Kassner, the idea that God is incarnate in Jesus Christ makes poetry impossible because "the Word being made flesh" fuses "reason and imagination."[39] Poetry, however, depends upon the gulf between reason and imagination. Poetry could be the literary domain of Old Testament prophets because they lived before the unification of reason and imagination in the "God-man" Jesus. That the God-man writes nothing suggests that the time of the need for poetry, with its metrical structures and fictions, is past: according to Kassner, parables are prose narratives, not prophetic verse, and more appropriate to the collapse of reason and imagination in the Word made Flesh.

To Auden's credit, he complains that for the sake of poetry, there must be an answer to Kassner's objection to it. That the question plagued Auden for years[40] is curious, for he had named the answer in "For the Time Being." While Kassner has truncated and collapsed the

---

37. Gustaf Wingren, *Luther on Vocation*, trans. Carl C. Rasmussen (Philadelphia: Muhlenberg, 1957), 117, 180, 185.
38. Oberman, *Luther*, 211.
39. Auden, "Postscript," 459.
40. Edward Mendelson, *Later Auden* (New York: Farrar, Straus and Giroux, 1999), 368.

relationship between "Word and flesh" and "reason and imagination," Auden in "For the Time Being" holds "finite and infinite," "eternal and temporal" in dialectical tension, as one might expect of one well-versed in mid-twentieth-century neo-orthodoxy. The answer to Kassner that Auden asks for but cannot find is christological, but it is not a narrow, rigidly articulated "Christomonism." The response to Kassner grows out of a far more profound understanding of God's nature as the God whom one encounters not simply as either the God of judgment or the God of salvation, but the creative and redemptive biblical God who is Trinity. This understanding of God does not collapse reason and imagination into one another, but expands and enlivens both, quickening the element of surprise and newness that is at the heart of all great poetry—and of parables that open the imagination to new possibilities. Oberman points out that when Luther says, "God is wonderful," he does not mean that God is "great" but that "God is astonishing."[41] When Auden's Luther "listens for the thunder" and a "fuse of judgment splutters in his head," even he reacts as much with surprise as with dread.[42]

The Theologian, the Writer, and the Dread Encounter

The place of experience in theology and art further challenges Auden's theological limitation of art and imagination in relation to Christian faith. According to Auden's biographer, while the poet's "radical neo-orthodoxy" was marked by strong personal and social moral rigor, it was not a "personal" religion.[43] The response to Kassner that Auden intuits but cannot articulate is that Christian art, if there is such a thing, does not depend upon concern for the subject of the poem, painting, or musical composition, nor the difference between imagination and reason, nor the distinction between prose rhetoric and poetic techniques, but recognizes that art emerges from the experience of encounter.

The contemporary American preacher and storyteller Frederick Buechner offers insight into the significance of religious experience for art. "At its heart, theology, like most fiction, is essentially autobiogra-

---

41. Oberman, *Luther*, 282.
42. Auden, "Luther," in *Collected Poems*, 301.
43. Mendelson, *Later Auden*, 153.

phy," he writes.[44] Even the most abstract theology, according to Buechner, emerges from a specific human experience that is neither quite
hidden nor quite reported in theological reflection, perhaps because
the experience has seemed less substantial than the propositions used
to explore the experience, or perhaps because the theologian by nature
is given to choose the traditional language and arguments of theological
discourse. In any case a great deal comes between the experience, reflection on it, and the articulation of it. But Buechner continues, there are
others

> —and at their best they are poets, and at their worst artful dodgers—for
> whom the idea and the experience, the idea and the image, remain insep-
> arable, and it is somewhere in this class that I belong. That is to say, I can-
> not talk about God or sin or grace, for example, without at the same time
> talking about these parts of my own experience where these ideas become
> compelling and real.[45]

Ultimately, Buechner's point is not about Christology as "the *Word*
made flesh," and therefore recognizable only in such uncompromising
particularity that it obviates all metaphor. For Buechner, when the Word
becomes *flesh*, it dignifies the capacity of all human flesh to encounter
God and to seek language to speak of the experience. Thus for Buechner, incarnation is not only about Jesus as the God-man, to use Kassner's
language. "I am thinking," Buechner writes, "of incarnation, breath
becoming speech through truth and tongue, spirit become word, the
holy face."[46] For Kassner, incarnation is conceptual. Buechner's understanding of what God does is dynamic, physical, sentient. When Buechner thinks of grace, he thinks of a "power beyond all power," which
"works through the drab and hubbub of our lives to make Christs of us
before we're done." Auden worries about the equation of the imagination and religious experience and claims that "the imagination is a natural human faculty and therefore retains the same character whatever a
man believes."[47] Buechner is concerned for the nature of God and the
human encounter with God. The experience is total, and the imagination is not abstracted from it but involved in it and transformed through

---

44. Frederick Buechner, *The Alphabet of Grace* (New York: Seabury, 1970), 3.
45. Ibid., 4.
46. Ibid., 11.
47. Auden, "Postscript," 459.

it. The alternative to transformation is destruction. Neither transformation nor destruction, Buechner writes, is a "painless" process. Transformation is not distinct from but essential to the making of the artist.[48]

For Luther it is as painful to become a theologian as it is for Buechner to become an artist. Veit Dietrich reports in the *Table Talks* that Luther said so himself. "I did not learn my theology all at once. I have had to brood and ponder over it more and more deeply; my *tentationes* have brought me to it, for one learns only by experience."[49] According to Wilhelm Pauck, *tentationes* are for Luther the faithful person's anguished sense of God's absence. He felt his *tentationes* as demonic attacks, which led him to second-guess his work. Pauck writes that Luther could speak of them as being due in part to a "psychological propensity for melancholy," but by and large he understood them as *Anfechtungen*—attacks from outside himself—and he was not always certain if the attack came from God or from the devil.[50] When they came, his first defense was to appeal to the first commandment, "I am the Lord your God," and to claim the command as promise. Because his *tentationes* always left him more confident in God's grace, Luther ultimately welcomed them. To be alive, according to Luther, is to know one's self always as a forgiven sinner. This is not spiritual stasis but a process of becoming—in other words, of transformation. *Tentationes* kept one from a spiritual arrogance that Luther considered the height of self-deception; thus the greatest of *tentationes* was "to know none at all."[51]

This understanding of the fundamental subjective experience of painful struggle and transformation is not limited to Luther. Ernest Becker identifies *tentationes* and *Anfechtungen* as essential to learning to live as adults without illusions, and traces the concept from Luther through Jakob Boehme and Søren Kierkegaard to William James.[52] Following Kierkegaard, Becker identifies the experience as one of anxiety. According to Becker, Kierkegaard holds that "the school of anxiety leads to possibility *only by destroying* the vital lie of character." Becker points out that for Kierkegaard the experience is terrifying, because "it seems like the ultimate self-defeat, the one thing that one should not do,

48. Buechner, *Alphabet of Grace*, 11.
49. *LW* 54:50.
50. Pauck, *From Luther to Tillich*, 7.
51. Ibid., 7.
52. Ernest Becker, *The Denial of Death* (New York: Free Press, 1973), 88.

because then one will have truly nothing left." But Kierkegaard concludes that it is normal and necessary that the self "be broken down in order to become a self." Becker finds that William James represents the tradition well:

> This is the salvation through self-despair, the dying to be truly born, of Lutheran theology, the passage into *nothing* of which Jacob Behmen [Boehme] writes. To get to it, a critical point must be passed, a corner turned within one. Something must give way, a native hardness must break down and liquefy.[53]

Becker finds this aspect of human religious and psychological development well represented by "the destruction of the emotional armor of Lear, of the Zen Buddhist, of modern psychotherapy, and in fact of self-realized men in any epoch."[54] With this experience in mind Luther writes, autobiographically, "A man becomes a theologian by living, by dying, and being damned, not by understanding, reading and speculating."[55] It is also in the spirit of Buechner to say "living, dying, and being damned" makes the artist.

"Living, Dying, Being Damned": The Prime Element of the Poet's Craft

Other modern theorists discussing what makes a poet echo Luther, Buechner, and Becker in their understanding of what makes a theologian, an artist, and an adult without illusions. Though American poet Edward Hirsch does not use Luther's words, "living, dying, and being damned," his writing on poetry repeatedly speaks of deep human experience as fundamental to poetic creativity. In "The Work of Lyric: Night and Day," Hirsch presents five aspects of poetry in light of a set of *horae canonicae* from one's predawn waking until one's late-night return to sleep.[56] Like all typologies, his is arbitrary, but it is useful because each category represents one aspect of the whole human experience. The stakes he sets for the "work of poetry" are high:

---

53. William James, *Varieties of Religious Experience: A Study in Human Nature* (New York: Mentor, 1958), 281, quoted in Becker, *Denial of Death*, 88.

54. Becker, *Denial of Death*, 88.

55. Cited in Douglas John Hall, *Lighten Our Darkness: Toward an Indigenous Theology of the Cross* (Philadelphia: Westminster, 1976), 117.

56. Edward Hirsch, "The Work of Lyric: Night and Day," *The Georgia Review* 57/2 (Summer 2003): 369.

> Poetry begins and ends in silence. It commences in darkness and speaks to vast reaches of night, to mortal panic and fear, to the infinite spaces. It is language in action against time, against death, language that talks back to oblivion. It faces effacement with a human image. The work of lyric is to confront the void with *poiesis,* which is to say, with human making.[57]

Clearly, poetry for Hirsch is *not* "small beer." Nor is poetry theology as articulated in classic discourse. But poetry does more than delight. Hirsch ascribes to poetry an instructive task that is profoundly theological, one that Luther might not have expected of poetry, but one that the theologian who so struggled with God would appreciate.

Hirsch identifies five categories that he sees as the "day's work of the poem": the "Dawn Song," "The Morning of the Poem," "The Afternoon of the Poem," the "Sundown Poem," and "A Clear Midnight." Hirsch uses the categories to delineate differences in tone and subject matter in a variety of poems, but they are also useful for exploring the relationship between poetry and Luther's theology. The "Dawn Song," or *aubade,* is the poem of awakening from sleep, of coming into individual consciousness, of growing from silence into speech.[58] Because it is also the poem of taking leave from the lover with whom one's individuality has been merged, the dawn song holds a sense of anxiety at the potential of fading from community into isolation and nothingness. The "Morning of the Poem" is poetry of extroverted joyfulness, a work of praise that "would awaken matter and show us the true face of awe."[59] It is poetry of Luther's first creedal article, celebrating the work of God in creation, expressing wonder, and giving thanks for divine providence.

"The Afternoon of the Poem" moves, Hirsch writes, from individual to civic consciousness, makes one aware that one's life is social and political, and speaks of work but also skeptically asks questions of reality.[60] Afternoon poems both express human experience as communal existence and speak prophetically of "individualist subjectivity" against "collectivist thinking." Such poems might be considered poems of the second and third articles of the Apostles' Creed, which are concerned, in

---

57. Ibid.
58. Ibid., 370.
59. Ibid., 374.
60. Ibid., 375.

Luther's explanation, with individual sin and evil and restructuring human community in light of God's saving work. Although making poems is solitary work, the poems of morning and afternoon face outward toward the world in celebration and criticism.

In contrast to the morning and afternoon poems, Hirsch's fourth category, the "Sundown Poem" moves back into the poet's subjectivity as the poet enters into the mysteries of night, darkness, and emptiness. At sundown, light is more intense and the shadows longer and deeper. At dusk one still sees, but not clearly. Because sundown is the end of daylight and the workday, the sundown poem may carry a sense of grief or satisfaction or both. But the primary experience of this time is one not of ending and finality, but ambiguity, liminality, potential danger, struggle, and ultimate transformation.[61] "A Clear Midnight," Hirsch's fifth category, is "the moment when lyric poetry, one of the soul's natural habitats, seeks to release something that dwells deeply within us. It seeks to contact the mysteries and shows us its deep kinship with prayer."[62] The characterization is reminiscent of the experience of letting go that follows intense spiritual struggle and that Luther, like Johannes Tauler before him and Jacob Boehme after him, summed up in the German word, *Gelassenheit,* or "relinquishment."

The sundown poem is particularly suggestive for exploring more deeply the relationship of Luther's theology and the poet's creativity. In his discussion of the sundown poem Hirsch explores Federico García Lorca's use of the idea of *duende,* which, according to the early twentieth-century Spanish poet, is "the obscure power and penetrating inspiration of art."[63] Hirsch writes: "For him, the concept of *duende,* which could never be pinned down or rationalized away, was associated with the spirit of earth, with invisible anguish, irrational desire, demonic enthusiasm, and a fascination with death."[64]

In a recent interview, Hirsch identifies a number of characteristics of *duende* that echo Luther's description of the Christian life as one of "living, dying, and being damned."[65] *Duende* is a "spirit of artistic

---

61. Ibid., 378.
62. Ibid., 380.
63. Ibid., 379.
64. Ibid.
65. Donna Seaman, "An Interview with Edward Hirsch," *TriQuarterly* 117 (Fall 2003): 61.

mystery," a troublesome "ineffable force" that the artist finds both "demonic" and "joyful"[66] because in the creative process the artist feels seized by something from outside the self and lifted to a new plane of creative excellence. In this alone *duende* resembles that aspect of Luther's *tentationes* that he called *Anfechtung* and described as being "attacked" from outside himself. And Lorca's *duende,* according to Hirsch, is

> tied to death, to being, metaphorically speaking, in the presence of death. . . . Lorca recognizes that in many great works of art there's an element of mortal panic or fear. There's some sense of our humanness, some sense of our strangeness, and some sense of our mortality. And he thinks that great works of art take their risks by being in the presence of their dark force, which for Lorca, is tied to the spirit of the earth.[67]

Lorca himself dismisses any connection with Luther: "I do not want anyone to confuse the *duende* with the theological demon of doubt at whom Luther, with bacchic feeling, hurled a pot of ink in [Eisenach]."[68] One can understand that an early twentieth-century Spanish Catholic poet might recognize no artistic kinship with a sixteenth-century German reformer. But Luther's *tentationes* are not simply abstract or intellectual "theological doubt." As Becker describes Luther's experience, it is closer than Lorca thinks to the experience of *duende.* Becker writes that education in one's humanity is confrontation with one's own mortality: "As Luther urged us: 'I say die, i.e., taste death as though it were present.'" Becker explains, "It is only if you 'taste' death with the lips of your living body that you can know emotionally that you are a creature."[69] To know one's mortality as a characteristic of sentiency, as Buechner pointed out, is basic to human self-understanding, and both theology and poetry emerge in response to it.

The literary work that most profoundly links mortality and sentiency, theology and poetry, biblical and pagan literature, is the *Divine Comedy* of the thirteenth-century Italian poet Dante Alighieri. In Western literature no poem has described living, dying, and being damned with

---

66. Ibid., 66.
67. Ibid., 67.
68. Federico García Lorca, *In Search of Duende,* ed. and trans. Christopher Maurer (New York: New Directions Bibelot, 1998), 49.
69. Becker, *Denial of Death,* 88.

greater precision of visual detail, emotional clarity, and measured technique than the *Inferno.* The epic journey in which Dante makes his way through hell and purgatory on his way to paradise begins in the middle of the poet's life, when he awakens in a dark woods unable to make his way forward. With Virgil as guide, he enters hell. There he meets both women and men whom he has known in Florence and women and men familiar to readers of the Bible and Greek and Roman literature. Together Dante and Virgil spiral downward through hell's circles until their final confrontation with Satan. It is for Dante a journey of increasingly paralyzing terror—Satan is not of fire but ice—but the pagan poet knows that there is no way to avoid the experience and leads him to the very center of hell in order to move beyond it by moving through it.

British poet Kathleen Raine argues that Dante's experience of descent into hell is every poet's experience and thus the experience out of which every great poem has its genesis. The downward movement she describes is analogous to that of Lorca's *duende,* and she makes the same claim for it as the experience that engenders the impulse to poetic creativity. Also, the epic's precipitous beginning shows the pilgrim Dante experiencing an attack like the *Anfechtung* that gives rise to Luther's theology. But her point is not simply that *The Divine Comedy* is the journey of every *poet,* but of every *person:* it is common to poetry and psychology because "the poet is the explorer, the opener of the way, who ventures, in a state of inspiration, into regions of consciousness which in most of us remain dark and unexplored."[70] As Raine points out, the goal of this journey is not simply awareness of "the hells within." At the point of confrontation with the source of his terror, the place into which Virgil leads Dante is one of "new orientation . . . that involves a new way of seeing even the hells."[71]

This theme is also common to theology. It is doubtful that Luther read Dante. Perhaps he would have found *The Divine Comedy* precious in much the same way that he regarded the work of Erasmus as too artful. He may have rejected it for its scholastic theology. But he would have delighted in Dante's placement of popes and bishops in hell and purgatory. More importantly he may have appreciated Dante's sense

---

70. Kathleen Raine, *The Inner Journey of the Poet and Other Papers,* ed. Brian Keeble (New York: George Braziller, 1982), 32.

71. Ibid., 29–30.

of the soul's struggle as a pilgrimage through terror to joy. Although Luther offers no visual aids to support instruction in *tentationes* and would have had his own cast of characters, he may have recognized Dante's landmarks. Luther's is a theology that does not constrain imagination by dogma but shapes it through experience. For both the poet and the theologian, the way to inspiration from beyond is the breakdown of the self, or the death of self that leads to the new self, which is an aspect of both Luther's *tentationes* and Lorca's *duende*.

Another aspect of Lorca's *duende* that emerges perennially in poetry and surfaces in Luther is that of wrestling. Hirsch observes that *duende* as a demonic force "inevitably inflected the counter figure of the angel." Angels, however, are not simply benevolent or benign, as they appear to be in the New Testament. In the Hebrew Bible Hirsch finds "a much more archaic idea of the angel, as exemplified in the story of Jacob wrestling with the angel." Hirsch finds this story analogous to Lorca's description of the "artist's struggle with the *duende*" and concludes that Jacob serves "metaphorically as the figure of the artist struggling with the dark, creative force." Consequently Hirsch writes "about moments of artistic possession, and encounters with demons and angels as experienced by various artists and writers."[72]

Hirsch's discussion of the inspiring angel with whom the artist wrestles places him in a significant poetic tradition. Emily Dickinson, who had her own quarrels with the God of her family, community, and church, wrote with a gentler voice about the Jacob-angel encounter where "the bewildered Gymnast, / Found he had worsted God!"[73] Herman Melville describes the work of the poet as a struggle, like that of Jacob wrestling in the night, in which a number of oppositions must unite with each other "And fuse with Jacob's mystic heart, / And wrestle with the angel: Art!"[74]

The German-speaking poet Rainer Maria Rilke uses the Jacob story several times, but with more ominous overtones. In "Imaginary Career," he suggests an outline of Jacob's life as one of arbitrariness and ambiguity until, as an adult, in solitude and longing for "the ancient one,"

---

72. Seaman, "Interview," 67–68.

73. *The Complete Poems of Emily Dickinson,* ed. Thomas H. Johnson (Boston: Little, Brown, 1960), 31.

74. Herman Melville, "Art," in *The New Oxford Book of American Verse,* ed. Richard Ellman (New York: Oxford University Press, 1976), 305.

he is stunned as "from His place of ambush, God leapt out."[75] Rilke does not relate an outcome for this match. But in "The Man Watching," an earlier poem that develops the theme, he suggests that defeat at the hands of the divine-demonic stranger is both inevitable and more desirable than victory:

> Whoever was beaten by this Angel
> (who often simply declined the fight)
> went away proud and strengthened....
> Winning does not tempt that man.
> This is how he grows: by being defeated, decisively,
> by constantly greater beings.[76]

Oberman argues that wrestling is also emblematic of the theologian. He applies Rilke's poem "The Man Watching" directly to Luther. Oberman interprets Luther as "Overwhelmed by God, at the mercy of His power," and observes that the Reformer understood himself as "an instrument in the hands of God, whose overpowering wisdom is hidden in history."[77] The application is apt, and absolutely related to the issue of Luther's understanding of God and the encounter with God that leads some to be poets and others to be theologians. According to Pauck, Luther understood God as "the life of every being. He determines everything. He is present everywhere. But he is impenetrable and inscrutable."[78] The power of God as the preserver of all creation is present in all things; the power of God as creator transcends all things. Nothing is closer to a person than God. Yet, Luther writes, "God is an inexpressible being above and beyond all that one can name or think." God, for Luther, is the energizing force that moves all things, "at work everywhere and in all, also in the godless, even in the devil." According to Pauck, it is the will and work of this God "to help the forsaken ones, to justify sinner[s], to resurrect the dead, to save the damned."[79] This

---

75. Rainer Maria Rilke, "Imaginary Career," in *Ahead of All Parting: The Selected Poetry and Prose of Rainer Maria Rilke,* ed. and trans. Stephen Mitchell (New York: Modern Library, 1995), 157.

76. Rainer Maria Rilke, "The Man Watching," in *Selected Poems of Rainer Maria Rilke: A Translation from the German and Commentary by Robert Bly* (New York: Harper and Row, 1981), 105.

77. Oberman, *Luther,* 318.

78. Pauck, *From Luther to Tillich,* 4.

79. Ibid.

is the God to whom, in Luther's understanding, the whole of creation is translucent. It stands to reason that the creative and sensitive artist or theologian whose creative impulse is engendered by struggle with this God who suddenly leaps out will make poems or paintings or music—even volumes of theological discourse—which are also translucent to the wild source of creative energy.

Luther's understanding of God as present and active in the world, engendering both faith and doubt in sensitive and creative theologians and artists who struggle to believe, is breathtakingly far from Kassner's troublesome assertion that the God-man makes poetry difficult. For Kassner the incarnation limits God and tethers poetic imagination.[80] For Luther Jesus is only one of many possible encounters with the God of the Bible. The God who comes in Christ is no less or other than the God of Hebrew Scripture, while Christ is the God of Israel present to men and women of the world in a new way, particularly in the child lying in the manger and the man suspended from the cross. Auden's concern for the significance of Jesus' particularity for Christian faith and for the artist's place in the Christian ethos is appropriate. But Luther's faith is not focused simply on Jesus, but on the God of judgment and grace revealed in Jesus through the power of the Holy Spirit. In other words, Luther's God is the Trinity, dynamically committed to the world, who "plucks up, breaks down, builds and plants" in this earthly place (Jer. 1:10). This activity is most transparent in Jesus—salvation through and in whom is the Trinity's proper work. The God who is Trinity also does God's alien work hidden behind Jesus, who is *translucent* to God. Luther's is the Cappadocian understanding of the Trinity as the dynamic tension of perichoretic interrelationship that, sometimes hidden and sometimes revealed, inspires struggle and spiritual affirmation in both theologians and artists. The theologian or poet who wrestles with such a God might well stand after defeat and walk both humbly and proudly, with new name and with new gifts of naming, blessed and able to bless as well.

Poets have found other ways to describe the intensity of experience that engenders poetry. "If I read a book [and] it makes my whole body so cold no fire ever can warm me I know *that* is poetry," Dickinson famously wrote to her friend and mentor T. W. Higginson. "If I feel physically as if the top of my *head* were taken off, I know *that* is poetry.

---

80. Auden, "Postscript", 459.

These are the only ways I know it. Is there any other way?"[81] Many of
Dickinson's poems also explore the intensity of experience that the poet
must be willing to explore. In poem 1247 she enigmatically conflates
experience, poetry, love, and God: "To pile like Thunder to its close /
Then crumble grand away / . . . This—would be Poetry— // Or
Love—. . . / . . . For None see God and live—."[82] Randall Jarrell also
uses storm language to describe the discipline of opening one's self to
the source of the creative impulse: "A good poet is someone who manages, in a lifetime of standing out in thunderstorms, to be struck by
lightning five or six times; a dozen or two times and he is great."[83] The
metaphor calls to mind the thunderstorm during which a terrified young
Luther determined to become a monk. Luther however counseled that
the Christian *not* seek out such experiences. There is no need for the
Christian to seek out *tentationes* or to wrestle with numinous strangers
in the night because God—or the devil, or *life*—will bring the experience soon enough.

This seems to set Luther at odds with Hirsch, for whom *duende* is
an aspect of the poet's craft and may be cultivated. But Hirsch and
Luther both recognize that the experience can be dangerous. Hirsch
does not "advocate madness" or "giving yourself over to irrational
forces." Nonetheless the experience is for Hirsch at the heart of the mystery of artistic creativity. This dimension of the craft of poetry is, as it
were, a "tapping into" something that one understands is larger than
one's self. Hirsch describes poetry as a "bodily art. . . . It inhabits you. . . .
And I think you feel it taking over." In other words, one is "attacked"
or "possessed." Hirsch continues, "There's a kind of transport in it.
You're taken somewhere else. And this is the root meaning of ecstasy,
to be beside oneself." But the cultivation of this ecstasy is only one aspect of the creative effort. Hirsch claims that there has been a tendency
to place in opposition the dynamic experience that engenders the poem
and the discipline of the craft by which the poem is accomplished. But,
he says, "there's another kind of vocabulary we can bring to this to think
about the way that the working intellect, what Keats called the working
brain, operates in tandem with this demonic force." The artist must be

---

81. Emily Dickinson, *Selected Letters*, ed. Thomas H. Johnson (Cambridge: Harvard University Press, Belknap Press), 208.

82. Dickinson, *The Complete Poems*, 547.

83. Randall Jarrell, *Poetry and the Age* (New York: Knopf, 1953), 148.

"at the service of other forces" while at the same time consciously "controlling one's art."[84] This is the real craft of the poet: to know techniques of which Horace, for instance, writes, and know them so well that when "the lightning strikes" or "the wrestler suddenly leaps out" or when one is caught up in ecstasy or overwhelmed by *Anfechtung* one is not destroyed by the experience but has the technical means by which to shape experience and make of it something new. Auden's friend and contemporary Stephen Spender wrote, "Our ideal was always to make out of experience artifacts—verbal objects as poems or fictions—which within themselves would have transcended their origins whether these were politics or sex or history."[85] Echoing Buechner, Hirsch describes a poem as an "incarnation of the spirit," "a form of verbal materialism" whose world is made of "aspiring sounds, consonants and vowels, black markings on a blank page."[86] From experience the poet uses language molded by discipline to construct an artifact by which others recognize and connect with the poet in a way that transcends time and distance. They may also see the poem as translucent to the source of the artist's disciplined creativity.

The Created Artifact: Translucent to God

Poems that wrestle like Jacob or that emanate from such a wrestling are about encounters with the Holy; they are about, in the language of Tillich, "Being grasped by the Ground of Being." Tillich writes, "In religious experience the Holy—or the ultimate—breaks into our ordinary world. It shapes this world, shakes its foundations, or elevates it beyond itself in ecstasy and transforms it after having disrupted its natural forms."[87] Again, art understood this way is not "small beer." Rather, Tillich observes, it has the power to move and transform the reality of the person who observes it. He illustrates his point with reference to Rilke's poem, "Archaic Torso of Apollo," which concludes, "for [on

---

84. Seaman, "Interview," 68–69.

85. Stephen Spender, "Looking Back in 1994: A New Introduction to *World within World*," in *World within World: The Autobiography of Stephen Spender* (New York: St. Martin's, 1994), xx.

86. Hirsch, "The Work of Lyric," 369.

87. Paul Tillich, "Religious Dimensions of Contemporary Art," in *On Art and Architecture*, ed. John Dillenberger and Jane Dillenberger (New York: Crossroad, 1988), 177.

the surface of this torso] there is no place / that does not see you. You must change your life."[88] Such art is revelatory: it is a translucent medium that mediates grace. At the very least this is because the given artwork is also deeply involved with human experience. Carl Braaten has written, "When the theology and the church address the deepest human questions, they are dealing with the theme of salvation even though the word is never mentioned."[89] This is also true of poetry.

To speak of art this way is to understand it sacramentally as a vehicle through which the nonmaterial holy breaks into our lives. Tillich offers several ways to understand art sacramentally. It is sacramental first of all because, like any created thing, it can be. Tillich writes, "The universe and everything in it both reveals and hides ultimate reality. . . . There is ultimate reality in this stone and this tree and this man. They are translucent to ultimate reality, but they are also opaque."[90] Here Tillich follows Luther and also Nicholas of Cusa,[91] who understand God as beneath and beyond all things, the finite and the infinite within each other. In "For the Time Being," Auden as a poet of neo-orthodoxy puts the question, "How can the infinite become a finite fact?" Tillich and Luther might answer with a play on the words of French poet Arthur Rimbaud: "because they *is!*"[92] According to Braaten the point is essential to Lutheran eucharistic theology: "the finite can contain the infinite" and "the infinite can comprehend the finite."[93] At the 1526 Colloquy at Marburg Luther argued against Zwingli for the "real presence" of Christ in the bread and wine of the Lord's Supper: Christ is present in the bread and wine of the Eucharist because he can be, even as God who is always Trinity is always present, however hidden, in all things, and revealed in the human creature, Jesus.[94]

---

88. Rilke, *Ahead of All Parting*, 67.

89. Carl E. Braaten, *Principles of Lutheran Theology* (Philadelphia: Fortress Press, 1983), 63.

90. Tillich, "Art and Ultimate Reality," in *On Art and Architecture*, 141.

91. Paul Tillich, *A History of Christian Thought: From Its Judaic and Hellenistic Origins to Existentialism*, ed. Carl E. Braaten (New York: Touchstone, 1968), 373.

92. French poet Arthur Rimbaud said, "Je est un autre" ("I *is* an other"). The phrase has become a touchstone for postmodern conversation on the multidimensionality of the individual personality. Cf. Edward Hirsch, "To Wrestle an Angel," in *Responsive Reading* (Ann Arbor: University of Michigan Press, 1999), 176.

93. Carl E. Braaten, "The Person of Jesus Christ," in *Christian Dogmatics,* ed. Carl E. Braaten and Robert W. Jenson, 2 vols. (Philadelphia: Fortress Press, 1984), 1:510.

94. Tillich, *History of Christian Thought*, 260–62.

From this Tillich develops four useful categories to recognize "the religious in art." In each of them he looks for religious content and religious style. By "religious content" he means a portrayal of figures or symbols that are recognizable within the context of a given religious tradition, such as a saint or a cross. By "religious style" he means indication of the encounter with the divine emerging from the depths of the work of art and breaking through its surface.[95] It is instructive to juxtapose these four types with the five categories that Edward Hirsch suggests as the task of lyric poetry. Certain poems from any of Hirsch's categories could meet the conditions for several of Tillich's four types, while Tillich offers language to explain how the poem may be recognized as more or less opaque, translucent, or transparent to the Holy that is breaking through from the depth behind the poem.

In the first of Tillich's four types there is neither religious style nor religious content, though some vitality of life is presented. Tillich suggests Brueghel's "Peasant Dance" as an example of this type. Many of the poems that Edward Hirsch regards as the morning poems that name and celebrate the world might also have neither religious content nor religious style, yet display created vitality.

Art that uses religious style but no religious content is Tillich's second type. No image in the work is recognized immediately as a religious symbol, but the style evokes some energy from beneath the artifact's surface that reflects the artist's transforming encounter with what Tillich calls "ultimate reality" or "the Ground of Being"—or what Luther would call God and what Edward Hirsch would call the demon/angel with whom the artist wrestles. Lorca would say such art has *duende*. Tillich finds this type most frequently in expressionist art but argues that expressionism is not simply a modernist movement in art. Michelangelo's secular sculptures, for instance, also exhibit this style. As for poetry, the *aubade* that hails the dawn and laments the isolation of the one who goes out into the day may express depth of struggle; the morning poem of pure ecstasy may display the transforming depth of wonder; the afternoon poem of work, community, and irony may offer a critique of the world from a deep, raw, wounded place; the poem of transformation and terror at dusk and in darkness will be a poem of religious

---

95. Tillich, "Existentialist Aspects of Modern Art," in *On Art and Architecture,* 92–93.

style, if not of content, and translucent to the creative force with which the artist has struggled.

Tillich's third category, by contrast to the second, is religious in content but not in style. It is, however, what most people think of when they think of religious art, and Tillich recognizes many of the artifacts of piety in this category. Auden has items in this category in mind when he looks into the window of a store selling religious objects and "can't help wishing the iconoclasts had won."[96] Tillich, too, cautions that art that is religious in content but not in style may lead one to be dishonest about the compelling places of anguish in the world—or to miss the places where the Holy is breaking through.[97] Such art may be merely religious, more opaque than translucent. Any of Hirsch's categories will include poetry that is well crafted and uses religious images in order to praise, even without transformative depth breaking through the surface.

The art of Tillich's fourth category exhibits both religious content and religious style. This is art made with recognizably religious images, manifesting the experience of one who has been grasped by God, the Ground of Being, and showing that this experience has been transformative for the artist and for the artist's world. Tillich does not recognize much twentieth-century art as religious both in style and in content. It is his category for the icons of Greek and Russian Orthodoxy, for Michelangelo's "Pietà," and for the Isenheim altar of Mathias Grünewald. From the end of the twentieth century one might add the bronze castings of the sculptor Paul Granlund and music such as the "*Passio*" of Arvo Pärt and Kryzstof Pendereck's "Passion according to Saint Luke." Much literature presents religious content but trivializes it, which is the danger of Tillich's fourth category. The best of twentieth-century religious poetry includes Rilke's "Duino Elegies," T. S. Eliot's "Four Quartets," and "For the Time Being," Auden's long oratorio text, which in spite of the poet's protest does what the poet says a poem cannot do.

The twentieth as a century of unbelief has posed a singular problem for religious art at the beginning of the twenty-first century. Yet for many artists our previous century has also been a time of longing for a

---

96. Auden, "Postscript," 460.
97. Tillich, "Existentialist Aspects," 98, 99.

transcendence that one cannot name. Nearer the beginning of the twentieth century Wallace Stevens wrote, "After one has abandoned a belief in god, poetry is that essence which takes its place as life's redemption."[98] Tillich reflects this attitude when he finds more theological significance in art religious in style but not in content, than he does in art that is religious in content but without religious style. Stevens stands diametrically opposed to the idea that, for the Christian, art is small beer, or to Luther's latent utilitarian attitude toward poetry. Yet Luther's theology warrants recognizing God's work in the art even of those artists who have abandoned a belief in God. Joseph Sittler once said that the reality of a thing may be witnessed to most profoundly by a precise articulation of its absence: "Hunger, unabated, is a kind of testimony to the reality of food. To want to have may be a strange way of having."[99] Emptiness, too, may be translucent to divine reality: consider the paintings of Mark Rothko, the stark and cynical poems of Philip Larkin.

The Poem as Revelation:
Signs of the Presence of Christ

How does one know if the gift—experience and artifact—is of God? Luther struggled with the question. His father, disappointed and angry after the young man precipitously decided to leave the study of law and to enter the Augustinian monastery, had put the question to him. It would be twenty years before Luther could say with confidence that God had been speaking to him from behind the terror that thunder and lightning had occasioned and that had driven him to become an Augustinian monk. Even after considering all the following—(1) Luther's humanistic training, which gave him an affinity and appreciation both for classical and sixteenth-century German poetry, music, and art; (2) how experience that gives inspiration to the artist compares to experience that engenders faith and finds expression in theological reflection; (3) God's creative, providential, revelatory, and transforming presence "in, with,

---

98. Wallace Stevens, *Opus Posthumous*, ed. Milton J. Bates, rev. ed. (New York: Knopf, 1989), 185.

99. Joseph Sittler, "The View from Mount Nebo," in *The Care of the Earth and Other University Sermons* (Philadelphia: Fortress Press, 1964), 87.

and under" creation; and (4) the sacramentality of art—we still have the question whether Luther indicates how art may be recognized as Christian. Luther teaches in his Small Catechism that we know Christ is present in baptismal water and eucharistic bread and wine because God's Word declares he is. Is there a comparable declaring word for a poem or a painting, or for music without words? Two further considerations are key.

Luther attends to individual human experience and the particularity of the incarnated Christ. This demonstrates the influence of Renaissance humanism on his thought and suggests in turn how he may help us understand art as translucent to the glory of God. The Renaissance brought the cult of the individual artist, in contrast to medieval art, which was almost invariably ecclesiastical and anonymously produced. The Renaissance artist sought to develop techniques that moved away from stylized portrayal to represent the artist's object as realistically and even idiosyncratically as possible: trees look like trees, dogs like dogs, and men, women, and children like people from the surrounding village (as they often were). Furthermore, in their particularity they are translucent to something beyond themselves. Michelangelo expresses this profoundly. He understood the human being to be, quite literally, the image of God, and the almost superhuman realism of his "David" and of the Adam on his ceiling in the Sistine Chapel testify to his vision of the individual inhabited by the spirit of God.[100] Luther, too, is preoccupied with the individual alone in the presence of God under judgment and in grace. His lectures on Genesis indicate that he shares Michelangelo's view of the individual as image of God. But Luther had become so overwhelmed by his own sinfulness that even ritual absolution and communal participation in the Eucharist was insufficient to allow him a sense of salvation. As an individual one is born, and as an individual one sins; one stands alone before God in terror of judgment and in need of mercy, and alone one dies. In many assessments of his theology, Luther's understanding of the human being as a fallen sinner has tended to override his amazement at the beauty of Adam and Eve created as image of God. It is as though sin has, in every particular instance, rendered God's creation utterly opaque.

---

100. Paul Johnson, *The Renaissance: A Short History* (New York: Modern Library, 2000), 158.

But as Luther grew to understand salvation as justification by grace—God's righteousness as Jesus' righteousness conferred on the believing sinner because of Christ's loving obedience in death—he grew to understood it individualistically as well: the grace of the individual Christ is given freely to the individual man, woman, child. This is not to say that Luther's theology has no sense of community: his understanding of the church is profoundly communal. But the community consists of individuals in their idiosyncrasy and particularity. As such they were painted by the Cranachs, for whom the actual faces of Luther, Melanchthon, and other Reformers and *Bürghers* of Wittenberg were featured. And the individual in life and in art is translucent to God's creating and redeeming grace.

As an individual the human being is in need of grace and mercy; as an individual Jesus offers—in fact embodies—God's grace and mercy. A striking characteristic of Luther's Christology is that he does not engage in the debates about Christ's person and work that have historically marked christological reflection. Luther simply saw a human being, and a not particularly remarkable human being at that: a helpless infant, a man unjustly executed. Yet this is the human being in whom God is most transparently revealed. This is a statement of trust that echoes Michelangelo's recognition of the human creature as the image of God. The difference is this: one looks at Michelangelo's "David" and is moved to awe by the image of a stunning human being translucent to God's grandeur. One looks with Luther at Jesus and is moved to pity and gratitude by the image of the vulnerable and suffering human being in whom God's passionate love is transparent. *Pace* Pazzi, this may be the greatest difference between the Latin cult of beauty and Luther's— although Michelangelo's work, too, moves one to pity and gratitude as well as awe: consider his "Pietà." Luther's Christology is a humanistic one of biblical realism: the Jesus of Hebrews, "like us in all things but sinless," and Isaiah's "suffering servant." These are not grand human images. A key concept for Luther is that God works "hidden," "under the sign of the opposite." Here Luther's medieval mysticism shows itself: not a mysticism of personal piety or devotion, but of recognizing God hidden "beneath and beyond" a translucent particular, so that even the cross's darkness and the child's helplessness are strangely luminous with God's glory. Luther's eucharistic theology is an extension of his Christology. Again, the attention is on individual particularity: Christ in his uniqueness comes to the woman in hers, to the man in his, in the idiosyncrasy of a particular bit of bread fresh from a specific oven, a glass of wine of a certain vintage, and in a particular place and time that constitutes a community of forgiven sinners living changed lives.

Ironically, the modern poet closest to Luther in focusing on God's earthly particulars is the Victorian Jesuit Gerard Manley Hopkins. Like Luther, he found Christology and eucharistic theology central to his art. Convinced that Luther the Reformer was a heretic, however, he took his theological cues from the late medieval theologian and philosopher John Duns Scotus. What Scotus and Luther have in common is what Scotus called *heccaity*, "this-ness": attention to the particular. In Hopkins's poetry, it comes out in a marvelous, even weird, and often self-conscious idiosyncrasy of line and meter. His preoccupation with this-ness is most apparent in his subjects. In one sonnet, "kingfishers catch fire," "dragonflies draw flame," and "tumbled in roundy wells / Stones ring"; the sonnet builds around the unique action of the specific thing. But unique action is in fact common to all in that each cries, "What I do is me: for that I came!" Then the sonnet turns to become at once both anthropological and christological:

> I say more: the just man justices;
>> Keeps grace: that keeps all his goings graces;
> Acts in God's eye what in God's eye he is—
>> Christ. For Christ plays in ten thousand places,
> Lovely in limbs, and lovely in eyes not his
>> To the Father through the features of men's faces.[101]

In this Christology, Christ is whatever or whoever does what it is that God intends him or her to do. Hopkins's anthropology is akin to Michelangelo's. Both consider the image of God powerful, the more so when the human creature fulfills God's design exactly. But while Michelangelo portrays it as strikingly awesome, not even he identifies the image of God with the Christ of God, as Hopkins so boldly does. Yet Luther, Michelangelo, and Hopkins all attend to the particular—to David, to Christ, to the individual man and woman thirsty for grace, to the kingfisher, to the dragonfly. They also see the individual as more

---

101. Gerard Manley Hopkins, "As Kingfishers Catch Fire," in *The Oxford Authors: Gerard Manley Hopkins,* ed. Catherine Phillips (Oxford: Oxford University Press, 1986), 129.

than what first appears: David is God's image, Christ is God's presence, the bread and the wine are Christ's presence, as are the dragonfly and human facial features. Luther's and Hopkins's theology is metaphorical in the deepest sense: bread and wine are not merely symbols that focus and recollect one's memory of a past event, as they were for Zwingli. They are metaphors: they *meta-phero*, they carry with them and bring into reality something other and deeper and truer than they first appear to be. In their own right they are not changed: David remains David, the kingfisher is always a kingfisher, bread is bread. But each bears—is inhabited by, is translucent to—something beyond itself. As Braaten has pointed out, the "Holy Other" is capable of entering the finite particular: *infinitum capax finiti*.[102] So Hopkins writes, "The world is charged with the grandeur of God. / It will flame out like shining from shook foil."[103]

In addition to the emphasis on profound particularity that poetry and Luther's theology share, Luther's theology of the cross immerses us in deep and honest sympathy for the world. The theology of the cross is the key signature of Luther's theology, and it derives from his recognition that the dying man on the cross must be recognized *under the sign of the opposite* as God's power made perfect in weakness in order to destroy death by dying. In his Heidelberg Disputation of 1518, Luther writes, "A theology of glory calls evil good and good evil. A theology of the cross calls the thing what it actually is."[104] In his quarrel with Erasmus, Luther's commitment was not to style, but to truth. Christian poetry's commitment is the same. Emily Dickinson's poem 1129 comes to mind: "Tell all the Truth."[105]

Art's truth-naming task is both difficult and necessary, and both more difficult and more necessary at the beginning of the twenty-first century than ever before. It is difficult because it is too easy to let an attempt to tell the truth degenerate into a banal or sadistic repetition of data that are as unbearable as naked truth may be, leading to a self-defensive numbing or world-denying frivolousness. Emily Dickinson's admonition to "Tell all the Truth but tell it slant" suggests that the truth is "too bright for our infirm delight":

102. Braaten, *Principles of Lutheran Theology*, 92–96.
103. Hopkins, *The Oxford Authors*, 128.
104. *LW* 31:40.
105. Dickinson, *The Complete Poems*, 506.

> The Truth must dazzle gradually
> Or every man be blind—[106]

Whether delightful or distressful, the point is that the truth told badly—which is to say, the truth told literally rather than metaphorically—is blinding, stunning. This is the difference between good poetry and bad (or even good) journalism. Larry Rasmussen and Walter Brueggemann both write that the theology of the cross, properly understood, is an antidote to numbing because it grounds Christian awareness in the earth and in the body, and invites sensitivity, empathy, weeping for others as well as for one's self.[107]

Like Luther's theology of the cross, poetry that tells the truth aims to move its listeners to love the earth and to weep for others. This is the purpose and power of Hirsch's afternoon poem, the poetry of civic consciousness. Such poems may be cynical and ironic in their willingness to doubt and to second-guess, and to speak of the individual against the collective. They acknowledge, however, that even the individual who works in solitude, as do most artists, is never fully human without community. Literary art as "truth-telling under the cross," expressive of the range of intense feeling, is also what Tillich considered art religious in style, if not always in content. Art that tells the truth about the human situation, but does not simply describe it literally, draws on the deep transforming struggle with some angel (or demon), with the Ground of Being or with God, and transforms that experience into something new: the truth told slant. Tillich considered Picasso's "Guernica" the "most Protestant painting" because, as an expression of the Spanish Civil War's horror, it tells a truth about war that protests war. It transforms war without glorifying it or ignoring its horror. So does poet Paul Celan's *Totenfuge*, which eerily describes the smoke and ashes of the Nazi death camps. Nietzsche said, "We have Art in order that we not perish from the Truth."[108] Or, to paraphrase Luther, "Naked reality, like 'inexpressible majesty,' will crush a person. 'Behold Christ lying on the lap of his young mother.' Behold the dead man on the cross, opaque but radiant.

---

106. Ibid.

107. Walter Brueggemann, *The Prophetic Imagination* (Philadelphia: Fortress Press, 1978); Larry Rasmussen, "Returning to Our Senses: The Theology of the Cross as a Theology for Eco-Justice," in *After Nature's Revolt: Eco-Justice and Theology*, ed. Dieter Hessel (Minneapolis: Fortress Press, 1992).

108. Auden, *Dyer's Hand*, x.

It is there that you see God most clearly."[109] Art that is instructed by Luther's theology of the cross honestly represents the human experience of negation: but it dares this because the artist, like Luther, knows that God's last word is not one of negation. It is translucent to a deeper truth: in Luther's words, "from above or from underneath the 'No' the deeply hidden 'Yes.'"[110] Poetry that tells truth slant "confronts the void," in Hirsch's words, and does "the lyric's work," which is always, finally, a work of hope.

Christian Faith and the Task of Poetry

In the incarnational experience of God in Christ, no human experience has been left untouched by God, and any earthly form can be tapped to mediate God's grace. Luther's theology is informed by his liberal humanistic education, with its attention to individuality and particularity. It is also informed by a profoundly intense religious experience that included the heights and depths of emotion. In the aftermath of the Reformation, however, there was a great distrust of emotion. The iconoclasm of the Genevan reforms included reducing hymn writing to Psalm paraphrases and eliminating musical instruments to support and embellish Christian praise. At the same time in Italy, an aging Michelangelo complained that the reforms of the Council of Trent left little room within Roman Catholicism for support of his dynamic, sensual portrayals of the image of God.[111]

The poet T. S. Eliot felt that most European poetry from Dante until the twentieth century had lacked an "objective correlative"—a phrase that produced the most exact correspondence between image and emotion.[112] The emotional range that Eliot found in Dante's *Divine Comedy*[113] and that one can recognize in Michelangelo's sculpture

---

109. Luther, "Nativity," in *The Martin Luther Christmas Book*, trans. and arr. Roland H. Bainton (Philadelphia: Fortress Press, 1948), 40.

110. Martin Luther, *Day by Day We Magnify Thee: Daily Meditations from Luther's Writings Arranged according to the Year of the Church*, comp. and trans. Margarete Steiner and Percy Scott (Philadelphia: Muhlenberg, 1950), 129.

111. George Bull, *Michelangelo: A Biography* (New York: St. Martin's, 1995), 395–99.

112. T. S. Eliot, "Hamlet," in *Selected Prose of T. S. Eliot*, ed. Frank Kermode (London: Faber and Faber, 1975), 48.

113. T. S. Eliot, *The Varieties of Metaphysical Poetry*, ed. Ronald Schuchard (London: Faber and Faber, 1993), 182, 220.

and frescos—which was also characteristic of the intellectual, emotional, and spiritual vitality of Luther's theology—was restricted through the theological formulations of Lutheran and Reformed neo-scholasticism and Tridentine Catholicism. The codified reduction of theology and worship also shriveled the emotional substance of visual and literary art (but not music), however brilliant the technical expression. Buechner points out that both artistic creation and theological reflection emerge from the same primal experience, but their modes of communication appeal to different human ways of knowing. Since the Reformation and Counter-Reformation, Western Christianity has privileged one of these, but Luther's theology does not justify the privileging of one over the other.

Art sensitizes and humanizes. Religious texts inspire faith and hope. This does not make one superior to the other, more translucent to God than the other, particularly when both are inspired by profound experience with something from beyond one's self that seizes one. In the *Iliad*, Priam before Achilles begging the return of Hektor's body moves the reader to tears. Homer does not let up on the pathos of his epic until the final scene, in which he shows Andromache holding the dead hero's body. The scene could be a prototype for Michelangelo's "Pietà" and thus another instance when an artist melds pagan image and Christian content to tell a truth slant, and draws on all a person's senses in the telling. In the "Pietà" the artist controls and is energized by universal pathos of both pagan myth and Christian story. The sculpture honors both and reduces neither—though the sculptor may not have been conscious of that.

And Luther? Sensitive to the art of his time and place, he teaches the artists of ours. He never lost his delight in earthly things, and he never lost a sense of God's presence, even when God appeared most absent. While he might not have said that "Christ plays in ten thousand places," he found it sufficient that Christ had played, and plays, in one. Poets tell people of faith—and those of no faith—what joy and sorrow we can anticipate and how to live well with what comes, trusting that God is present in both anguish and ecstasy. Like powerful theology, poetry effects transformation of human particularity and individuality, though it uses, not propositional rhetoric, but formed language translucent to God to tap emotion and imagination through image and sound, to show more sensately how God makes of something, something other than it seems. Much of my argument has been with W. H. Auden, but his elegy, "In Memory of W. B. Yeats," seems an apt description of the Christian poet's task. In tightly cadenced couplets he gives the poet direction: "Follow poet, follow right / to the bottom of the night." He gives purpose: "With your unconstraining voice / Still persuade us to rejoice." And he hopes for great consequences:

> In the deserts of the heart
> Let the healing fountain start,
> In the prison of his days
> Teach the free man how to praise.[114]

---

114. Auden, "In Memory of W. B. Yeats," in *Collected Poems*, 247.

5

The Translucent Word

Religious Imagination in the
Literature Classroom

CAROL GILBERTSON

Classroom Religious Discourse and Translucent Literature

"God is here," proclaims the elderly Englishwoman Mrs. Moore to Dr. Aziz in E. M. Forster's 1924 novel *Passage to India*. She has newly arrived in India and has surprised the Muslim Indian doctor standing in a mosque's darkness. He is startled by a non-Muslim's boldness in entering this holy place. Even if the Christian Mrs. Moore has removed her shoes like a good Muslim, he has scolded that she has no "right" to be there. Aziz sees the mosque itself as symbolizing his faith: its dualism is represented in the black frieze on white stone, on which are inscribed "the ninety-nine names of God." For him the mosque "alone signified," and he, as believing viewer, "decked it with meanings the builder had never intended." "So few ladies take the trouble," says Aziz, speaking of the British wives of Anglo-Indian officials. "I think you are newly arrived in India."[1]

First-year students, newly arrived at college, may find dorm life and printed syllabi as foreign as Mrs. Moore finds India. Yet these students

---

1. E. M. Forster, *Passage to India* (1924; New York: Harcourt, Brace & World, 1952), 19–21.

know some things deep in their instinctive psyches after years of school-ing, much like the other English people in Forster's novel, who arrive in India and soon learn to keep "to the accredited themes" and to "snub" those outside the Anglo realm. Our students have learned that their high school textbooks rarely speak of God, except perhaps to note quaint religious customs in faraway lands or to explore Puritan intolerance in *The Crucible*. Public education's studied avoidance of religion as part of life—combined with the contemporary American cultural climate, with its emphasis on quick flashes of interest and the white noise of media "information"—results in college students who not only need guiding to be more ruminative, but also need urging to spend intellectual and imaginative energy on theological matters.[2]

Yet many university classrooms are inhospitable to religious dis-course: one extreme ignores the subject, while the other is openly dis-missive.[3] American church historian George M. Marsden argues that the historic "disestablishment of religion" has instead "led to the virtual es-tablishment of nonbelief."[4] Susan Handelman, a Jewish academic who has written widely on pedagogy and spirituality, quotes the comment of a Smith College religion major referring to her religion classes: "We talk about spiritual experiences as if no one in the classroom could possi-bly have had one."[5] "The question for me," writes Mary Rose O'Reilly,

---

2. I am grateful to all my students, who continue to reveal texts to me and teach me about how faith and learning inform each other. Special thanks to present and for-mer students who responded to my request for some reflection on how they encoun-tered the religious dimensions of literature in the classroom (only some of them are quoted in this chapter): David Aanestad, Kari Black, Kimberly Brathol, Heidi Gericke, Sue Gilbertson, Bonnie Gunzenhauser, Kristie Van Batavia Halvorson, Brent Heibner, Tyler Hesseltine, Emily Johnson, Sarina Moser, Laura Ostrander, Alissa Reeves, Sarah Rouse, Gwen Rudy, and Jacqueline Smith. My colleagues in the Luther College English Department have been especially helpful readers of this essay, as has Robert Cording of the College of the Holy Cross.

3. For a personal account of the indifferent and sometimes chilly climate for reli-gious discourse on campuses, see Anne Ruggles Gere's "Articles of Faith" in the larger context of a symposium on how literary and composition theory intersects with personal lives, in "The Politics of the Personal: Storying Our Lives against the Grain," ed. Jane E. Hindman, *College English* 64/1 (September 2001): 46–48.

4. George M. Marsden, *The Outrageous Idea of Christian Scholarship* (New York: Oxford University Press, 1997), 23; see also Marsden's *The Soul of the American Uni-versity: From Protestant Establishment to Established Nonbelief* (New York: Oxford Uni-versity Press, 1994).

5. Susan Handelman, "'Stopping the Heart': The Spiritual Search of Students and the Challenge to a Professor in an Undergraduate Literature Class," in *Religion, Scholar-*

"is, how do we teach people who are profoundly, even stubbornly, spiritual [beings]? I think we assume that spiritual beings is the last thing they are (because it is perhaps the last thing they will let us know)."[6] Mark Browning shows how writing teachers implicitly signal that "religious thought is inappropriate and without value," warning students to omit any religious references in their writing "because many readers will not accept religious content as authoritative." His claim perhaps becomes more controversial when he discusses how the same teachers allow students to use other non-authoritative sources and subject "religious content to far more severe scrutiny than they would material from a government organization or the NRA."[7]

Eliding classroom religious discussion and discouraging written use of religious vocabulary conflict with the liberal arts college rhetoric that we help students synthesize diverse learning and that we educate the whole person. Students need our invitation to bring their religious understandings to the fore for critical examination. By not inviting them to voice religious questions or theological insight, we encourage them to bifurcate their lives, to see their sexual selves, faith journeys, mental lives, and professional endeavors as separate, parallel tracks.

Though I am arguing for a classroom atmosphere that welcomes religious discourse, our pedagogical vocabulary for such discourse is still in its infancy. My purpose therefore is to invite further conversation as much as to venture strategies. I offer here some thoughts about the teacher's role in classroom religious discussion. I also offer some student responses to literary works I have taught in the last ten years, some presented orally on final class days and others written—some of these during the semester and some retrospectively. Because of the courses I teach, most of my examples relate to religious works from the Christian tradition (although *Passage to India* explores both the Hinduism and Islam of India, its author's British citizenry classifies it as written in a Christian context). But I have had opportunity to teach the African traditional oral epic *Sundiata* and Cheikh Hamidou Kane's modern Sufi novel *Ambiguous Adventure*, the eighteenth-century Chinese classic *The*

ship, and Higher Education: Perspectives, Models, and Future Prospects, Essays from the Lilly Seminar on Higher Education, ed. Andrea Sterk (Notre Dame, Ind.: University of Notre Dame Press, 2002), 206.

6. Quoted in Handelman, "Stopping the Heart," 209.

7. Mark Browning, "Your Logos against Mine," *Dialogue: A Journal for Writing Specialists* 6/1 (Fall 1999): 9–11.

Dream of the Red Chamber and Ba Jin's twentieth-century novel *Family*. In each case, I found that teaching these so-called non-Western, non-Christian works raised the same pedagogical questions. Teachers of works with religious content—regardless of the faith's particulars—face similar teaching questions.

In some senses, all instructional choices—course design, reading, theoretical approach, class time allocation—imply political stances toward the canon, social and intellectual values, and student-faculty relationships. Yet to encourage fair and open discussion, teachers can avoid making the classroom a polemical space. A literature teacher can intentionally work to make the classroom atmosphere friendly to religious content—inviting communal discourse about belief, theology, and religious practice without caricaturing, politicizing, or proselytizing. The hope is that this can be done without making either religious or non-religious students feel silenced.

This book's translucence metaphor offers an illuminating way to navigate this difficult territory. Literary works are textual constructs that may reveal ideology, but the reader always views such ideology through the texts' linguistic ambiguity and discursive contradictions. Typically, a literary work does not, and is not intended to, transmit transparent truth or belief, analyze abstract theological ideas or moral values. Rather, it is the translucent written product of a person situated in historical time and place and bound by his or her absorption—and also intentional and unintentional reading—of that context. When we assess the reliability of a narrative voice and its relationship to an authorial viewpoint, read the psychology and choice of highly realized characters, or unfold the rich suggestiveness of metaphor and symbol—we are reading a poem, novel, or drama as a translucent rather than a transparent vehicle.

In fact, one might say that translucence is the central subject of the literary discipline. Through its linguistic texture, ambiguity, and multiplicity, its rhetorical choices and generic tensions, a literary work both reveals and conceals its relationship to tradition, history, idea, and context, just as a translucent stained glass window transmits filtered light but also calls attention to itself as picture, color, or design. Language and form obscure direct spiritual insight but give a literary work power to move readers: we are always aware of the medium through which we see, and any discoveries we make about human life or supernatural possibilities are filtered by the artwork's textuality.[8] By inviting our students to enter vicariously into literature's human experience, we can focus on the literary work as a way to expand students' insight. We already do this with other cultural issues, but if the scholarly foci are any indication, we do it less with religion than with political, economic, racial, and gender issues. Some classrooms discuss such cultural issues as religious history, discipline, and practice and the narrative implications of biblical texts and stories. Teachers are less comfortable with discussion of worship styles, propositional beliefs, spiritual affect, theology, prayer, mysticism, and desire for self-transcendence.

My argument offers some ways to bring warmth to the academic climate for religious conversation. Though debate about the classroom as political or politicized site continues, I argue that we as individual teachers can transform our classrooms into more hospitable places for fair religious discourse. We can face religious literature squarely and without apology, without advocating its authors' or characters' beliefs or losing our critical edge in excessive sympathy. Rather than averting our classroom eyes, we can openly discuss a literary work's construction of sin and evil, spiritual longing, or revelatory vision just as we discuss its construction of gender, race, class, or empire. In doing so, we might deepen students' religious imagination: empower them to develop more nuanced religious vocabulary, engage in complex theological thinking about a fictive world, increase their understanding of other religious expressions, and encourage them to see connections to their lives. In the process, they may even be spiritually moved.

Creating Interpretive Communities

How, then, do we as literature teachers approach theological literary content? No one tactic will transform the teaching of religious literature; I suggest here only some possibilities. I certainly do not think that only committed believers can give religious content a fair hearing. Nonreligious teachers can approach such works sympathetically and with fresh eyes, and many fine scholars of Christian works are devout Jews,

---

8. For an illuminating but controversial argument that all language, and all art, is a "wager on the meaning of meaning, . . . a wager on transcendence," see George Steiner, *Real Presences* (Chicago: University of Chicago Press, 1989), 4.

Muslims, or other non-Christians, and vice versa.[9] Religious and non-religious teachers need to be aware of the hazards of gravitating toward works that reflect their own biases or of hyper-interpreting a text's religious content. William H. Moore, writing about the classroom teacher, views such interpretation as putting theologizing before reading. Kate Narveson, discussing scholarly work in early modern devotional literature, calls it "the imperialist act of imposing our critical or theological schema on the religious text."[10] A teacher's hostility to religious content, on the one hand, views the work as opaquely self-referential, not pointing beyond itself to religious insight or truth-value. Simplistic religious affirmation, on the other, considers the work as transparent dogma rather than translucent art.

One strategy focuses on how we as teachers model a literary work's classroom reception. In the early nineteenth century, poet and critic Samuel Taylor Coleridge urged in the literary reader a "willing suspension of disbelief for the moment," a willingness to have "poetic faith" enough to entertain a text's fictive constructions with sympathy and credulity.[11] Such a model is helpful for the classroom. But I am wondering whether a teacher might go farther, fostering in students not

---

9. For a discussion of the difficulties of a (self-proclaimed) nonreligious person teaching conservative Christian students, see Robert Johnson, "Teaching the Forbidden: Literature and the Religious Student," *ADE Bulletin* 112 (Winter 1995): 37–39. Rebecca Ann Bach describes how her Jewishness is particularly helpful in teaching Bible Belt students who are unfamiliar with Jews. Her students simply find her "presence in the classroom ... educational," partly because of her "outsider perspective," which helps alert students to religious differences in Renaissance texts by Catholics and Protestants; see "Teaching the Details of Race and Religious Difference in Renaissance Drama," in *Approaches to Teaching English Renaissance Drama,* ed. Karen Bamford and Alexander Leggatt (New York: Modern Language Association of America, 2002), 127–33. In the last couple of years, the Milton listserve has seen some emotional debate on the issue of the scholar's or teacher's own religious faith and tradition, including a particularly heated discussion of whether Stanley Fish, a Jew, can rightly interpret Milton's Christian epic *Paradise Lost.*

10. William H. Moore, *Sermons from Literature: A Reader/Teacher's Experience* (Lanham, Md.: University Press of America, 2001), 27; Katherine Narveson, "New Thoughts on Hobby-Horses, or Herbert Criticism and the Role of 'Interestedness' in Reading Religious Verse," *Christianity and Literature* 48/3 (Spring 1999): 310. See also Jean Bethke Elshtain, "Does, or Should, Teaching Reflect the Religious Perspective of the Teacher?" in Sterk, *Religion, Scholarship, and Higher Education,* 193–201.

11. Samuel Taylor Coleridge, *Biographia Literaria,* ed. James Engell and W. Jackson Bate, 2 vols. (Princeton: Princeton University Press, 1983), 2:6.

only a "suspension of disbelief" but a "willingness to believe" as the speaker or the characters do—perhaps what Peter Rabinowitz calls "genuine listening" or what rhetorician Wayne C. Booth calls "the rhetoric of assent."[12] A teacher can model how to read texts with an intelligent, sympathetic posture toward what that fictive world holds up as holy. Viewing the work, then, as translucent rather than opaque, she may open the way to students' spiritual introspection, to more critical readings, and to healthy religious discourse in the classroom. Building "habits of genuine [critical] conversation," Booth argues, is a crucial pedagogical aim: to develop "the kind of person who can criticize others not just negatively but productively."[13] To apply Booth's terms to this discussion, we would aim to develop in our students religious resistance as well as religious respect.

To develop this kind of critical thinking, we need, of course, to keep the classroom from becoming a venue for personal testimony or indoctrination. This is the issue whether we are focusing on a text's production, formal attributes, cultural realities, psychoanalytic implications, changing reception, or gender constructions. All these approaches come to bear on classroom discussion of religious texts. Critique of a literary text's religious content can be historical or cultural criticism; literary depictions of religious ecstasy can be explored psychologically. But a teacher needs to be sensitive to the unique place of religion in human culture and of religious faith in individual experience: she must be careful not to reduce faith in transcendent realities and spiritual presence to mere invention or delusion.

Translucency is a powerful metaphor for the teacher's role too: the teacher needs to let the content shine through her pedagogy, but she also needs to be aware that she is part of that content's effect, that her role inevitably alters the student's vision. When I asked my former students to reflect on their classroom experience with religious texts, one of my student respondents, a self-identified "lesbian nonchristian," commented on how teachers, as well as other students, shape her classroom experience: "I'm a lesbian, and every day I walk into a classroom where

---

12. Rabinowitz quoted in Wayne C. Booth, "The Ethics of Teaching Literature," *College English* 61/1 (September 1998): 49; see also Wayne C. Booth, *Modern Dogma and the Rhetoric of Assent* (Notre Dame, Ind.: University of Notre Dame Press, 1974).
13. Booth, "Ethics of Teaching Literature," 52.

most, if not all, of the other students are straight. A straight professor teaches about literature written by, for, and about straight people." This student's description of her sense of classroom unease is instructive for teachers' sensitivity to gay students' concerns and to gender content, but it is also instructive for our treatment of spiritual content and of religious or nonreligious students. If students are accurate when they cite professors' critiques of their views as "too conservative," "knee-jerk liberal," "racist," "sexist," or "evangelical," they are right to resent the politicization of the classroom and the degradation of academic discourse to transparent name-calling and invective.[14] Most illustrations of professorial insensitivity on sensitive issues seem to me professional misjudgment in treating students, allocating class time, and narrowly focusing discussion, rather than off-limits content.

Given the present sensitive atmosphere surrounding the issue of classroom ideology, it may be important for a teacher to disclose her confessional stance, at least at some level, even if it includes skepticism and nonbelief. Of course, a teacher's stance of belief should not lead to single-minded foci or intolerant comments any more than a white instructor should be intolerant of students of color or restrict discussions of race (though the pedagogical issues about discussing race seem to me quite different from those about religious faith). Handelman bases her argument in etymology, pointing out that the word *professor* denotes one who "makes open declaration of his . . . opinions, . . . who makes public his belief" and even his "faith, love, or devotion."[15] This may be more teacher transparency than some would be comfortable with. However much an instructor chooses to reveal about personal belief, what is crucial is the teacher's integrity in treating religious faith, and in acknowledging that some texts finally hold more religious value for him

---

14. See Sara Hebel, "Patrolling Professors' Politics," *The Chronicle of Higher Education*, 50/23 (13 February 2004), B12, where she describes situations such as a teacher announcing his liberal political views on the first class day and advising conservative students to enroll in a different class. In the same *Chronicle* issue, David Horowitz, president of the California-based Center for the Study of Popular Culture, makes a more polemical and extreme argument that state legislatures and Congress should adopt his "Academic Bill of Rights," which includes the right "not to be indoctrinated or otherwise assaulted by political propagandists in the classroom or any educational setting" ("In Defense of Intellectual Diversity," B12). See also Stanley Fish's answer to Horowitz in that *Chronicle* issue, " 'Intellectual Diversity': The Trojan Horse of a Dark Design," B13.

15. Handelman, "Stopping the Heart," 203.

than others. A reflective believer keeps open the final question of truth with a humility appropriate to a temporal, mortal being.

Exactly how much of one's own life and belief should enter class discussion varies with teacher personalities, but it seems to me that neither the teachers' nor the students' religious and moral lives should be entirely off-limits any more than are their political lives. The more delicate issue is how much the instructor's ideas and approaches, through force of personality and position, might transparently inform the students' ideas. Writing teacher Lynnell Edwards argues that a teacher should model a "theology of *humility*,"[16] and here Handelman's notion of teacher as "sympathetic facilitator" is useful. She uses the model of the Jewish mystical idea of *tzimtzum*, or "God's 'self-contraction,' a concealing or withdrawal of the infinite divine light in order to leave an 'empty space' . . . , a space which can allow for finite beings, who otherwise would be overwhelmed and nullified by this light." Handelman applies this analogy of God's self-contraction to the teacher-student relationship: the teacher first must pull back her "intellectual light" to the student's absorption level, and the student is then empowered to explore his own way to the more complicated idea.[17]

Though many of us might smile at the teacher as god-figure in Handelman's analogy, her point is useful. The teacher's attempt to (more transparently) *transfer* her religious values would restrict the intellectual process and overwhelm the student, as well as being ethically questionable. As in *tzimtzum*, the teacher who discloses her religious perspective should aim—using this book's metaphor again—at translucence rather than transparency, leaving only a "'trace' *(reshimu)*" of her own values in "the space" she creates for her students.[18] This trace might be a germ that grows and finds fruition (or mutates) in a student's mind, but this is not necessarily the goal; the trace might also be a catalyst to effect in the student's mind a chemical change to a very different discovery. Quoting Rabbi Nachman of Bratslav, Handelman writes that just as stories use indirection to "'garb' and 'enclothe' the light so it can be received" and readers can "'find their face,' without the light

---

16. Lynnell Edwards, "Writing, Religion, and the Complex Site of Evolution," *Language and Learning across the Disciplines* 5/2 (September 2001): 12–15; emphasis mine.

17. Handelman, "Stopping the Heart," 221–22.

18. Ibid.

overwhelming and blinding them," so teachers need to teach by in-direction. A teacher's translucent pedagogy creates an atmosphere of expectation that students will move toward adult independence of thought, feeling, and judgment; it allows students to discover and then claim their own authority—affirming, testing, or resisting the teacher's views and values.

Creating intellectual and religious space for students, then, is cru-cial to developing a supportive, collaborative atmosphere that fosters fair religious discourse. Literary theorist Stanley Fish long ago used the phrase *interpretive community,* a term that emerged out of his early reader-response theory.[19] Both *interpretive* and *community* are relevant words here. Students need to become capable *interpreters.* We need to help them recognize a work's ambiguity as well as its clarity (its translu-cent quality of paradoxically both concealing and revealing) and provide them with certain tools: careful reading; active intellectual engagement; knowledge of hermeneutical skills, methods, genres, and conventions.

Community is also integral in this dynamic synergy: Fish argues (or argued; he has since moved away from this theory) that a written work only becomes a "text" when a community of readers, sharing beliefs about what constitutes meaning, together create its meaning. Fish writes that such a community, implicitly agreeing to a set of mutual interpre-tive strategies, is "objective, in the sense that it is the result of an agree-ment, and subjective, in the sense that only those who are party to that agreement (and who therefore constitute it) will be able to recognize it."[20] Though my argument relies on Fish's term and general notion, my primary purpose is not to define what constitutes a text. Rather, I focus on the collective interpretation. Only when disciplined and in-formed reading becomes collaboration will students work in dialectic, revising and supporting each other. As Christopher C. Weaver says about interpretive communities in the literature classroom, this collaborative

---

19. Stanley Fish first used this term "interpretive communities" in 1980 as a cor-rective to overly subjectivist reader-response critical theory (some of it Fish's own), which saw readers as individually creating texts' meanings as they read and interpret on the basis of their own experience and prejudices. Fish argued that common themes emerge in readings because readers often share "interpretive strategies" and even values, particularly when they read and discuss in the classroom. See *Is There a Text in This Class? The Authority of Interpretive Communities* (Cambridge: Harvard University Press, 1980).

20. Fish, *Is There a Text in This Class?* 178–79.

work helps students learn that "knowledge is always a matter of consensus arrived at through persuasion and negotiation."[21]

Ideally, the classroom can evolve, over time, into a trusting atmosphere, a respectful climate in which to explore a literary work's religious content. Sometimes it can even become a place where students take each other's faith positions seriously but also fairly critique them. The teacher initiates this atmosphere's creation, though most of us will openly admit how much class chemistry varies with each new group. Still, a teacher can set a tone of hospitality as well as model respectful disagreement, intellectual discipline, and intentional critical method. At the end of a recent course called "Poems for Life," when the students had formed a particularly lively and thoughtful team, one woman commented on the class community: "We read poetry not to admire other people's literary monoliths, but instead to enter into the poem which is the space between poet and audience. All poems are functional poems, and all poems are poems for life."

What Literature Makes Possible

How, exactly, does literature relate to our students' lives, particularly their spiritual and theological lives? In the following pages, I would like to suggest various ways that intelligent and sympathetic study of literature can enlarge students' religious imaginations. In my experience, such study (1) fosters ecumenical understanding by allowing students to vicariously live inside religious faiths other than their own; (2) invites imaginative exploration of theological possibilities; (3) nurtures sympathetic involvement in others' religious ideas and practices (which may lead to a student's private spiritual epiphany); and (4) nudges them to reflect on their own faith formulations when they perform, or ventriloquize, poetic speakers' arguments of doubt and devotion.

Forster's *A Passage to India* enables readers to see through the text's lens in order to isolate and critique particular religious worldviews. The story portrays the idiosyncratic religious postures and practices of Christians, Muslims, and Hindus. The novel's plot demonstrates that none

---

21. Christopher C. Weaver, "Interpretive Communities: Making Use of Readings and Misreadings in the Literature Classroom and Elsewhere," in *Teaching in the 21st Century: Adapting Writing Pedagogies to the College Curriculum*, ed. Alice Robertson and Barbara Smith (New York: Falmer, 1999), 202.

holds the spiritual answer to life's horrors and injustices.[22] Yet Forster holds out hope for a universal ecumenical stance—cherishing life's wholeness and holiness. Although it may sound naive in such a brief paraphrase, for him this affirmation runs deeper than any political attempts at racial understanding. *A Passage to India* not only suggests the social and moral value of religious tolerance but also works to flex readers' religious muscle, allowing them to face each faith's limitations as well as its richness by living inside disparate religious thinkers who are sympathetic characters despite their personal flaws.

In one well-known example of ecumenical understanding, Forster presents the instinctually spiritual Mrs. Moore encountering a wasp on a coat hook. She acknowledges it, imagines its life in India, and then instinctively blesses it: "Pretty dear."[23] Later in the novel, the devout and wise Hindu Professor Godbole, who has admired Mrs. Moore as a kindred spirit, enters the rich chaos of an outdoor Hindu worship festival and suddenly is vaguely reminded of "an old woman he had met" years earlier and also of the wasp scene, of which he has no direct knowledge:

> Chance brought her into his mind while it was in this heated state, he did not select her, and she happened to occur among the throng of soliciting images, a tiny splinter, and he impelled her by his spiritual force to that place where completeness can be found. Completeness, not reconstruction. His senses grew thinner, he remembered a wasp seen he forgot where, perhaps on a stone. He loved the wasp equally, he impelled it likewise, he was imitating God. . . . "One old Englishwoman and one little, little wasp," he thought, as he stepped out of the temple into the grey of a pouring wet morning. "It does not seem much, still it is more than I am myself."[24]

---

22. Critics of the novel sometimes argue that Forster, though highly critical of British colonial attitudes and administration, was too situated within early twentieth-century imperial British culture to see beyond its racist colonial assumptions about India, Muslims, and Hindus. I find it interesting, however, that when Pakistani-born Akbar Ahmed—Ibn Khaldun Chair of Islamic Studies and professor of international relations at American University in Washington, D.C. and, according to the BBC, "probably the world's best-known scholar on contemporary Islam" as well as an active participant in interfaith dialogue—gave a recent lecture on "Islam and the West—Clash or Dialogue of Civilizations?" he held up Forster's vision in *Passage to India* as a hopeful model for contemporary interfaith and intercultural understanding (lecture, Luther College, Decorah, Iowa, March 10, 2004).

23. Forster, *Passage to India*, 35.

24. Ibid., 286, 291.

In his fictional portrayal, Forster implicitly distinguishes religious *discourse* (articulated propositional belief); *practice* (human actions inspired or required by religious belief); *institutions* (the organizational structure that codifies those beliefs and in which such actions take place); and a *community* of believers (those who share discourse and practice).[25] He depicts a Christian English woman and a Hindu Indian man through their internal religious discourse and external social interactions. Each is at times spiritually imaginative and compassionate, at times limited and self-centered. By presenting these complex believers as sympathetic characters, the novel educates the reader to see them as appealing anomalies in a dysfunctional world of multiple English and Indian communities, with their absolute categories of chauvinistic patriotism, colonialist domination and subjection, religious bigotry, and misogyny. When Mrs. Moore tries to convince her son, Chandrapore's City Magistrate Ronny Heaslop, that his colonialist notion of "hold[ing] the wretched country by force" is ill conceived, he retorts: "We're not pleasant in India, and we don't intend to be pleasant. We've something more important to do." Mrs. Moore responds that "the English *are* out here to be pleasant," and she articulates a profoundly simple principle of religious ecology: "Because India is part of the earth. And God has put us on earth in order to be pleasant to each other. God . . . is . . . love. . . . God has put us on earth to love our neighbors and to show it, and He is omnipresent, even in India, to see how we are succeeding."[26] In her subsequent dive into India's profound complexity, however, Mrs. Moore finds her unquestioning institutional Christianity shallow. Ironically, later, when the dead Mrs. Moore has become a symbol of interfaith understanding and even the focus of a folk cult, her phrase becomes a sacred mantra for the Hindu crowds at the festival, where one inscription mistakenly reads, "God si love."[27]

In *A Passage to India* Forster turns readers' eyes toward the refracted light of his story so that a reader temporarily wears another's faith or nonbelief, assesses it, calculates its significance, and compares it to other characters' faith positions. The whole reflective process enlarges the

---

25. For these four "domains" that define "religion," I am indebted to Stephen Healey's paraphrase of Bruce Lincoln's argument in his review of Lincoln's *Holy Terrors: Thinking about Religion after September 11* (Chicago: University of Chicago Press, 2003), in *The Christian Century* 120/11 (31 May 2003): 25–29.

26. Forster, *Passage to India*, 50–51.

27. Ibid., 285.

reader's imaginative wardrobe. Such a novel invites discussion of the difficulties of interfaith understanding. In other words, it exercises the student's *religious imagination*. I use the term as an analogue to what philosophical ethicist Martha Nussbaum calls the "moral imagination." She argues that novels elicit in readers a way of seeing that develops "habits of empathy and conjecture," "sympathetic responsiveness" to others, and respect for a fictional character's "rich inner life," enabling a reader to see "its importance in defining a creature as fully human."[28] Nussbaum calls this process "empathetic identification." Speaking of Whitman's poetry, she writes that "the ability to imagine vividly, and then to assess judicially, another person's pain, to participate in it and then to ask about its significance, is a powerful way of learning what the human facts are and of acquiring a motivation to alter them."[29] Nussbaum's argument about literature widening our sense of the possibilities for *moral* experience, by extension, suggests that the vicarious experience of reading literature's also enlarges our *spiritual* repertoire.

In Forster's narrative, readers enter a new, religiously pluralistic fictive world, which allows them to see its tensions more readily than in their own world. They enter the spiritual consciousness of a character of a different faith and learn how that person thinks, talks, and acts religiously. They watch how the institutionalized machinery of church or state rolls across individual response. In narrating characters' internal self-examination as well as external dialogue of other-criticism, the novel nudges readers to recognize limited human perception and the shape of religio-racial prejudice. Such imaginative thinking invites readers to reflect on their own faith expressions; it helps them to think about how tolerance and even fellow feeling might coexist with spiritual conviction. Forster's novel invites readers to imaginatively reflect on interfaith ecumenism.

Literature can also expand a student's sense of what is theologically possible within his or her own faith. Several years ago two senior students in their last semester enrolled in my "Literature by Women" course in order to fulfill English prerequisites for medical school. These male biology majors felt awkward in a class of mostly female English

---

28. Martha C. Nussbaum, *Cultivating Humanity: A Classical Defense of Reform in Liberal Education* (Cambridge: Harvard University Press, 1997), 90.
29. Martha C. Nussbaum, *Poetic Justice: The Literary Imagination and Public Life* (Boston: Beacon, 1995), 91.

majors, but they stuck with it. On the final class day, one of these bright seniors, who had been fairly quiet all semester, gave his testimonial. Though he had taken the college's required two religion courses, he admitted that he had never imagined that thoughtful people could envision God in what he saw as startling, new ways—God as female or God as embodied in deep human love. He was fascinated with Celie's religious struggle in Alice Walker's *The Color Purple,* her quest for a new God who is not male like the men who have abused her, and her discovery of a God who is "inside you and inside everybody else," who can be discovered in the trees, the air, and the birds.[30]

This student compared that realization to his theological discovery in reading Mary Gordon's *The Company of Women.* The novel portrays a group of pious Catholic women friends and their diverse, idiosyncratic faiths. In a 1960s youth culture very different from theirs, Felicitas, the daughter of one of these women, struggles to find her way to adulthood, to her own clumsy faith, and finally to a rather unusual but happy marriage.[31] This senior wished he had read these life-changing books earlier so that he might have enrolled in contemporary theology courses: he was fascinated by such untraditional conceptions of God. I think he, a reflective but secular kid who was perhaps raised Lutheran, would have been exhilarated by studying contemporary theology, but it might not have been as concrete to him—as "incarnational"—as these deeply physical, socially embedded stories of people he was made to care about and whose lives resembled a life he might, in some sense, live. "It is in stories, in narratives large and small rather than in coded commandments, that students absorb lessons in how to confront ethical complexity," Booth writes. "It is in stories that we learn to think about the 'virtual' cases that echo the cases we will meet when we return to the more disorderly, 'actual' world."[32]

Different kinds of literary works bring light at different intensities and angles, which effect varying responses. Sometimes, as we have seen, literary works lead students to ecumenical understanding or theological reflection. Another reception brings a lightning-bolt epiphany. In a recent course in British Romanticism, a nineteenth-century period in

---

30. Alice Walker, *The Color Purple* (New York: Washington Square, 1982), 177–78.

31. Mary Gordon, *The Company of Women* (New York: Ballantine, 1980).

32. Booth, "Ethics of Teaching Literature," 48.

which poets sought nature's transcendent meaning and saw divine potential in the human heart, my large class—despite my best effort to create community—seemed a rather impersonal group. At semester's end, I felt that we had failed not only to plumb Romanticism's philosophical depth but also to have profound literary discussion; I felt particularly dismayed at our treatment of the texts' religious dimensions. On the final class day, one particularly bright junior—whose mix of countercultural dress and politically conservative views I had never been able to figure out—bared her soul. She told how she had grown up in a Christian home but had become a "skeptical agnostic." She had read with interest the poets who tried to articulate a new spirituality. These texts' unorthodox religious views broke through this young woman's skepticism. All of her semester's writing, she admitted, had been indirectly about her spiritual struggle.

The student's favorite work was *The Marriage of Heaven and Hell,* a visionary, late eighteenth-century satiric work in which the poet William Blake ironically reverses conventional notions of good and evil, heaven and hell, angels and devils. Unlike Forster's novel, which offers a fiction about socially embedded characters who struggle when their faiths clash with their experience, Blake's work is meant to hit readers directly with puzzling images, surreal visionary dream-scenes, and ironic paradoxical pronouncements. The student told about reading the "Memorable Fancy" in which an "angel" shows the poetic speaker what Hell is like, with monsters and torturous punishment in a dark cave. The bold speaker refutes the angel's "metaphysics," and when the angel flees in terror at his blasphemous tongue, the speaker finds himself in an Elysium of restful meadows and beautiful rivers; the fearsome Hell, he suggests, is an illusion conjured up by an institutional church that maintains power through fear. Blake's poem critiqued the hypocrisy and legalism of his era's institutional Christianity. But its revolutionary spiritual message—which affirms human desire and energy, and rejoices that "Jesus was all virtue, and no rules"—spiritually enlightened my student.[33] She explained that the poem helped her to clarify her beliefs and move her beyond a religion based in fear. And then she stunned the room: the course had helped her decide to study for the ministry.

---

33. William Blake, *The Marriage of Heaven and Hell,* in *Blake's Poetry and Designs,* ed. Mary Lynn Johnson and John E. Grant (New York: Norton, 1979).

In that case, the student's literary epiphany had the pragmatic effect of leading to a decision. Sometimes students' experience of a literary text can become a way to re-see or re-affirm the choices they have already made. In my course on John Milton's seventeenth-century epic *Paradise Lost,* we focus not only on Milton's poetic structure, narrative method, tropes, and political context, but also on his constructions of gender, class, science, and governance, at times comparing them with twenty-first-century views. My hope is to help students see this Puritan classic of the Christian intellectual tradition not as a work with curious, antiquated ideas. Instead, through the translucent medium of religious story, image, and idea, this epic simultaneously plunges readers into seventeenth-century English theology and church polity and raises crucial theological questions still fascinating to twenty-first-century readers.

Paradise Lost's narrative, of course, is not realistic fiction like Forster's novel but rather the imagined recreation of the biblical Fall story, the re-scripting of the traditional War in Heaven, and the rewriting of Old Testament history. It is told by a theological narrator who lives in the fallen world, comments on the actions, and contrasts the Eden narrative with postlapsarian life, highlighting the loss. In addition, Milton's stated purpose, "to justifie the wayes of God to man," gives the narrative a more didactic function than many literary works.[34] Still, the epic is not transparent creed or exemplary parable. The narrative voice explicitly nudges the reader, beyond identifying with characters, to *reason* about the characters' actions and arguments, including the limits on human knowledge: are they actual (the limits of human intellect) or ethical (to clone or not to clone). The text raises issues about the quest for knowledge and the nature of evil in a world created by a good God, about whether gender roles represent divinely inspired hierarchy, about sexuality's role in love. Although we cannot answer all our questions, our class's interpretive community helps students to engage in religious conversation, to rigorously question Milton's (and our) theological and moral logic, and to develop reflective religious sensibilities.

When the Milton students write their formal class papers, they confront the interpretive issues raised in the class, but they rarely discuss

---

34. John Milton, *Paradise Lost,* in *The Riverside Milton,* ed. Roy Flannagan (Boston: Houghton Mifflin, 1998).

religious discoveries inspired by the text. Informally, however, they sometimes write about being pained and quietly calmed by *Paradise Lost*'s ending. The first two humans reluctantly leave the Garden and enter the wilderness outside with terror and grief, wiping their tears as they make their "solitary way" "with wand'ring steps and slow." Still, they are holding hands, and they have "Providence [as] thir [*sic*] guide."[35] After the semester was over, I asked class members to reflect in writing on their experience studying literary works with religious content. One student wrote about her emotional response to Adam and Eve's final predicament:

> "Hand in hand"—the poetry is breathtaking, but the image is heartbreaking. Page after page I've followed their story. I saw them meet. I saw them work together, hand in hand. I, just like the earth, "felt the wound" when Eve first tastes the forbidden fruit. I felt their loneliness as Adam and Eve sat apart, cold and alone with their sin. I watched them leave the garden, with one last look behind, as their hesitant feet step onto unfamiliar ground. Adam and Eve are Everyman and Everywoman; their story is my story. Every day, I'm given Paradise, and every day, I eat the apple. When I read Milton's words, I see myself, I see humanity, I see forgiveness, and I feel humbled.

This student elevates her language to a stylistic sublime to convey her powerful affective response to the poem's poetic power and her theological response to its illuminating parallels to her spiritual life. She sees the work as a poetic dramatization of her already developed theology.

The student goes on to describe this poem's particular relevance for her life, especially as she looks forward to her coming marriage. In doing so, she synthesizes Christian faith, ethical ideals, and literary understanding with her thoughts about her future:

> God's message of hope and forgiveness for all humanity seems particularly applicable to the married couple. Who more needs to know how to forgive, to know that he or she is forgiven? In just over two months, Peter and I will stand in front of God and become one as Adam and Eve were one. We will relive the story of Adam and Eve every day in our lives together. We will have moments where we taste the fruit, moments we feel separated from each other. We, too, must find our way through the world, and it will probably be with "wandering steps." However, like Adam and Eve, we will do it "hand in hand," and not just Peter's hand in mine.

---

35. Ibid., 645–49.

> God's hand, Providence our guide, will lead us through life. Even when Peter and I let go of each other's hands, God will not let go.

This student came to the epic already religious and biblically literate, and the class's interpretive community allowed her to become what some might consider Milton's ideal reader. Few of us expect such eloquence about faith to be nurtured in our classes, and it seems to me that teachers should view it as a byproduct of class discussion rather than a goal. It also must be said that even this confident student did not voice this view in class but rather wrote it in a personal summing-up that her classmates would not read.

Not every student, of course, would respond this way to *Paradise Lost:* my lesbian student regularly resisted the text because she felt that the epic's divinely created, normative heterosexual coupling excluded her experience. It is also true that not everyone would regard the other student's spiritual declaration as appropriate in an academic class. Yet I cannot keep from wondering what other spiritual and intellectual reflection—oral and written—we have discouraged in our elision of classroom religious discourse.

Different literary genres differently affect readers' religious selves. Dramatic works, and narrative texts such as Forster's novel, invite reflection as we experience unfamiliar cultural worlds and virtually live in the consciousness of fictional characters unlike ourselves. A longer study would need to look at Forster's shaping narrative voice, which sometimes more directly nudges readers to look skeptically on religious certainty and institutional rigidity. Other realistic fictional worlds present characters who declare their doubt or belief or make ambiguous gestures that might be groping toward faith (the agnostic father on his deathbed in Evelyn Waugh's *Brideshead Revisited,* who may be crossing himself) or forgiveness (in Robert Penn Warren's *All the King's Men,* Jack Burden's implicit final discovery that living peaceably in an imperfect world demands a loving forgiveness). In O. E. Rolvaag's *Giants in the Earth,* what the preacher believes is a failed sermon to the Norwegian immigrants on the Dakota frontier offers a theological frame for interpreting the characters' difficult choices.

In a novel, the characters and action are compelling, but the conclusion rarely gives a clear theological statement: any lesson is suffused with ambiguity, and authorial position is difficult to determine. Lyric poems use different means and elicit different responses. In Blake's poem, the neon images and proclamations shock us into thought, but the ironic storytelling makes its meaning richly ambiguous. The scope of Milton's epic and its narratorial commentary urge speculative thinking but reveal nuance and contradiction. Short lyric poems, usually with a first-person speaker expressing thought, feeling, or idea, appear to state the poet's own position more directly, though most poets adopt a fictive lyric voice. In any case, as students read the poem, they become the poem's voice: the poem's medium, as poet Robert Pinsky argues, is the reader's breath.[36] Lyric poems, then, force readers more directly into another's mental deliberation and emotional anguish.

Students are drawn into the words of poets who sometimes write in response to their own experiences, both mundane and epiphanic: their poetic voices beg dying fathers to "rage against the dying of the light" (Dylan Thomas's "Do Not Go Gentle into That Good Night"), render up a dead child to God but yet grieve him as my "best piece of poetry" (Ben Jonson's "On My First Son"), imagine Christ gently insisting they sit and eat his eucharistic love feast (George Herbert's "Love [III]"), muse on the power of Jesus' crucifixion image (John Donne's "Good Friday, 1613, Riding Westward"), reflect on whether faith is possible in the modern world (Wallace Stevens's "Sunday Morning," Sylvia Plath's "Black Rook in Rainy Weather"), explore their alienation from the institutional church (Philip Larkin's "Church Going," Richard Garcia's "Why I Left the Church"), or attempt to find new language for modern or postmodern faith (T. S. Eliot's *The Four Quartets,* Carl Dennis's *Practical Gods,* Louise Glück's *The Wild Iris*). In an essay about teaching Renaissance metaphysical poetry, Gene Edward Veith Jr. writes about how students become involved even in the foreign world of Renaissance religious poetry: "By beginning with the poem's particular emotional or aesthetic content and then explaining the religious concepts involved, rather than vice versa, a teacher can effectively present almost any religious poem, even to people who do not share the poet's religious vocabulary."[37] Poetic works intentionally give direct utterance to the quest for spiritual certainty, the outpouring of gratitude, the

---

36. Robert Pinsky, "Poetry in the Real World" (lecture, Luther College, Decorah, Iowa, September 16, 2003).

37. Gene Edward Veith Jr., "Teaching about the Religion of the Metaphysical Poets," *Approaches to Teaching the Metaphysical Poets,* ed. Sidney Gottlieb (New York: Modern Language Association of America, 1990), 55–56.

self-conviction of sin, the midnight *angst*. Poetic utterances range from spiritually devotional to agnostically philosophical, from tonally gentle or cerebral to cynical or impassioned.

When reading John Donne's Holy Sonnet #14, "Batter My Heart, Three-Personed God," the reader ventriloquizes the speaker's plea that God take violent control of his spiritual life. As a way to heighten the powerful urgency that the speaker begs from God, Donne develops the military metaphor of a battering ram besieging a castle. In the act of reading, the reader must momentarily suspend disbelief in both atheism and unquestioning faith—the reader *becomes,* for a moment, the doubting believer-speaker, who longs to be rescued from the sin that holds his "Reason" captive. The rough metrics and violent imagery heighten the octave's urgency, which shifts suddenly to the sestet's sweet love language: "Yet dearly I love you, and would be loved fain," the speaker whispers. But the softness is short-lived: the speaker's continuing desperation intrudes, and the final metaphors deftly combine love and violence: "for I, / Except you enthrall me, never shall be free, / Nor ever chaste, except you ravish me."

In a recent poetry class, one student in her final reflection recounted a long breakfast talk with a friend about her own dismissive treatment of another student, her best friend. Their discussion turned to human weakness and "spiritual warfare," and she left feeling depressed and hopeless. In class an hour later, as she recounts, we discussed Donne's sonnet:

> When we went through the poem's argument, I welled up inside. I felt exactly like the poem's speaker. No matter how hard I tried, I could not "Reason" my way out of my apathy and unkindness. It was so ironic that my friend and I had been talking about spiritual warfare, and then I heard Donne talk about being "betrothed unto [God's] enemy" and needing God to "Divorce" him from the devil. Everything about the poem struck home with me. I left the class very affected and immediately shared the poem with my breakfast buddy and the best friend I had been snubbing. I could not get over the feeling of knowing that John Donne, a man who lived four hundred years before me, felt the same weakness I felt.

The student responds to the sense of spiritual helplessness that Donne's speaker expresses: she longs for self-transcendence and like him wants God's direct action to effect it. Interestingly, she does not appropriate (or at least does not mention) what some see as Donne's images of military and sexual violence for God's decisive intrusion into a believer's heart. For some readers, the sonnet has disturbing theological implications as it models the God-human relationship in metaphors of rape and imprisonment. Others counter that Donne's hyperbolic wit and urgent rhetoric requires extreme language; they point out that seventeenth-century connotations of "ravishment" suggest "enraptured embrace" rather than forceful sexual assault.

When poetry students compare Donne and his contemporary religious poet George Herbert, they encounter very different devotional styles and different theologies. Veith points out that Donne's "Arminian synergism"—the notion that the human will must choose to accept and to cooperate with the grace of God—was a challenge to the "divine monergism" of such thinkers as Herbert, "the view that God accomplishes everything necessary for salvation, that God is the active partner and the initiator in the relationship between human beings and God." Perhaps if I had devoted more class time to the theology of Donne's sonnet, we might have critically explored its metaphors' implications. After studying Donne and Herbert, Veith notes, students often realize "that their own religious tradition is richer, more complex, and more intellectually open than they had dreamed."[38]

A teacher will be more effective, perhaps, if he is aware of students' personal circumstances. In many of the cases I present here, I was unaware of the student's particular history and even sometimes oblivious to individual receptions of a particular text. Life situations, of course, lead individual students to particular emotional responses. One student recalled how, when she learned of a sixteen-year-old friend's sudden death, she "needed the assurance that God was still watching over me and that he knew what I was going through." At that traumatic time, she did not seek a broadening of her religious universe; she wanted the comfort of religious certainty. She writes that when she read Mary Herbert's sixteenth-century versification of Psalm 100 (*Jubilate Deo*) in

---

38. Ibid., 57. For other discussions of classroom pedagogy and religion, see Bach, "Teaching the Details of Race and Religious Difference," 127–33; Irena S. M. Makarushka, "A Picture's Worth: Teaching Religion and Film," *Journal of Religion and Film* 2/3 (December 1998); Robert N. Minor and Robert D. Baird, "Teaching about Religion at the State University: Taking the Issue Seriously and Strictly," *The Council on the Study of Religion Bulletin* 14 (1983): 69–72; M. D. Walhout, "Beyond the Wars of Religion: How Teaching the Conflicts Can Desecularize American Education," *Profession* (1996): 139–45; and Gerald Graff, "Response to Mark Walhout," *Profession* (1996): 145–48.

sonnet form, "I was reminded that all my beliefs were true. It tells us that God is always with us and will provide for us. The poem's powerful voice encouraged me that this was the truth [because] the speaker does not hesitate, but states the truth about God with an unquestioning voice." Though we may say that "poetry makes nothing happen," as W. H. Auden's ironic line goes, teaching students actual poems belies the assertion.[39] Devotional poems' rhetoric effects more than emotional satisfaction in the reader, but it can offer a solace that emerges from aesthetic as well as spiritual dimensions, as Denis Donoghue—a Roman Catholic literary scholar-teacher—suggests:

> The consolatory power of a work of literature is real, because it lets us see that a mess of conflicting feelings can be brought to order, though not to heel. . . . The desired end is poise, the feelings brought into equilibrium. A poem is, at its best—its most achieved—what Robert Frost called it, "a momentary stay against confusion."[40]

A teacher's modeling of suspended disbelief, willingness to be moved by religious content, and sensitivity to others' reception of texts are surely first steps. But as the class walks deeper into that literary-religious space, the discussion must probe the work's issues more critically; we need to balance sympathy (Coleridge's "poetic faith") with a resistance that tests ideas and values. A teacher cannot predict when students will be drawn by story, rhetoric, or image to appropriate a fictive religious struggle, sometimes in disturbing ways. This is true for political, social, and domestic issues as well, even when we use care in facilitating and responding to student comments. If we create a knowledgeable and trusting classroom community open to such spiritual revelations, we might more carefully challenge easy acceptance of literary faith statements that may be poetically powerful but theologically problematic. As Booth argues, students need to be taught not only how to be moved by a literary work but also "how to *think* about, and possibly reject, values of the story world they first 'took in' . . . [so that] our own aspirations and habits of thought are changed."[41] Such critical religious

---

39. W. H. Auden, "In Memory of W. B. Yeats," *Another Time* (New York: Random House, 1940), line 36.
40. Denis Donoghue, "Questions of Teaching," in Sterk, *Religion, Scholarship, and Higher Education*, 179.
41. Booth, "Ethics of Teaching Literature," 49.

thinking should involve imaginative growth for nonreligious as well as religious students, whether Jewish, Muslim, or Christian.

As teachers we need to enable students to wander in the text's literary goldmine. We need to prepare them with a topographical map and some notion of what to look for, to allow them, in other words, to explore with both curiosity and caution—critically but also openly—the literary work's labyrinthine caverns of religious (as well as other) space. Sometimes they will discover different veins from those they set out to find; some will resist the map and explore in their own way. Most of my examples cite students who are happily affirmed or transformed by religious texts, yet students do and should also resist texts, as I have suggested. I have fewer such examples and sometimes worry that I am perhaps not as receptive to them as I think. The "lesbian nonchristian" I quoted earlier, who was a thoughtfully resistant and sometimes hostile reader in class, explains her resistance, which she argues led to an unfortunate sense of social alienation: "[My] nonchristian perspective leads me to encounter [religious] works in a different way, and I sometimes feel alienated knowing that I don't have the same connection to the work's themes as other students. However, there are certainly works which I find moving and can relate to my own spiritual life." Some readers are resistant in other ways, at times less for ideological reasons than for disinterest, as in the following case:

> I generally do not think of religion at all when I am in a class because I am not an excessively religious person. I found Satan the most enjoyable character in [*Paradise Lost*], for Milton's Savior figure seemed rather distant and maybe even cold.... I have written a diary every single day for eleven years, and a lot of Blake's quotations found their way into those pages. I ascribe to his practical ideas far more than his religious ideas, as common sense always appeals to me more than theology or abstract faith.

Sometimes students absorb their classmates' different modes of resistance and find it instructive. One former student's letter reflecting on her classroom experience was heartening:

> I often felt my most valuable class time was spent weighing the words of others against each other's and my own. I would get so caught up in listening to the class discussion that I often forgot to speak my own ideas. This strikes to the core of how the classes I took from you affected my religious faith. Some of the poems we studied expressed an attitude toward faith. You fostered an atmosphere of intellectual exchange without allowing us to take others' comments personally. Nothing could have served me better.

This atmosphere and my love for poetry allowed my mind to open and soak up the interpretations of my classmates. In class discussions with non-believers, agnostics, and believers, I know, looking back, that my faith continually expanded.

Some instructors are more comfortable than others with the notion that classroom study might lead to a student's "growth in faith." But the student is using conventional religious language to describe a deepening of what I have been calling "religious imagination." This can happen without our knowledge, but when a student privately articulates a faith position to us, we can try to help the person explore to what extent it emerges from careful, imaginative reflection.

To Martin Luther the Word, the *Logos,* was more than biblical Scripture: it was preaching and teaching, but it was also daily, spoken language that somehow, miraculously, became a translucent vehicle for God's message. God's workings in the world, as Lutheran theologian Darrell Jodock reminds us, are "incarnational," not codified.[42] They are embodied in people, in things, and in nonbiblical texts. Thus God's workings are as complicated and ambiguous as human beings are, and that complexity and ambiguity is the stuff of literary art. The philosopher George Steiner argues that "all good art and literature begin in immanence" and that

> it is the privilege of the aesthetic to quicken into lit presence the continuum between temporality and eternity, between matter and spirit, between man and "the other." It is in this common and exact sense that *poiesis* opens on to, is underwritten by, the religious and the metaphysical. The questions: "What is poetry, music, art?", . . . "How do they act upon us and how do we interpret their action?", are, ultimately, theological questions.[43]

Steiner's is an extreme position, set out as a response to postmodern doubt. But even if we do not see literature (and, in Steiner's view, all language) as self-evidently pointing to spiritual transcendence, we can agree that writers portray religious worlds and voice faith pleas, and that teachers can help students to delineate them. Luther valued deep

---

42. Darrell Jodock, "The Lutheran Tradition and the Liberal Arts College: How Are They Related?" in *Called to Serve: St. Olaf and the Vocation of a Church College,* ed. Pamela Schwandt, Gary DeKrey, and L. DeAne Lagerquist (Northfield, Minn.: St. Olaf College, 1999), 28.

43. Steiner, *Real Presences,* 227.

questioning and dialectical paradox, so a mix of classroom responses to religious literary works—compliance, resistance, and hostility; intellection and abstraction; faith, indifference, doubt, and unbelief; compassion, empathy, and ecstasy—facilitates meaningful education.

What happens in a literature classroom, as some of these illustrations suggest, can at times go beyond intellectual and imaginative growth. Certainly, the classroom should not become a prayer meeting or an occasion for either spiritual witness or iconoclastic manifestos. Still, its climate can be temperate to allow students' voicing of faith positions as well as skepticism or secularism, and we can be ready to deal with the implications. Sometimes something miraculous—a kind of spiritual turning, or "conversion"—can happen while teacher and students look together at a compelling story or poem. Sometimes no one wants to talk about it aloud: we should be open to silence or voiced response. A translucent revelation can happen when there is no Bible in sight and no one is transparently preaching or witnessing or moralizing—except the magical black marks on the page, with all their flawed and multiple meanings. Sometimes in the classroom we can look at the book and find ourselves thinking, as Mrs. Moore says in the mosque: "God is *here.*"

The Larger Interpretive Community

Nurturing a climate for careful religious discourse takes continuous calibration. The classroom becomes an interpretive community not only because of the teacher and her particular students, but also because of the surrounding institutional culture and ethos. A working macro-community is a fertile environment in which classroom micro-communities thrive. Here I assume a liberal arts college small enough to share a common purpose. Yet even in such a place, faculty and staff who intentionally articulate to each other the college's mission are crucial, and that, I am convinced, presupposes considerable collective discussion of the college's mission of educating the whole person. We need to remember to come together as a collective body—our professional specialists, isolated scholars, maverick teachers, and fund-raising administrators—to become an interpretive community. Faculty need to move beyond a business agenda, to regularly gather as a group to talk. In an earlier era, collective faculty deliberation was assumed, at least at small colleges. In our world—dominated by privatized flurries of emails and voicemails, publication pressures, family needs, and heavy teaching loads—deliberation has not disappeared, but we need to intentionally create opportunities for it to happen. A faculty community is crucial to effective liberal arts education in which students sharpen their critical skills and deepen their understandings. Without that faculty community, we have no student or classroom community, and without either, we cannot build a campus focused on its institutional mission. Together, a faculty can reflect on how to build students' qualities of mind, how to become not only expert disciplinary guides but also nurturers of fragile self-development.

This call to nurture students' development includes developing their religious imagination: we can help each other articulate how we might elicit respectful and tolerant classroom religious discourse and how our work—in different ways for different disciplines and personalities—might touch on students' spiritual growth without becoming indoctrination. The atmosphere of extreme, politicized views in the culture as well as some parts of the academy makes deliberative faculty discourse rarer even in schools where it should be cultivated—at church-related colleges such as the one where I teach. Given the larger culture's paucity of critically reflective religious discourse, colleges that explicitly see themselves as church-related—committed to a "dialogue of faith and learning" (to use my institution's phrase)—have a greater responsibility to nurture the religious imagination. Lutheran institutions model themselves on Luther's notion of faith that unflinchingly encounters the world. These schools' traditions embrace open inquiry, the rigorous pursuit of truth with no fear of shattering faith or offending God. With their missions of engagement with and service to the world as well as ecumenical hospitality, Lutheran colleges should be leaders in developing careful academic vocabularies for religious discourse and content both within and outside of religion departments.

At some church-related institutions like mine, the place where the mission is underlined most palpably is the chapel service, where the campus faith community gathers to hear the Word. Here a different kind of literary incarnation can happen—words spoken by a known community member whose professional role is distinct from this shaped religious utterance but yet enlightens its insights. Chapel can be a place where academic content, intellectual probing, disciplined reading, and careful logic meet the constituents of spirituality—aesthetics, reverence, love, intimacy, and awe. It is where some faculty members, more transparently than in the classroom, model for students their weaving together of these strands of their daily living, including personal relationships, spiritual faith and doubt, political and economic realities.

One former student who sent me an email reflecting back on her college career points out a danger of the classroom teacher's paralysis in the face of religious discourse—unchallenged declarations of orthodoxy. She reported that as a student she had been put off by students using "experiences of fictional characters as springboards to testimony or proselytizing." But she went on to argue that more religious transparency was appropriate in the chapel talk:

> I think I had an unconscious sense that chapel talks were a different kind of discourse; in this forum, it seemed okay for people to use characters or stories as moral exempla, or to use poetry to voice a personal conviction. I remember a chapel talk you gave my freshman year. In your Drama class we had recently read *The Duchess of Malfi*, and you used something from that play to illustrate something you were saying. I remember the moment: it was one of the first times I started to think that maybe literature could enhance/enrich/complicate the way I thought about religious or moral questions.

Chapel is where the faith-learning "community of discourse," as Jodock calls it, comes together to "discover depth and beauty and truth and freedom and mystery," which gives them perspective "to serve human beings and steward the world."[44]

As this essay's first sections argue, aesthetic sensibility, spiritual depth, and commitment to service are fostered not only in the chapel. A classroom as open to truth and mystery as to idea and clarity honors the glowing translucence of human creation. But such a classroom arises more readily within a college community that humbly holds up the model of *translucence* as a reminder of the limits of human understanding as well as its achievements. And if we can show our students how to seek humble wisdom that embraces a religious imagination, it will benefit us all, even beyond our campus community.

Some of us shudder at the use of the term "outcomes" to name the complicated people our graduates have grown to be. But as educators, we do need to think about the people our education will shape. I have talked about trying to develop students' religious as well as their moral imagination in the classroom, which seems important to an educated student body but also to a thoughtful church and an informed public

---

44. Jodock, "The Lutheran Tradition," 16, 30.

discourse. Stanley Fish views "citizen building" as "a legitimate democratic activity," but surely he is wrong when he argues that it is "not an
academic activity." I think Nussbaum rightly sees our education of the
moral imagination as "essential to citizenship."[45] In arguing that traditional and postmodern scholar-teachers use very different language but
in fact have similar ethical aims, Booth suggests a long view when he
writes that as teachers and faculty members we need to intentionally

> *think* about the ethical aims of education: *what kind of person pursuing
> what kind of ideas and practices and social improvements do we hope to see
> emerging from our labors?* . . . What ethical improvements *in ourselves* should
> we seek, in or out of the world of story, that will help our students create
> selves most useful to them—useful not just in the utilitarian sense but in
> the sense of yielding an ultimately rewarding life, working for an ulti-
> mately rewarding and defensible society?[46]

Developing the religious imaginations of students and faculty will enrich our campus cultures. With an enlarged sense of what it means to
be religious, our graduates will lead more reflective lives. They will be
better able to influence their commonwealth's response to the violent
injustice and sectarian extremes of our time. And they will strengthen a
Christian church that is grounded and flexible because it has at its heart
the religious imagination.

---

45. Stanley Fish, *Professional Correctness: Literary Studies and Political Change*
(Cambridge: Harvard University Press, 1995), 3; Nussbaum, *Cultivating Humanity*,
85.
46. Booth, "Ethics of Teaching Literature," 45.

6

Faith Comes from What Is Heard

Oral Performance of Scripture

JAMES S. HANSON

When I heard that the British actor Alec McGowen would be performing the Gospel of Mark in Princeton, where I was attending graduate school in biblical studies, I went to the theater more out of curiosity than anything else. I was, to be honest, more excited about seeing an actor whose work I had admired than about the content. After all, I had read the Gospel dozens of times and studied it in advanced classes; it was, in fact, the focus of my dissertation. What could I hear that I did not know already? But when the lights dimmed and the actor took the almost bare stage, beginning to intone the words I knew so well—"The beginning of the gospel of Jesus Christ, the son of God"— I was utterly transfixed, completely taken into the world his performance created.

It was as though I was encountering the story for the first time. The characters, which on the written page seemed flat, mere instruments for illustrating theological ideas, took on flesh and blood: the paralytic and his friends who lowered him through the roof; the man with the withered hand; the woman with the flow of blood; Jairus's daughter; not to mention the disciples and Jesus himself—all of them came to life before my eyes. The conflict between Jesus and the religious authorities, his struggle to create faithful followers of these sometimes comically but ultimately tragically dull, fearful disciples, his anguish from the cross over his suffering and betrayal—I experienced these for the first time as real suspense and drama. Along with the rest of the audience, I laughed at places I had never seen as humorous, as when the disciples, having seen Jesus feed the five thousand and then the four thousand (not counting women and children), worry about having one loaf of bread in their boat as they crossed the sea of Galilee with Jesus. I was on the edge of my seat during Jesus' trial. I wiped away tears when they crucified him, and shared the women's fear and awe at the angel's announcement that he was alive.

In short, I left the theater transformed in a way I had never experienced from a biblical text. And more than ten years later, I still have access to that experience. What was going on? What made this encounter with Mark's Gospel so distinctive, imprinting it so indelibly on my mind, heart, and spirit?

On the one hand, perhaps the answer is obvious: there is a tremendous difference between reading (and reading about) a work and experiencing it in the fullness of a performance. But what makes this an issue worth exploring is that, while it may be evident that this is the case, the church by and large has not experienced Scripture this way. That is certainly the case in the critical guild. I attended McGowen's performance of Mark as one whose training in conventional, historical-critical biblical studies had shaped me to view Mark's Gospel—indeed, Scripture as a whole—as an ancient written artifact to be mined for its historical and theological significance. I learned to approach the Gospel as a work of and for its first-century context: Mark was writing, for example, to address a community disoriented and confused by the disastrous Jewish revolt against the Romans, and undergoing persecution for its adherence to the good news. This context helped shape his reworking of the Jesus tradition into the first Gospel, which emphasized Jesus' own suffering and his call to those who would follow him to take up their cross. His famous secrecy motif likewise had a historical explanation: to square the non-messianic character of Jesus' ministry with the early church's proclamation of him as Israel's Messiah, the Son of God.

Such an approach to Mark had indeed afforded me valuable insight into its meaning for its first-century audience; but it rendered the

Gospel incapable of speaking a living word to me, or perhaps more accurately, it rendered me incapable of experiencing it as a living, transforming word. I was caught up in the world of secondary discourse about the Gospel, which choked off the possibility of a primary encounter with the One whose presence Mark's story attempted to evoke.

What is perhaps ironic about my experience, though, is that for most of my life I have had an avid avocational interest in the arts—especially music and theater—and was keenly aware of their power to affect and transform an individual or community. But somehow that interest remained separate from my interaction with Scripture; my engagement with the biblical text was characterized by critical acumen and argument, not by the fuzziness of experience.

Though this may be a particular occupational hazard for those who engage in historical-critical study of the Bible, in my experience it is not limited to the critical guild. If my teaching experience in the college classroom and in churches is a reliable measure, we are a culture still shaped by the Enlightenment's insistence on the empirical basis of truth claims (especially religious ones), as well as by the desire to rely on experts to explain to us what a significant text or work of art *means*. The result is that we too often rush to substitute a discursive exposition of a text or artwork for an encounter with the work itself. (This propensity is also visible in the way we get our news: we are often much more interested in expert commentary on a political speech or debate, for example, than in hearing and digesting it as a live event.)

The consequences of this for the church's relationship to its scriptural witness are potentially serious. Rather than experiencing Scripture as a translucent instrument through which we encounter a living Presence, the Bible becomes opaque, or at least limited to the realm of the intellect, its capacity to shape us as individuals and as community severely diminished.

Here I will argue that oral performance of Scripture can help us recover its transforming power. It does so, I will suggest, in three ways: (1) it causes us to recognize Scripture as a dynamic artwork rather than as a static container of historical or theological ideas; (2) it encourages the interpreter to become a servant of Scripture's goals rather than a master of its meaning; and (3) when these components come together in a performance, it affords the audience a fresh, immediate, and potentially transforming experience of the biblical text.

From Reading to Hearing: The Text as Oral Literature

At the heart of Christian faith lies its Scripture, the written record of the experiences of Israel and the early church. The common understanding of the Bible by both Christians and Jews is that it is a written artifact—a book; a text to be read, studied, and interpreted for the community's life and faith. Indeed, the very word "Bible" comes from the Greek word meaning "book" (or "books"). For Christians especially, the Bible has functioned as a primary source for theological ideas, for ethical norms, and for discerning God's will for communities and individuals. Outside the faith community, moreover, it has become common in academic institutions to teach the Bible as literature, to study it in much the same way one would study a novel, a play, or a poem: analyzing its portrayal of character, literary themes, symbolic images, and rhetorical or narrative structure.

Biblical scholarship over the last century has shown, however, that the individual documents of the Bible, with few, if any, exceptions, had a long life as *oral* tradition before taking written form, and that the process of telling and retelling the stories, poems, hymns, and laws has left an indelible mark on the writings' final forms. What is more, most people in ancient cultures were not literate, so it is likely that even when the traditions took on written form, they were intended primarily to be experienced aurally by the communities for which they were composed. This is the case even for Paul's letters, which he composed orally, dictating to a scribe; he commanded that they "be read to all of the brothers and sisters" (1 Thess. 5:27).

Interest in the Scripture's oral aspects has proliferated in the last decade or so, as indicated both by the scholarly literature and by the increasingly regular presence of oral performances of Scripture at churches, scholarly conventions, and academic institutions.[1] Especially popular have been presentations of the Gospels, most often the Gospel of Mark. This interest has been generated both by performing artists—

---

1. See, for example, Werner Kelber, *The Oral and the Written Gospel* (Philadelphia: Fortress Press, 1983); Mary Ann Tolbert, *Sowing the Gospel: Mark's World in Literary-Historical Perspective* (Minneapolis: Fortress Press, 1989); and most recently Elizabeth Struthers Malbon, *Hearing Mark: A Listener's Guide* (Harrisburg, Pa.: Trinity Press International, 2002).

Alec McGowan's performance of the Gospel of Mark in the 1980s was a landmark—as well as by biblical scholars—David Rhoads's more recent performance of Mark's Gospel. These and others have recognized that such oral presentations actually replicate much more closely the experience of Scripture in early Christianity.

The early Christian writings were profoundly shaped by the fact that they were formed in an almost exclusively oral/aural culture. The importance of orality in interpreting ancient traditions has been widely noted in studies of Homer, Herodotus, and other classical works. Orality's significance is at least twofold. First, some aspects of the texts become clearer when one recognizes the oral shaping that underlies them. Oral presentation helps explain the repetitions, structure, intended wordplay, rhetorical patterns, and various other structural features. Considering orality has led to important new insights into how to understand certain features of biblical texts, as well as how to interpret the texts as wholes. Second is the recognition that when we hear a work we experience it very differently than when we read it, partly because of the obvious differences between seeing and hearing, and partly because the audience experiences the text embodied in the interpreter. The interpreter incarnates the text in a particular way, and that fleshly particularity is the translucent revelation of the text's fullest meaning.

The combination of the text's orality and its embodiment in a particular performer makes interpreting and experiencing Scripture from this perspective exciting. On the one hand, this experience brings one closer to how the authors intended their works to be received; and on the other, it acknowledges how contemporary culture receives the textual meaning. Cultural analysts have observed that our own culture is in a post-literary age, one in which the visual and aural have regained primacy. Thus, oral scriptural interpretation is important both for our general understanding of the texts and for allowing them most fruitfully to affect a contemporary audience.

Oral performance of Scripture brings three points to the interpretive triangle. When one reads a text, only two parties are explicitly involved: the text and the reader. Inserting an oral interpreter into the structure affects more than just the audience's experience of the text. If done competently, a performance alters the work's very nature; it requires of the performer a very different relationship to the text. And people who gather to make up the audience for a scriptural performance can experience it in profoundly new ways.

What difference does it make to approach a biblical text as something essentially oral rather than written? How does it alter the text's
nature and our reception of it? As noted above, the predominant approach for scholars has been shaped by the idea that the Bible is essentially a written work. This approach's primary goal is generally exposition, analysis: to attempt an interpretive articulation of what and how
the author is communicating. The historical-critical scholar tries, for
example, to interpret a biblical text's theological or christological ideas:
How does the author of Mark see Jesus' significance? What does Mark
mean when he calls Jesus "Son of God"? How has the author shaped the
story to bring out his ideas? Or, if her concerns are more historical, the
scholar may mine the text for what it discloses about the life of Jesus or
the early church: To what extent does the Gospel accurately reflect the
intentions, words, and deeds of the historical Jesus of Nazareth? What
developments in the early church does the book's composition reflect?

The Christian who reads Scripture instead for devotion or inspiration
also attempts to extrapolate something from the text, but in a different
way. This reader will look for the ways the text communicates God's
guidance for one's faith life, the beliefs and behaviors that are com-
mended through the text: belief in Jesus as God's Son, whose redemptive death cleanses us from sin and whose life models the fundamental
dual commandment to love God and neighbor.

These are both legitimate approaches to Scripture. Especially given
the ancient and foreign context in which biblical texts were generated,
historical and literary explanation is often necessary for a fuller understanding and experience of the text: What would it mean in Jesus' time
and place, for example, that he addresses a woman in public (Mark 7)?
Who were the Sadducees? What are Paul's argumentative moves in his
letter to the Galatians?

But these approaches also have their limits, and these limits need to
be acknowledged. First of all, any approach to Scripture that attempts
to render the text in other words—exegetical observations, summary,
paraphrase, identification of the story's moral—places an intermediary
between the text and the audience, obscuring a direct encounter. As
George Steiner has observed about artistic works in general, we have
developed an intellectual culture in which the critic, rather than the literary work itself, plays the central role.[2] The critic is the hero who elicits

---

2. George Steiner, *Real Presences* (Chicago: University of Chicago Press, 1989).

the text's meaning, substituting her learned interpretation for a direct encounter with the work. In often rather caustic terms, Steiner attacks the critical guild for creating a "secondary city" in which the experience of an artwork—literature, music, visual arts—is held hostage to a group of professionals who offer their interpretations as the text's indispensable mediators. But at stake for Steiner is the disappearance of the "real presence" that underlies artistic expression: the experience of the transcendent, of God. The ironic outcome of centuries of secondary discourse on artistic works—and here, of course, we could substitute the Bible—is that "the very methodologies and techniques which would restore to us the presence of the source, of the primary, surround, suffocate that presence with their own autonomous mass. The tree dies under the hungry weight of the vines."[3]

Further, refashioning a text into secondary discourse reflects a *static* view of the work; the interpretation renders it present all at once, as an unchanging, transparent container of meaning. Conversely, a direct textual experience—reading, but especially listening and watching—takes place in time and space; it is dynamic, with the listener sequentially assessing the text, revising, and then reassessing as the work unfolds. As a central character's new traits are revealed, for example, the audience's perceptions of him or her have to be renegotiated; the connections between important plot events become clear often only in retrospect. The reader-response critic Robert Fowler describes this dynamic, temporal experience as "looking forward and looking back":

> As we read we are constantly looking back and re-visioning what we have already read, while at the same time looking forward in anticipation of what might lie ahead. We review and pre-view constantly to make as much sense of our experience at each individual moment.... This obviously visual metaphor invites us to consider how our view of the whole literary work changes ceaselessly, as we proceed step by step on our way through the reading experience.[4]

In other words, a literary or dramatic work emerges in the temporal process of reading or hearing; it can never be grasped in its entirety by the audience or reader. In this sense, the reader can never be the master

---

3. Ibid., 47.
4. Robert Fowler, *Let the Reader Understand: Reader-Response Criticism and the Gospel of Mark* (Minneapolis: Fortress Press, 1991), 45.

of it, never clearly convey to an audience in discursive language the text's meaning. To restate a text's central ideas, to explore themes, and to analyze the plot—none of these things can substitute for an immediate engagement with the work.

Moreover, regardless of how effective an interpretation might be—how correct or illuminating of a text's content—it remains fundamentally a form of cognition; we emerge from a secondary encounter with the text with new knowledge about it, but with little sense of how or why to put that knowledge to use in our lives. A distinctive feature of Mark's portrayal of Jesus, we may learn, emphasizes his suffering and the call to follow him (for example, Mark 8:31-37). But if we separate that idea from the vehicle through which it is conveyed—Mark's powerful and moving story—we rob the text of its potential capacity to move and empower us to shape our lives around its reality. That is, the Gospels, Paul's letters—indeed, all the canonical works—are fundamentally *rhetorical* texts that attempt not merely to convey information to their audience, but to *do* something to them. Their language is what scholars of rhetoric term "performative"; that is, it does not simply denote or connote but claims the capacity to effect something in those it encounters. The "I do" of the wedding ceremony is an oft-cited example of such language; it is an utterance that effects a change in the reality of the person saying it and of the one about whom it speaks. One could also point to understandings of the Eucharist, such as Martin Luther's, in which the words "the body and blood of Christ broken and shed for you" effect a change in the communicant's reality.

In other words, an oral interpreter must view and convey the biblical work as a rhetorical whole, rather than focus on a specific passage, theme, or idea. The biblical books are designed to compel the audience into the narrative world, to bring them to share its values, to react to its characters by imitation or rejection of their traits—in short, to subject the listener to the story's claims. As Gabriel Josipovici puts it, the Gospels

> force us to enter the world of the narrative. And they do this...not because of any excess of detail but by forcing apparent contradictions upon us and yet giving us the confidence that this and no other way was how it was.... We assent to narratives, as we do to people, to the degree that we grow to feel we can trust them.[5]

---

5. Gabriel Josipovici, *The Book of God: A Response to the Bible* (New Haven, Conn.: Yale University Press, 1988), 229–30, 234.

The Gospel of Mark intends to cultivate just such trust. It attempts to move its audience, for example, to embrace a Messiah who is such through his suffering and death and through his understanding that power is service rather than domination. To accomplish this goal, Mark needs to draw his readers into his symbolic world, to change their perception of how God works in theirs. Mark begins with an event with which the audience is likely to feel largely comfortable: At Jesus' baptism, the heavens are "torn apart," and a voice from heaven declares Jesus to be "God's Son" (Mark 1:9-11). Things become more complicated, however, when Jesus enjoins those who experience his power to keep his identity a secret. Scholars have long recognized this "messianic secret" as a clue to Mark's Christology. But here the question becomes what that motif does to its audience. As the story unfolds, the audience experiences a dissonance between a Jesus who obviously possesses God's power and one who submits himself to the world's powers, which results in his suffering and death. This movement's climax comes when the secret is finally broken, at the foot of the cross by the Roman centurion, who, in response only to Jesus' anguished cry of dereliction, declares him to be God's Son.

To underscore this hidden revelation, immediately prior to the centurion's confession the temple curtain is "torn apart"—recalling the tearing of the heavens at Jesus' baptism. Mark's intention seems clear: if the audience still wishes to embrace that confession, it must do so also in that place—the cross—and it must embrace as well the implications of following such a Messiah: taking up one's own cross in suffering service to the world. Intellectually understanding this theological crux is vastly different from living through its story. Cognition is one thing, experience another. The biblical text must be viewed in its capacity to empower its audience members to shape their individual and communal lives around it.

Another way in which oral Scripture performance can be illuminating is in clarifying textual features that, when approached from a purely literary perspective, seem baffling. For example, most who read Mark's Gospel find it a puzzling piece, full of repetitions (two feeding stories), cryptic scenes (the "naked young man" at Jesus' arrest, 14:51-52), and a Jesus who conceals as much as he reveals. When one reads the Gospel informed by biblical historical and literary scholarship, some features do become more intelligible. The feeding stories most likely came from two different sources: one on the Jewish side of the Sea of Galilee, the other on the Gentile side. The naked young man may be the one who appears at Jesus' tomb, announcing his resurrection, and the secrecy motif serves Mark's idea of a crucified Messiah. It is possible, then, to discern a meaning for these narrative problems and thus to achieve a better intellectual understanding of Mark's Christology.

When one experiences these narrative knots in an oral presentation, however, one comes to grasp not only what they mean but what they accomplish in and for the story's hearers. The effect of the double feeding stories, for example, becomes quite painfully obvious: Mark uses it to shape his audience's reaction to the disciples. It is both comical and tragic that, even after witnessing Jesus' miraculous feedings of a total of nine thousand people, the disciples are concerned when they find themselves with only one loaf of bread in the boat (8:14ff.). It is puzzling, to say the least, that Jesus would choose as his followers men of such little promise. Interpreters of Mark have long debated whether Mark uses the disciples to discredit a faulty Christology—one based on Jesus' miracles—or to portray more sympathetically, even pastorally, the difficulties of following a crucified Messiah. But when a performer brings this story to life orally, the issue becomes less a matter of trying to discern the correct way to interpret the disciples, and more a matter of emotionally investing in the Gospel's ultimate fate. In Gospel performances I have seen, the disciples' obduracy induces laughter, but it is a knowing laughter: the audience members can see themselves in the disciples' struggles to understand, and they can also genuinely sense how the disciples' obtuseness might actually impede Jesus' goals. The audience sees the conflict between Jesus and the disciples, then, not as a clue to Mark's ideas, but rather as a visceral experience that embodies the fundamental conflict between the divine plan and our human incapacity to grasp it.

Another puzzling feature of Mark's Gospel that receives new light through oral performance is the ending, over which scholars have also spilled much ink. Though the canon gives us three possible endings, most scholars agree that the best evidence points to the shortest one: after the women have come upon the empty tomb and have heard the young man proclaim that Jesus has been raised, Mark tells us, "They went out and fled from the tomb, for terror and amazement had seized them; and they said nothing to anyone, for they were afraid" (16:8). Curtain. Here again, scholars have long debated what this cryptic ending means. What is Mark trying to say? That the disciples are denied (in the story world, at least) a reconciliation scene with Jesus may lend support to the polemical view of the disciples noted above: this ending thoroughly discredits them and the understanding of Jesus' messiahship that they reflect—one based solely on his miracles, rather than on the cross. Or the abrupt ending may mean that Mark does not want to move prematurely to resurrection and victory, which might rob the cross of some of its scandalous power.

These observations are not beside the point, but as with the previous examples, the difference lies in the question we bring to the text: What does this ending *do* to the audience? What effect does it have on them? Quite frankly, the impact of this abrupt ending in a well-wrought performance is absolutely stunning. Even though when I first experienced it I had explored it in a whole dissertation chapter, I was completely taken aback. Part of me protested: This is not the end of the story! Our longing for a scene that ties everything together is strong indeed: the disciples would be reconciled to Jesus, his unjust crucifixion suffering vindicated. But the dramatic performance led me to realize the text's concluding power: the story does not, in fact, end with the resurrection. Its resolution lies ahead, in a dramatic moment not narrated but rather predicted: a time when Jesus returns and is publicly vindicated, and the world's suffering and evil are vanquished for good. For an audience, an oral performance of Mark viscerally imparts the sense of being in the heart of a narrative, in the middle of time.

These examples lead us to another observation: While literary and hermeneutical theory has acknowledged that any text has the potential for multiple interpretations, in practice much biblical interpretation still strives for the best or even the correct interpretation. Familiarizing oneself with the literature on Mark's disciples, for example, reveals vociferous defenses of one view or another—that Mark attacks their false understanding of Jesus or that he uses them pastorally to address the failures of his audience. In oral performance, by contrast, the interpreter must recognize that the text will be apprehended differently by each of its hearers. The goal, in fact, is to facilitate this pluralism. Seeing the text as something to be brought to life in a particular, performed moment and acknowledging that it will strike people differently—to relinquish, in other words, control of the text's meaning—has the potential of transcending any individual interpreter's claims to meaning.

In sum, approaching the biblical text with the goal of bringing it to life through oral performance radically alters how it is understood. Such an approach seeks to let the translucent text work its own wonders as it encounters an audience directly, rather than letting it be reduced through secondary discourse. Performance recognizes that the text consists not only of words on a page to be mined for meaning, but also of powerful events waiting to be experienced in an encounter with the whole.

I am not suggesting that we toss all of our commentaries and critical essays into the trash bin (though Steiner would perhaps have it so). We must engage in critical inquiry into the text, both to illuminate features obscured by its different culture and to evaluate critically its theological perspective. A realization of the biblical text such as Mel Gibson's *The Passion of the Christ,* for example, demands critical reflection, both about the historicity of its presentation and its understanding of the story's implications for salvation. Rather, I am urging our recognition that if we limit our scriptural experience to solitary reading, to hearing bits of it in worship, or to reaching for expert commentary on the text's meaning, we short-circuit an experience that has the potential to affect our whole being: a dramatic encounter with the word in the flesh.

The Interpreter/Performer as Servant

We turn our attention, next, to the question of what difference it might make when the interpreter's goal is not to produce a close reading in order to shed light on a text's literary, historical, or theological dimensions, but to prepare and create a dramatic experience of the text. At the heart of the matter is a performer's paradoxical and complex relationship to a text: he must bring his whole self and presence to the performance and yet serve the text's goals. In other words, the actor's goal is to become a translucent vehicle for the text's goals and designs, to allow the audience to view and experience its dynamics, its claims to truth, its reality as embodied in a particular human being.

Emerging from this observation, I would suggest, are three principal differences between conventional exposition of the written text and an oral, dramatic approach. The most fundamental is a basic shift in the interpreter's relationship to the text; rather than attempting to become the text's *master,* a performing interpreter must become its *servant.* Second, the interpreter must fully—and bodily—inhabit the story-world the text creates, thus collapsing the critical distance generally required of discursive interpretation. And third, in creating an authentic, effective character (or characters), the interpreter, rather than bracket her own life in the service of objectivity, must instead draw, explicitly and intensely, from that living experience. The truth of the performance requires it.

Although both exposition of the written text and dramatic performance are engaged in interpretation, they differ both in the conception of the interpretive act and in the way that a work's meaning comes to expression. A significant dimension of the exegetical interpreter's task is to discern and offer in her own formulation some aspect of the text's meaning—historical, literary, or theological. If it is to be taken seriously by fellow interpreters, this work requires mastering both text and context: the interpreter stands over the text and presents herself in full command of the expressed ideas. In most cases—and again, if she wishes to be taken seriously—the interpreter must engage in an argument or dialogue, often to show what previous interpretations lack, where others have failed to sufficiently master the material. Any dissertator knows of the obligatory history-of-research chapter, which attempts to show how everyone else addressing the topic has distorted or limited the text. The dissertation is, in fact, designed to display the degree candidate's mastery of the disciplinary conversation. Such work is legitimate and important; it has deeply enhanced our understanding of the biblical texts. Certainly, historical-critical and literary interpreters can approach the text in a spirit of humility and service. Nevertheless, the culture of secondary scholarship will demand, to some degree, a posture of mastery over the text.

To approach a text in order to realize it in performance demands something else. The performer must become the translucent vehicle through which the author reaches his audience; thus, by definition, she stands subordinate to the text and its designs. In drama, the actor's goal is to communicate the play. That is not to say that an inept performer cannot get in the way of this communication by somehow calling attention to himself, or by rendering characters in ways clearly contrary to the author's goals; but properly conceived and executed, the actor's job is to make the text's goals his own, realized in his performance. And the performance's success will be judged largely by the degree to which he is able to make himself translucent, to become the character without disappearing into the character. A successful performance demands the actor's intellectual understanding of the text; still, this intellection should not be visible to the audience, who should instead see someone undertaking the actions necessary to make the author's plotted journey come alive.

The actor must, in other words, become the servant of both author and text. I find it hard to conceive of a more appropriate and effective stance for the biblical interpreter. If, as Luther put it, the goal of biblical interpretation is to bring the Bible into our daily lives (*"die Bibel in das Leben ziehen"*) and to transform written into living words (*"Leseworte zu Lebensworten machen"*), the analogy—and indeed the actual practice—of an actor who realizes a playwright's text seems very fruitful indeed.[6]

Actors can approach this venture in a variety of ways: the acting craft includes a secondary discourse every bit as intense (though perhaps not quite as voluminous) as biblical interpretation.[7] It is worth noting that there are approaches to performing that result in a greater degree of transparency than others. The method acting approach, for example, focuses on techniques that are meant to help the actor become the character he is portraying—through emotional memory, sense memory, and substitution. In its most radical form, this approach results in a detailed mapping out of a character's emotional and dramatic arc; the performance runs the risk of losing immediacy and transparency, and often encourages an audience to respond to the actor's incredible skill rather than to the play itself. According to some (for example, Sanford Meisner or David Mamet), such work can actually get in the way of the actor's basic task, since it turns the audience's attention back to the performer rather than to the play's goals.

The approach I find most helpful as both actor and biblical interpreter focuses only minimally on preparation for the role in this sense. Meisner, who represents the more realistic, practical branch of the Stanislavsky legacy, describes the foundation of acting as "the reality of doing."[8] Mamet, whose approach has come to be known as "practical aesthetics," reduces the actor's task to its most basic elements: delivering the lines the author penned clearly and distinctly, and actually undertaking an action that corresponds to what the character is trying to accomplish in the scene:

---

6. Tim Schramm, "Bibliodrama in Action: Reenacting a New Testament Healing Story," in *Body and Bible: Interpreting and Experiencing Biblical Narratives,* ed. Björn Krondorfer (Philadelphia: Trinity Press International, 1992), 58.

7. A helpful overview of the different schools of acting can be found in Uta Hagen's *A Challenge for the Actor* (New York: Scribner, 1991), 3–28.

8. Sanford Meisner, *On Acting* (New York: Vintage, 1987), 16.

Learn to read a script to ferret out the action, to read it not as the audience does, or as an English professor does, but as one whose job is to bring it to the audience. It's not your job to *explain* it but to *perform* it. Learn to ask: What does the character in the script want? What does he or she do to get it? What is that like in my experience?[9]

Acting is, in other words, living truthfully under the play's imaginary circumstances, rather than attempting to become the character through a feat of imagination. The goal is not to convey *meaning*, but reality. When one witnesses an effective, even revelatory performance, inevitably it stems from the actor's ability to find the character's real humanity; she is not pretending to be the character, but faithfully and truly enacting the character's goals and desires, having made them her own. As Mamet says, "Invent nothing, deny nothing is the motto."[10]

Of course, this is more difficult to achieve than it sounds. Two fundamental components are key: the *action* and the *moment*. The actor must determine what a character in any given scene wants from another character—all drama is susceptible to such essential analysis. The next step involves translating what the character wants into a playable or doable action—for example, to find the truth, to persuade someone to act, to win an ally. When an actor on stage actually engages himself in the action as he defines it, using the words of the script to cajole, entreat, encourage—whatever means, or tools, he finds necessary to achieve what he wants—his performance achieves a real immediacy often described as "the truth of the moment"—that is, a real human being responding with real human characteristics, at any given moment, to real human happenings on stage. As Melissa Bruder puts it, one must learn to embrace each moment and act on it according to the dictates of one's action.[11]

In this sense, a truthful performance includes improvisation, since the actor does not pre-determine his actions, reactions, and emotional states. Knowing what the character wants, the actor in performance responds in a way that will actually help the character achieve it. The

---

9. David Mamet, *True and False: Heresy and Common Sense for the Actor* (New York: Random House, 1997), 42.

10. Ibid., 41.

11. See Melissa Bruder et al., *A Practical Handbook for the Actor* (New York: Vintage, 1986), 40.

dramatic interest, of course, results from the fact that, as in life, a significant obstacle stands in the way of achieving a goal—another character with conflicting desires, or sometimes a flaw within the protagonist herself. The audience is drawn into the unfolding story, pulled into genuine human struggle.

To approach a biblical text with these questions and objectives dramatically alters the interpreter's role. An example will help elucidate the difference. As I have noted, one of the most puzzling, even disturbing aspects of Mark's Gospel is the sharp conflict between Jesus and his disciples; much more so than in the other Gospels, the disciples consistently reveal their ignorance of Jesus' identity and, once they do achieve insight into this identity, clash stridently with Jesus over its significance. The conflict reaches one of its most intense moments when the disciples are crossing the Sea of Galilee with Jesus (8:14-21), having just witnessed his two miraculous feedings. Despite having experienced these wonders, they are still concerned that they have only one loaf of bread in a boat containing thirteen people. When Jesus warns them about the "yeast of the Pharisees and the yeast of Herod"—having just been accosted by the former for his failure to produce a sign to authenticate his ministry—they respond: "It is because we have no bread." Jesus proceeds to unleash his pent-up exasperation:

> "Why are you talking about having no bread? Do you still not perceive or understand? Are your hearts hardened? Do you have eyes, and fail to see? Do you have ears, and fail to hear? And do you not remember? When I broke the five loaves for the five thousand, how many baskets full of broken pieces did you collect?" They said to him, "Twelve." "And the seven for the four thousand, how many baskets full of broken pieces did you collect?" And they said to him, "Seven." Then he said to them, "Do you not yet understand?" (8:17-21)

If one interprets this text in commentary or exegesis, the result will, inevitably and naturally, be a lengthy attempt to explain this puzzling story. Why are the disciples so slow, and so fearful? What does Jesus mean by his warning about the Pharisees and Herod, and why does he bring it up here? What *is* the significance of the number of baskets the disciples collect? What, in other words, does this text *mean*? It is a legitimate question, and it yields various answers in commentaries or exegetical essays. Explanations usually focus on how Mark uses the disciples to convey his idea of a suffering Messiah, on how healing stories surround this scene (the healing of a deaf-mute, 7:31-37, and the two-stage healing of a blind man, 8:22-26), and on the symbolism of the numbers themselves.

Though legitimate and helpful, such attempts to render discursively the meaning of this dramatic encounter miss the boat, so to speak, in that they are unable to get at the truth the scene reveals. To the oral interpreter, it actually matters little what connections the author makes to the surrounding scenes or what the numbers symbolize; if the author has made the connections relatively clear, the audience will discern them. The performer's task is to discern what each character (or character group) in the scene *wants*, and to translate that desire into a concrete action that can be played on stage in a particular moment.

Jesus, for example, wants nothing more than for his followers to grasp his identity and message and become true allies in his larger goal of inaugurating God's kingdom. To render this into a playable action, I would perhaps choose something like "to get someone to come through for me," or "to startle someone into reality." My goal as interpreter would be to find tools or techniques to achieve this action, rather than to attempt to translate or paraphrase its general meaning. The disciples, on the other hand, desperately want from Jesus an unambiguous clarification of his identity and the security that would accompany it. An action such as "to get an ironclad guarantee," or "to get reassurance" would help bring the scene alive in a way that makes the disciples' desire a genuine human longing with which an audience could easily identify.

Of course, one has to account for the fact that, unlike most plays, in which different characters are played by different people, a one-person performance of text requires a single performer to play many roles, including the narrator. The only other participants in the scene are the audience members. So it may be that a performance must chiefly focus on the narrator's goals vis-à-vis the audience—what does this scene's narrator want from the audience? But the same principle applies: the immediacy, the *in-the-moment-ness* of the performance, no matter how many players are on stage, always includes the audience; in any effective performance, they contribute to a scene's actual dynamics as much as any character. As Mamet puts it, "the so-called Fourth Wall is a construction of someone afraid of the audience. . . . There is not a wall between the actor and the audience. Such would defeat the very purpose of the theatre, which is communication and communion."[12] Indeed,

---

12. Mamet, *True and False*, 58.

acknowledging with the audience what is actually happening in the moment often makes the difference between a true and false performance. The example of the squeaky door is a common one: If an actor is to sneak unnoticed into a room, and the door squeaks as she opens it, her first impulse is simply to ignore it, since it is not appropriate to the scene. But the audience knows it has happened, too, and so the actor must, if the truth of the moment is to be preserved, somehow acknowledge it.

It is, then, by approaching a biblical text as a performer—willing to accept the text's goals as one's own and to portray them truthfully— that one becomes, quite literally, the text's servant. Such an approach, moreover, can in many ways come much closer and be more faithful to the author's intentions than traditional exegesis. When I wrote my book on conflict in Mark's Gospel, I attempted to explain how Mark uses the disciples—and conflict in general—rhetorically, that is, to "address the experience of conflict in Mark's implied audience between God's promises and the reality of the seemingly unredeemed world inhabited by the audience."[13] But nothing I wrote as discursive explanation takes the place of actually living through the dramatic conflict in performance. Mark does not simply use the disciples to make a point he could have made by other means (for example, a theological argument); rather, the disciples' very human desires for understanding, for safety, for assurance—for salvation—become the means to address his audience's own needs. The scene's truth comes not through correct interpretation, no matter how masterful, but emerges rather when audience members reenact their own struggles in those of the disciples in the moment that they are truthfully realized in performance. It's that aha! of recognition that all of us have experienced in viewing an effective performance of a worthwhile play—that uncomfortable laughter, that terror at our own fears. Mamet articulates how deeply the audience internalizes a dramatic performance:

> Acting is not a genteel profession. Actors used to be buried at a crossroads with a stake through the heart. Those people's performances so troubled the onlookers that they feared their ghosts. An awesome compliment. Those players moved the audience not such that they were admitted to a graduate

---

13. James S. Hanson, *The Endangered Promises: Conflict in Mark* (Atlanta: Society of Biblical Literature, 2000), 1.

school, or received a complimentary review, but such that the audience feared for their soul. Now that seems to me something to aim for.[14]

The second principal way the interpreter's role changes when the goal is to fully realize the text in performance flows directly from the first. When one agrees to commit fully to the text's goals, the critical distance generally deemed necessary for discursive interpretation collapses almost completely. Of course, the degree of, and indeed the very nature of, objectivity required for interpreting texts in a literary or historical-critical mode has been hotly debated for decades; postmodern approaches claim that any such distance is a fiction. But when postmodern practitioners speak of performances of the text, they mean those that spring from the interpreter's radical subjectivity: the performer literally creates the text's meaning. When I speak of collapsing critical distance, I mean, on the one hand, that it is possible to discern an author's—or perhaps better, a text's—goals and intentions, but on the other hand, that an effective oral rendering compels the interpreter to identify with those aims and to commit to them.

Both literary and historical-critical approaches, as noted in the first section, tend to treat the text as an artifact, so that the interpreter's job becomes to critically examine the text from a safe distance in order to explain its meaning, its context, or its genesis. That distance often prevents texts from laying any claim on the interpreter, something that, by their rhetorical nature, they are designed to do. When Mark's Gospel portrays Jesus proclaiming, "The time is fulfilled, and the kingdom of God has drawn near; repent, and believe in the good news" (1:15), Mark wants his hearers' lives to be changed by the newly proclaimed reality.

Dramatic oral performance compels the interpreter to fully embody, inhabit, and believe the biblical text, its world, and its goals in a way conventional exegesis simply cannot. The comments of biblical scholar Walter Wink are helpful here; as he puts it, the critical approach to Scripture results in the interpreter's "getting 'stuck' in an alienated distance"; what is called for instead is an approach in which the text can "rebound on the exegete and call the exegete's life into question," an approach that allows, indeed compels, the interpreter to read the text "not to

---

14. Mamet, *True and False*, 6–7.

dominate it by means of our technical skill but to be changed."[15] It is the difference, I suggest, between a judge and a defense attorney; the judge attempts to stand at a critical remove from the defendant in order to render a fair decision, one that is as unbiased as possible. But the defendant's attorney must argue the defendant's case as if her own life were on the line; as any attorney can attest, such identification with the client does not leave one unchanged.

As I write this essay, I am developing my own one-person performance of Paul's letters—a monologue that takes excerpts and weaves them together to convey a sense of the actual human character behind the letters, which have for so long been interpreted solely in light of their theology or history. The task involves not only analyzing but also fully committing to, Paul's point of view, his values, and his goals. I must become, in effect, an advocate for Paul's perspective and his goals. It is a remarkable experience. It involves first, of course, internalizing the text through memory work; this alone creates a fundamentally different relationship, as the text virtually becomes a part of the interpreter. I need to analyze each section of a letter to determine what Paul wants from the congregation to whom he is writing; I then must translate that desire into an action that I can embody in performance.

In Galatians, for example, it is quite clear what Paul wants from the community: for them to desist from their potentially disastrous flirtation with a "different gospel," one that suggests one needs more than trust in the crucified Christ in order to be right with God, and to orient their lives around their foundational experience, which came by "believing what you heard" (Gal. 3:2). As a New Testament interpreter steeped in the Lutheran tradition, I understand Luther's concept of justification by faith—I have analyzed its theological implications and problems, tried to determine how it fits into Paul's overall theology, and experienced its power through word and sacrament. But my attempt to realize in performance what is at stake for Paul—that is, to bring it into truthful reality—has made possible a whole new apprehension of what Paul was after; it has indeed changed me.

To speak of *apprehending* of course risks losing a crucial element of this collapse of critical distance. A large measure of what happens when

---

15. Walter Wink, "Bible Study and Movement for Human Transformation," in Krondorfer, *Body and Bible*, 125; Schramm makes a similar point in the same volume: "When we restrict ourselves to analysis, we remain who we are" ("Bibliodrama in Action," 83).

one comes to the biblical text in this way arises out of the fact that, unlike most critical exegesis, the approach involves not just the mind, but the body as well. To achieve the goals of the character one is playing—and thus communicate to the audience—requires more than just the text's words. It requires moving my limbs through specific postures and gestures as well as my whole body through space and time. One thus quite literally incarnates the text. Rather than the disembodied—one might say *docetic*—quality of biblical exegesis, one achieves a bodily intimacy with the performed text that opens one, again, to the possibility of being fundamentally changed.

It is worth pointing out once again that I am not calling for the demise of a critical approach to Scripture; critical reflection on biblical language is necessary and valuable, especially when, as performer, one is called to embody and advocate for values and goals that may, in fact, be in tension with the gospel—for example, the attitude toward the Jews in John's Gospel, or the dehumanizing patriarchal structure reflected in some of the letters attributed to Paul. Even with such unsettling considerations, though, there is value in identifying and realizing their perspectives through performance; one does not simply argue against them conceptually or dismiss them altogether, but feels the resistance to them in one's body. At a recent chapel service, I asked our female pastor to read the infamous section of Paul's letter in First Timothy that suggests, among other things, that women should have no authority over a man, but must keep silent—for woman was made from man, and it was woman who disobeyed God in the garden, not man (1 Tim. 2:8-15). Not only did she register her discomfort with the text before reading, but her body language and voice manifested it very clearly during her reading.

Unlike traditional critical interpretation, which generally compels one to bracket one's own experience in the service of attempted objectivity, oral performance, to be effective and truthful, requires that the interpreter draw explicitly on her own experience. In this way, the interpreter forges connections to the text that go well beyond what traditional interpretation can accomplish.

In speaking of experience I refer not to generalized human conditions, such as oppression, alienation, and longing, but to the particular experiences an individual performer brings to a role. Crucial to creating that recognition moment that is the performance's truth is the performer's ability to be *real*—that is, to embody authentic human reactions and emotions. One accomplishes this by linking what the portrayed character wants—or, more specifically, the action that will get the character what she wants—to one's own life experience. "What is that action like in my own experience?" Mamet wants actors to ask, as we saw above. This is again where I think Mamet's practical aesthetics proves extremely valuable: the goal is not to pretend to be the character, or to draw on a sense memory so that, when the situation calls for it, one can be sad or angry; the falseness of such a performance is readily discernible to the audience and fails to serve the text's meaning.

Rather, attempting to achieve what the character wants calls for the performer to imagine and play out a situation from his own life that requires an action analogous to the character's. I might determine, for example, that Paul's goal in Galatians is to reorient the community to the truth of the gospel that brought about its saving relationship with God. What concrete, playable action can help Paul achieve this goal? "To get someone to seize a great opportunity" would be one example— especially appropriate for the letter's rhetorical climax in chapter 3:

> In Christ Jesus you are all children of God through faith. As many of you as were baptized into Christ have clothed yourself with Christ. There is no longer Jew or Greek, there is no longer slave or free, there is no longer male and female; for all of you are one in Christ Jesus. And if you belong to Christ, then you are Abraham's offspring, heirs according to the promise. (3:26-29)

No matter how hard I try, I cannot convince myself that I *am* Paul addressing a first-century congregation. But I can ask, What action from my own experience is appropriate to demonstrate "getting someone to seize a great opportunity" so that I can act it truthfully as I perform this passage? It would be, for example, as if I were trying to convince my teenage daughter that transferring to the performing arts high school would have life-changing benefits, when she would rather stick with her familiar friends. In preparing for my performance, I rehearse the scene with this *as-if* real-life situation in which I have a serious stake in order to pursue the action the scene calls for in a situation with which I can identify. I entreat, cajole, encourage, prod, needle, use humor, sarcasm—whatever tool it takes to persuade. One might object that there is not nearly as much at stake in this *as-if* as in Paul's letter, but the connection is in the action, not in the ideas. In actual performance, I use the words of Paul's text to pursue the action that will get Paul what he wants. In other words, I am acting out Paul's role in ways that resonate with my own experience so that it will resonate with the audience's.

In a well-executed instance of this technique, the audience senses the character's humanity and recognizes the truth of the character's desires—this is what life is like. For the interpreter/performer, the result is an intertwining of the character's humanity with his own and the ensuing sense of intimacy with the text's larger meaning. I will never be Paul, but by breaking down scene by scene what Paul wants from the Galatians, determining what action it will take to achieve that desire for Paul, and truthfully playing that action in the performing moment, I vicariously experience what Paul experienced, and emerge changed by it.

In these three ways, then—by shifting the controlling metaphor of the interpreter's relationship to the text from master to servant, by collapsing the critical distance between text and interpreter seen in traditional exegesis, and by bringing the performer's experience to bear on the interpretive task—oral performance of biblical text fundamentally alters the interpreter's role. The result can be a profound, rich, intimate, and dramatically deepened understanding of the biblical text, an understanding that encompasses the mind, heart, and body. While I have focused on the approach appropriate for an actor preparing a public performance of a script, there are various other techniques designed for anyone interested in this type of experience—that is, workshops and classes with the goal of facilitating a similar relationship to Scripture. One of the most interesting and increasingly popular is "Bibliodrama," in which participants act out various roles in order to achieve the intimacy and full-spectrum knowledge of Scripture outlined here.[16]

Putting It Together: The Audience's Role

The house lights dim, and the audience quickly quiets; an aura of expectation hangs in the air. The audience is prepared to give itself over to the event that is about to unfold, to place itself in the performers' hands in the fervent hope of being led on a journey away from this life and to return in some way changed. This is theater's magic and potential. As

---

16. See, for example, the essays in *Body and Bible* by Schramm (57–84), Wink (120–32), and Gerhard Marcel Martin, "The Origins of Bibliodrama and Its Specific Interest in the Text" (85–101).

Mamet puts it, "When you come into the theater, you have to be willing to say, 'We're all here to undergo a communion, to find out what the hell is going on in this world.'"[17]

We have thus far examined two of the components of oral performance of Scripture: text and performer. The audience completes the triad; without it, of course, the first two would be, if not pointless, at least less than fully realized. In discussing both text and interpreter, I have emphasized performance's temporal and experiential nature; it is for the audience's sake, primarily, that the event takes place at all. Indeed, it was as an audience member that I first encountered the power of oral Scripture performance and its profound and lasting impact. What can we say about the reception of dramatic performance?

In a basic sense, the audience's reception forms the obverse of the oral performance features for text and interpreter that I have already pointed out: the experience takes place in time and space; it creates a world the audience inhabits and thus compels, or at least makes more difficult to resist, the text's claims and values; it helps collapse the distance between text and audience; and it is an experience that affects not just the mind but the heart and body as well, depending on the experiences the audience members bring to the encounter. Moreover, it is a communal experience not unlike worship (in which, of course, the origins of theater reside). It has the capacity, in other words—as Karen Black points out about music in her contribution to this volume—to create and sustain a connection among audience members, as well as among the author, performer, and audience.

The temporality and spatial circumscription of this experience distinguish oral performance from most other ways of encountering Scripture. The British actor Patrick Stewart recounts how, when he was a young boy, he attended a matinee theatrical performance; when it was over and he was leaving the theater, he saw people lined up to get into the theater (for the evening performance, of course). But he failed to understand how this could be, since he had already seen it. "For me," he says, "the play had already happened. How could it possibly be going to happen again?"[18] His naïve insight captures performance's temporal and

---

17. David Mamet, *Three Uses of the Knife: On the Nature and Purpose of Drama* (New York: Vintage, 2000), 19.

18. Patrick Stewart, "An Actor's Contract with the Audience," *Minneapolis Star Tribune*, March 25, 2001.

spatial reality. As an event that unfolds in time, it is unrepeatable and unique; though the words may be fixed in writing (and thus susceptible to various discursive interpretations), any particular realization of them is one of a kind.[19]

This fact fundamentally alters what it means for a text to mean—or rather, what it means for an audience to find meaning in the text being performed. As anyone who has tried to describe a powerful theatrical experience knows, we cannot render in words what the experience meant for the one who was there. One simply has to be present. Someone else can describe the basic plot and some of the themes, but the experience becomes a memory fundamentally embedded in the person who underwent it.

Ten years later, I still remember the climax of Mark's Gospel in the crucifixion. I had a deep familiarity with the story, and was aware of the debates surrounding Jesus' last words—did he mean the whole of Psalm 22 when he quoted the anguished first verse? Are the other allusions to Psalm 22 in the narrative—the mocking and the dividing the clothes by lot—ex post facto, or genuine prophecies? Did the centurion at the foot of the cross represent Mark's true Christology, breaking the secret of Jesus' identity? All of those interpretive debates about the story's meaning faded away in the face of the drama unfolding before me. I especially remember that I felt the centurion's words not as meaningful phrase for Mark's Christology, but as recognition: this was a human being at the very moment of a new insight that would radically change his life. There, at that moment, text, performer, and audience came together to form an event that revealed a truth, one that penetrated far deeper into my being than anything I had read about the passage. Such is the power of a live performance.

This experience touches as well on the second observation: the way the viewers are taken up into the story's world, the way they allow themselves to be moved and shaped by it in a way that reading or researching the text simply cannot approximate. "Were you there when they crucified my Lord?" goes the old spiritual. Well, yes, in fact, I was. I was also with the disciples in that boat, feeling their insecurity, fear, and confusion. I was there as they struggled desperately to comprehend

---

19. As Stewart says, "Someone does not just see 'Virginia Woolf.' They see the Wednesday, March 28 'Virginia Woolf' and the afternoon performance, not the evening" (ibid.).

what it meant that Jesus the Messiah, the Son of God, was also destined for suffering and death. And I was with the women at the empty tomb and felt the fear that compelled them to run away. Jesus was indeed "on the loose," as my teacher Donald Juel used to say, and I half expected to encounter him in the theater lobby. In a compelling performance, no safe, critical distance between text and audience is possible. I was at the mercy of the text: it not only addressed me but molded me into the shape of its conceived reality, and I emerged from the theater a changed person.

It is true that the result of such an experience is not always a positive, life-giving one. One can also feel manipulated, even abused by a heavy-handed performance or insistence on an idiosyncratic reading. Such was the case for me, in fact, after experiencing Mel Gibson's version of *The Passion of the Christ*. Here was violence and suffering shoved down our throats, which, it was clear, was supposed to turn us inward into our dark souls and force us to recognize and confess that we were its cause, and that Jesus was getting what we deserve (not to mention the possibility that we might be tempted to blame the Jews in a special way). That is, a performance can induce one to feel things that degrade rather than ennoble or enlighten the human condition. Such a possibility helps make clear, as I have suggested at several points in this essay, that critical reflection on the text and on the experience of it is, in fact, essential; at the same time, my experience of Gibson's vision underscores the undeniable power of a dramatic rendering of Scripture.

Like the actor who brings her experience to bear on realizing the text in performance, an audience also brings both particular and shared experience to the theater. This stock of experience will influence how the performance affects them—what it will mean—and how they, in turn, will affect the players. In this way, the audience participates fully and meaningfully in creating a unique and powerful event. An audience member who is ill or physically disabled will identify strongly with Mark's healing stories. Those who struggle with their spiritual orientation will resonate with the cry of the possessed boy's father: "I believe; help my unbelief!" (Mark 9:24). Those who are materially well-off will be especially struck by the story of the rich young man who is unable to part with his possessions to follow Jesus.

Likewise, the entire audience will have shared experiences that will shape the performance's meaning, impact, and dynamics. If you have seen the movie *Godspell*, you may recall that one of the final numbers—

"All for the Best"—was shot largely on the roof of one of New York's World Trade Center towers. When I showed this movie to a class on Jesus' life and teachings, we felt together the horror of September 11 as we watched the aerial shots of the players on the roof, which lent a tragic irony to the song—"When you feel sad, or under a curse, your life is bad, your prospects are worse." The September 11 event would now, no doubt, also shape our experience of Mark's Gospel, which is particularly concerned with evil and suffering. This experience an audience brings not only transforms what it receives from a performance, but also, of course, profoundly alters the performance itself. A perceptive performer—one engaged in the moment—will sense where the audience is in any given realization, and will react accordingly.

Inevitably, when audience members reflect on a performed text such as Mark's Gospel, their comments will revolve less around the text's meaning than around the connections they experienced with the unfolding event. In other words, the text will have penetrated the cores of their being—mind, body, and heart—in ways only possible through such an experience. Thus the performed text has the power to shape their beliefs and actions—to return them to the world changed in significant, perhaps even fundamental, ways.

Finally, a performance of a biblical text for an audience has the capacity to create a community of the individuals who gather to experience it. The performance event is shared. That communal dimension has implications both for the experience itself and for the way the event illuminates the participants' continuing lives. Performance creates community because the audience is brought, as a group, into the world of the play. Though each member has a unique experience of the event, those experiences become part of a larger whole. During the performance, the audience shares the world with the players and each other; their individuality is taken up into the mysterious unfolding event as they share the protagonist's struggle to reach his goal and overcome the obstacles that impede him. When all audience members laugh, gasp, or cry together, they are experiencing the play's action as one. Anyone who has performed on stage knows that each audience has a collective personality—they tend to respond communally to particular moments in the play, and which moments those are can vary considerably from performance to performance. But the result in each case is that, for the event's duration, each individual feels knit together with the others, sharing a common humanity. Indeed, this communal dimension, it is often pointed out, is precisely what brought the theater into being.[20]

Moreover, this experience can create a contact point for each participant that has the potential to continue binding them together long after the event itself. Insofar as the experience's commonness enlarges the participants' humanity, they can reengage the real world with a sense of connectedness to those around them. When what is performed is a biblical text, of course, the result is a deepening and enriching of our sense that together we are part of a story—one that defines for the community its identity and its vocation in the world. Having together lived that story in performance, the community is in a better position to discern and live out the will and grace of God reflected in it, as well as to identify aspects of the story that are problematic and need reshaping. In short, the audience both experiences the biblical work in a completely different way and contributes substantially to its particular dramatic realization. In this way, the word becomes flesh in both performer and audience.

Translucence and Transformation

If the arts are translucent to God's glory, approaching Scripture as a work to be performed can result in a powerful and transforming experience of that glory, both for performer and audience. Such an approach has the capacity to transform our understanding of Scripture itself, doing justice to its living, breathing character. It offers a means to experience the biblical text, as Paul puts it, as words "written not with ink but with the Spirit of the living God, not on tablets of stone but on tablets of human hearts" (2 Cor. 3:3). It recognizes that the words of Scripture find their intended mark when they penetrate the heart, mind, and soul of those whom they encounter, taking them up into a profound and life-giving vision of reality. The Christian faith is much more than a set of propositions; it constructs a symbolic world within which human activity finds meaning and purpose. Performing Scripture can render that symbolic world powerfully to an audience.

The interpreter who approaches the Bible as an artistic work to be performed has the potential to become an embodied vehicle of that

---

20. See, for example, Victor Turner, *From Ritual to Theatre: The Human Seriousness of Play* (New York: Performing Arts Journal Publications, 1982).

symbolic world in a way that both provides a helpful model for biblical interpretation and affords the possibility of a deeper textual understanding and experience. The performer must make himself a servant to the work's rhetorical goals to find a means to render it faithfully and effectively to a particular audience. If interpretation is a "fusion of horizons," as Anthony Thiselton suggests,[21] a performer/interpreter becomes a locus of that fusion, discerning those points of connection between the text's horizon and the horizon of contemporary experience. This should, of course, be the goal of any form of faithful biblical interpretation. But an effective performance of Scripture—much like effective preaching—has a special capacity to make that point of fusion immediate and specific, such that it becomes an *event*, an encounter with a real presence.

In order to realize the biblical material effectively, as I have suggested, the performer must connect with it in mind, body, and spirit. I highlighted the way in which an approach to Scripture as performance helps collapse the analytical interpreter's critical distance, thus opening the way for the performer himself to be transformed. The task of acting requires us to be immediately present to and for the text—to allow it to have its way with us. As Mamet puts it, to be effective, an actor must "give oneself up to the play."[22]

And this involves not just one's mind but one's body as well—and it is here especially that performance brings a new dimension to biblical interpretation. As Walter Wink has observed, both biblical exegesis and, in many ways, faith itself have in Western culture been cut off from our physical beings. Yet we live out our faith in and through our bodies. And as Paul makes clear, God intends for us to "glorify God" in our body (1 Cor. 6:20) as well as to live life in a posture of hope for our body's redemption (Rom. 8:23). From my own work I have seen how the physicality required in performing Scripture allows these spiritual realities to be experienced in a powerful and transforming way. To connect bodily with the words of Scripture—to "bear the marks of Christ" in our body (Gal. 6:17)—can contribute significantly to an experience of God's creative and redemptive activity in and through our body, and help us grasp what it means to present our bodies as "living sacrifice" to God.

---

21. Anthony Thiselton, *The Two Horizons: New Testament Hermeneutics and Philosophical Description* (Grand Rapids: Eerdmans, 1980).

22. Mamet, *True and False*, 32.

Finally, the audience that attends a performance of Scripture puts itself in a position to experience it in profoundly new and fresh ways. In its contract with the performer, it is a full participant in creating the performance. It openly agrees to being shaped by the drama that unfolds. But it also—by the way it reacts to and interacts with the action in any given moment—assists in shaping the performance into a unique, unrepeatable creation. As Tom Driver has observed, an effective performance takes both "the actor and the audience to a level in which something is risked and accomplished—a level in which the performance does not only pretend and show but actually does something valuable for both the performer and the spectator in the moment of its realization." Such an occurrence, he says, "moves theater close to ritual, that is, to performance having transcendent quality and import."[23]

Indeed, to return to my initial encounter with Scripture performed, it was just such transcendence that I experienced in a double sense: the performance compelled me to transcend my previous, rather limited comprehension of Mark's story, in ways that I have attempted to articulate here, and it brought me as well into the Presence of a transcendent reality in a way that left an indelible mark on my mind, body, and soul. That it was Mark's particular realization of the story of Jesus—characterized by "secret epiphanies" and a Jesus "on the loose," one who is present for us, yet can never be fully apprehended—reminds us, in keeping with the theme of this volume, that we cannot claim too much for this experience. We do still see in a mirror dimly, not face-to-face, much as an artistic work itself allows us only to infer things about its creator.

Nevertheless, the arts are translucent vehicles through which we can encounter God and God can encounter us. In ways that rational thought and discourse alone cannot, the arts can be a powerful manifestation of the image of God in us. And Scripture itself is most fruitfully engaged—and allowed to engage us more fully—when we attend to its own artistic and imaginative dimensions.

---

23. Tom F. Driver, "Performance and Biblical Reading: Its Power and Hazard," in Krondorfer, *Body and Bible*, 159–174; 164.

Part Three
Reflections on Translucence

7

Musical Gifts for
the Worshipping Body

KAREN BLACK

If I ask someone to tell me about a time she felt the power of music, she will have a story. If I ask a believer to tell me about a time he felt the presence of God through music, I have no doubt he also will have a story. I remember singing as a college junior in the chorus of Bach's *St. Matthew Passion* and feeling that I was somewhere other than in the very familiar Boe Chapel at St. Olaf College in Northfield, Minnesota. I remember the three hours seeming, at the same time, like a few moments and an eternity. And I remember the momentary silence after the performance feeling necessary and right—not uncomfortable.

This was a powerful religious experience for me, but I cannot describe exactly how. I was not "born again." I was not really a different person after that night. But now, twenty years later, I can picture the chorus, orchestra, soloists, and congregation. I can hear the music with its halo of strings around the words of Jesus, the arias' personal responses to the Passion story, and the chorus acting as both crowd and believer. I remember the experience as a time when I knew God's existence, trusted what I could not understand, and experienced something otherworldly, something ineffable.

Probably few present at that *St. Matthew Passion* performance even remember it, and perhaps no one else remembers it as one of their most memorable religious experiences. But I believe that most Christians can remember a time when music illuminated for them the nature of God, linked them with others across time and place, and were nurtured on a journey of faith in ways that words alone could neither provide nor explain.

Participating in music as performer or as listener reinforces our humanness and yet takes us beyond ourselves. Knowing what music can inspire, we as church musicians need to be intentional about how we plan music to enhance worship. In shared music, particularly in worship, we as a congregation unite with others who listen or perform with us, and a traditional hymn tune or liturgical chant can even unite us with its long history among believers who lived before us. But the self-transcendence effected by music is more profound than the feeling of social unity it can impart: at times as we sing or play, we experience the real presence of God. Music's very temporality affirms the stages of human life and at the same time, paradoxically, transports us beyond this world to the timeless, eternal reality of God. This divine gift provides a reality that cannot be fully articulated or understood through reason. Still, church musicians need to reflect on how the music they select and use can enlighten worship and deepen worshippers' lives.

Music as God's Gift

To say that music is a "great and glorious gift from God" is not new. But the statement is more than a catchy phrase to adorn a wall hanging or bumper sticker; it asserts that God offers humanity musical sound as a wonder of creation. If music is God's gift, it becomes more than a sensory experience or a pleasant pastime by and for ourselves: music calls us back to the giver. Christians have not always understood music as divine gift. Although Augustine believed in music's power to draw the heart to devotion, he also worried, because of the danger of getting caught up in the pleasures of melody, that music might become a distraction from true devotion. Reformers such as Zwingli, while appreciating music, saw it as a purely worldly phenomenon and so denied its place in worship.[1] For these and others, music is a human invention that,

---

1. For a brief overview of Augustine's ambivalence about music and Zwingli's place in a Reformation understanding of music, see Paul Westermeyer, *Te Deum: The Church and Music* (Minneapolis: Fortress Press, 1998), 86–89, 149–53.

while perhaps pleasurable or even devotional, is not a divine gift as are Scripture and the sacraments.

For others, however, music's divine genesis means that it is something that deserves a privileged place in life and in worship. Martin Luther's emphasis on music as God's gift to enable Christian faith caused him to place music next in importance to theology. In his preface to Georg Rhau's 1538 collection of chorale motets, *Symphoniae iucundae,* Luther explained the difficulty of defining music's effects:

> I would certainly like to praise music with all my heart as the excellent gift of God which it is and to commend it to everyone. But I am so overwhelmed by the diversity and magnitude of its virtue and benefits that I can find neither beginning nor end or method for my discourse.... Next to the Word of God, music deserves the highest praise.[2]

When one considers Luther's rhetorical skill and the voluminous pages of writings he left, it is somewhat surprising that he struggled with words to praise music. Yet he understood that music has a unique place in God's creation to benefit God's people in ways that defy description. As God's gift, music for Luther should be studied and used for the benefit of God's people.

Luther recognized music's value in providing insight into a fuller understanding of the Christian story than words alone could provide. In his commentary on the Psalms of David, Luther wrote:

> The Book of Psalms is a sweet and delightful song because it sings of and proclaims the Messiah even when a person does not sing the notes but merely recites and pronounces the words. And yet the music, or the notes, which are a wonderful creation and gift of God, help materially in this, especially when the people sing along and reverently participate.[3]

Again, the emphasis is on music as created by God and bequeathed to believers in order to proclaim God's Word. While the words of the Psalm alone proclaim the Messiah, Luther believed adding melody and rhythm enhanced the message.

Luther's view represents a change in thought, as the composer Carl Schalk points out in *Luther on Music: Paradigms of Praise:* "From the

---

2. Martin Luther, *Luther's Works,* ed. Jaroslav Pelikan and Helmut T. Lehmann, 55 vols. (St. Louis: Concordia; Philadelphia: Fortress Press, 1955–1986), 53:321, 323 (cited hereafter as *LW*).

3. *LW* 15:274.

time of the early church through the Middle Ages, two especially powerful paradigms or models for the role of music in the life and worship
of the church had been music as teacher or pedagogue and music as
guardian of morals."[4] Music had been used to teach doctrine and instruct believers in right belief and correct living. As the early and medieval church struggled with doctrinal issues, music became a vehicle
for teaching doctrine and combating heresies. Philosophers from Plato
on believed in the power of music to shape human character and moral
behavior, and the church had inherited those views. Schalk argues that
Luther "did not deny the importance of either of these models," but
preferred to view music as even more central to Christian life:

> He chose instead to point to a more basic and primary paradigm that
> simultaneously encompassed and superseded them both. For Luther, that
> paradigm, that glowing center of awareness and comprehension that was
> for him the basis of understanding music in the life and worship of God's
> people, was *music as creation and gift of God.*[5]

Schalk's "glowing center of awareness and comprehension" suggests
this volume's focusing metaphor of art as translucent. Luther understood music as paradigmatic gift that remains itself an aural art form of
great beauty, both temporal and temporary, but that also—by pointing
beyond itself to God as source of infinite beauty—allows divine light
to shine in and through its earthly sound.

Exploring the nature of gift itself helps us to think about music and
its effect in our lives and, more importantly, to better plan our worship.
If music functions in worship as divine gift, it will engender different
effects than it would as a human product or invention. Gifts imply particular relationships between giver and receiver: we give gifts to those
we love or those with whom we have a relationship. Rarely do we give
a gift to someone we do not know. In fact, gifts are often given to those
with whom we desire a deeper relationship: an engagement ring is given
as expression of a desire for a lifelong relationship; a housewarming gift
is given to welcome new neighbors. Gifts are reflections of the giver
and the giver's understanding of the receiver. We try to give a gift we
think the receiver will enjoy and use, and we are pleased when the re-

---

4. Carl Schalk, *Luther on Music: Paradigms of Praise* (St. Louis: Concordia,
1988), 32.
5. Ibid., 33.

ceiver seems to truly take pleasure in the gift. Yet we also use gifts to share something of ourselves. As any parent will attest, the favorite gift from one's child is that plaster handprint, the crudely made clay vase, or the drawing of a happy family—something the child alone created.

A true gift is one that is neither earned nor deserved. In giving and receiving a gift, the exchange does not express a commercial transaction. Even if we offer a gift in thanksgiving for something, we do not give it as an equal exchange or as payment, but as outward sign of inward gratitude. Sometimes gift-giving entails personal sacrifice, either in saving money to buy the present, working many hours to make it, or as in O. Henry's "The Gift of the Magi," sacrificing something one values in exchange for it. All of these characteristics point to gift's role in expressing, creating, and strengthening a relationship between giver and receiver.

The giving and receiving of music also involves, of course, the human act of making music. Each piece of music, as it is composed and performed, is constructed from human ideas, experience, and work. Both creation and presentation require human skill, effort, and interaction. A composer may believe the work is inspired by God, yet such inspiration only becomes reality through putting notes on paper, with a performer (whether a professional musician or congregation member in the pew) bringing notes to life with voice or instrument. We speak of composers and performers as "gifted" when they possess the skill and talent to bring the gift to aural fruition.

As the intermediaries between God as giver of music and listener as receiver of the gift, composers and performers are full participants in a gift exchange. Remembering this reciprocal quality may help us approach the composing, performing, and listening with humility and gratefulness. Johann Sebastian Bach's signature "Soli Deo Gloria" suggests that he saw his compositions as offerings to God's people, given in recognition of God as source and the one who deserves glory. This is a crucial recognition for church musicians yet today: in bringing music to life in worship, they are bearers of a holy gift. If church musicians see themselves as actors in a gift exchange, as carriers of God's gift to people, then their work becomes holy work.

The culture of gift-giving also helps describe music's unique role in community life. In his book *The Gift: Imagination and the Erotic Life of Property,* Lewis Hyde uses the anthropology of gift exchange to find a language for art. In his analysis of ancient cultures, folk tales, and tribal communities, Hyde describes the relationships formed when commerce is based on giving gifts rather than selling commodities. Hyde lists several characteristics that mark the gift exchange. First, a gift is used but not used up, and even increases in material, social, and spiritual ways as it becomes a return gift or is passed through a community. Hyde comments that this increase is not profit: "Capital earns profit and the sale of a commodity turns a profit, but gifts that remain gifts do not *earn* profit, they *give* increase."[6] Secondly, gifts can transform the receiver and bring new life: "A gift passes through the body and leaves us altered. The gift is not merely the witness or guardian to new life, but the creator."[7] Lastly, gifts create bonds between the giver and receiver and can establish and maintain community.[8]

While a gift culture still exists in many families or communities today, the modern world operates mostly in a market economy. Only in *It's a Wonderful Life* do banks *give* us money to buy a house and then hope for a return gift. Rather, when we sign a mortgage, the bank maintains ownership of the house as collateral. Hyde writes, "Equitable trade is not an agent of transformation, nor of spiritual cohesion" as is art, which Hyde argues belongs in the gift world.[9] For Hyde, music as gift means that it will "give increase," perhaps in spiritual ways by changing the receiver and even creating new life. This increase is not interest, but a benefit that transforms the receiver. Musical experience, by shaping us into givers and receivers, forms and maintains relationship.

If God is the giver of music as gift to humans, the exchange involved in the musical medium creates profound relationship. Composer, performer, and listener exchange gifts, but an exchange is also taking place between God and God's people: music expresses, sustains, and deepens people's connection to each other and to God. God freely gives this gift in love for us to use and enjoy. Our pleasure in melody, harmony, counterpoint, cadence, and rhythm is given so that the receiver will enjoy and use it.

Our deep aesthetic satisfaction in music's combined components is rewarding human pleasure in itself. But this musical gift is translucent, pointing to itself and also beyond itself: God's light shines both into

---

6. Lewis Hyde, *The Gift: Imagination and the Erotic Life of Property* (New York: Vintage, 1983), 37.

7. Ibid., 45.

8. Ibid., 78.

9. Ibid., 137.

and through the musical moment. As a gift tells us something about the giver, we discover through it a divine truth. God gives us a reflection of God's self, one that we ourselves do not create out of nothingness. Music can have transforming power that changes us and our understanding of the Divine Other in ways impossible through other means. Entrusted with God's gift of music, we must work to make the best use of it in worship and other religious occasions, for ourselves and for all of God's people.

Music's Gift Values

If we view music as God's gift, then, with the musical exchange between composer, performer, and listener, we—as church musicians and worshippers—may deepen our thinking about music's value, benefits, and use. Music as an art form expresses the divine-human relationship. Music in worship can strengthen this relationship by its gift values, enriching worshippers' lives and sustaining a worshipping community.

Despite today's competitive music market economy, with music a commodity that is sold or purchased—including lucrative compact disc sales and lawsuits over music-downloading software—the musical gift exchange cannot be measured by its usefulness or market value. In an attempt to compete, musicians and music teachers often grasp at ways to validate musicians' roles, to convince others of music's usefulness, to assure its place in education and, for many, its essential place in worship. While music is important in many of these ways, its most valuable benefits are those that result from giftedness: creating relationship and community with others and with God, transforming our lives with a reality unknown any other way.

I can only begin to discuss here what Luther called "the diversity and magnitude" of music's "virtue and benefits." Of all music's *effects*, society perhaps most commonly cites music's *affect*—its power to influence the emotions. Ever since Plato made his arguments about music's power, it has been thought to powerfully affect the listener's psyche and emotions. Luther speaks of music's ability to alter one's emotional and moral states:

> Here it must suffice to discuss the benefit . . . of this great art. . . . But even
> that transcends the greatest eloquence of the most eloquent, because of
> the infinite variety of its forms and benefits. We can mention only one
> point (which experience confirms), namely, that next to the Word of God,

music deserves the highest praise. She is a mistress and governess of those human emotions.... For whether you wish to comfort the sad, to terrify the happy, to encourage the despairing, to humble the proud, to calm the passionate, or to appease those full of hate—and who could number all these masters of the human heart, namely, the emotions, inclinations, and affections that impel men to evil or good?—what more effective means than music could you find?[10]

Earlier in the same passage, Luther struggles to find words to praise music. Here, he describes music's power, as "mistress and governess" of human emotions, to alter emotional states, the "masters of the human heart," which in turn affect moral behavior. Luther believed that God's gift was to be used to temper human passions and give solace to God's people.

Today, descriptions of musical effects on the emotions are common. When people describe their reactions to a performance, they often describe the feeling it elicits. We can attempt to delineate particular feelings that music evokes—pathos, joy, anger, surprise, tedium—but none completely expresses the holistic way music affects us. People turn to their favorite music in various psychological states—to relieve stress, to celebrate, to mourn. Although music can be psychologically healing, some argue that sociopaths have been reported to commit acts of violence after listening to specific musical pieces. This debate over music's power to affect our moral character and behavior, which has gone on for centuries, continues today. Just as Plato believed in music's power to elevate the mind, today's critics argue that violent rap music has harmful effects on emotions and character.

Some would claim that music even has an influence on intelligence, pointing to music's usefulness in the so-called "Mozart Effect." The evidence from one controversial study suggests that students who listened to classical music, specifically Mozart, scored better on math tests than those who listened to other music or to none at all. Scientific proof, some say, that music will make you smarter, better able to think and reason, solve problems, and do math. The assumption is that if scientific methods prove that music can be used to make us better at scientific endeavors, then music has value. Playing or listening to music may indeed have an effect on brain development. But even if music makes one more

---

10. *LW* 53:323.

intelligent (if true intelligence can be measured), this still does not explain the unique or primary value of music.

Music's value extends beyond the individual and binds us with others, creating community in secular society as well as in religious communities. Thousands unite in singing the national anthem in a sports stadium; the crowd claps along with folk and gospel performances. Many will remember how, following the tragedy of September 11, the House and Senate members on the steps of the Capitol spontaneously joined and sang "God Bless America." And in church, collective hymn singing joins everyone in mutual gesture, as does the Eucharist. I have felt this sense of community in worship that included simple, unaccompanied, unison chant; I have also felt it in worship that included a massed choir singing Tallis's forty-part *Spem in Alium.*

Making music provides a sense of unity between performers and audience or among members of an ensemble. Musicians often report feeling a connection with the audience; listeners feel their bodies move in sympathy with the performer, and the music's high points quicken the listener's heartbeat. In a different way, orchestra and chorus members are aware of the collective power of their unified mission of music-making as they play or sing together: the whole creates more than the sum of its parts. Each section in an ensemble works toward sounding as one voice, and yet the sound is very different from that of a solo instrument or vocal performance. The voice of one section counters or dovetails that of another, and the result is harmony or counterpoint. Making music together forms a community within a performing ensemble, between performer and audience, or even among strangers brought together in one place.

In that singing of the *St. Matthew Passion* years ago, my connection with others worked on several levels to make the experience powerful for me. I felt united with others in the room—the chorus with whom I had rehearsed for months and the audience members for whom, I imagined, the performance was deeply resonant. As an organ student who had studied Bach, I linked with the composer as I helped to bring the music, in all its complexity, to life. While our performance ensemble was likely quite different from Bach's (and we sang in English), I sensed that music could indeed cross centuries and come alive again in another time. Not only could I hear the story in words, but the music helped me to put myself into the story, both as crucifier and as mourner. I witnessed the whole Passion story, and it felt as real to me as my daily life.

Through music, we also sense union with the church's history, with past saints and musicians. We transcend ourselves and our time by joining this even wider community through music. When we participate in the church's liturgy and hymns, we join those who have sung the same throughout the centuries. We are a part, but only a part, of something much larger than ourselves. In his "Treatise on the Last Words of David," Luther suggests that as we sing in worship, we become the Church Universal:

> David calls his psalms the psalms of Israel. He does not want to ascribe them to himself alone and claim the sole glory for them. . . . In that light we Christians speak of our psalmists. St. Ambrose composed many hymns of the church. . . . They are called church hymns because the church accepted them and sings them just as though the church had written them and as though they were the church's songs. Therefore it is not customary to say, "Thus sings Ambrose, Gregory, Prudentius, Sedulius," but "Thus sings the Christian church." . . . For these are now the songs of the church, which Ambrose, Sedulius, etc., sing with the church and the church with them. When they die, the church survives them and keeps on singing their songs.[11]

To Luther's list we would add the hymns of Watts, Wesley, Vajda, Haugen, and Luther himself as well as others. Centuries from now, even more will be added. When we think of ourselves joining in the song of the whole church, we belong to the great company of saints of the past, present, and future.

The strong union with centuries of Christians singing the church's song became real for me during the Triduum in my first position as a full-time church musician at a large urban Catholic parish. Holy Thursday Mass began with a procession, accompanied by the congregation's a cappella singing of *Pange Lingua* in Latin (the English text begins, "Of the glorious body telling, O my tongue, its mysteries sing"). Though the congregation rarely sang hymns in Latin, they knew this hymn as an important and meaningful part of their tradition and knew that day as a central festival of their faith. As the large assembly solemnly sang this medieval hymn in unison in the quiet church, the tall priest prostrated

---

11. *LW* 15:274.

himself before the altar. The hundreds of worshippers in the church singing together, symbolic of all believers joining in a hymn sung for centuries on previous nights like this around the world, was deeply moving. In that specific time and place we sensed a spiritual unity with each other but also, through song and ritual, felt one with Christians of all times and places.

Knowing more about the history of the church's song not only puts our own limited lifespan in perspective; it deepens the honor and privilege of joining our own voices with saints past and future. It is hubris to believe that Christian song begins and ends with our generation. We are privileged to have words of Ambrose and Prudentius, Luther and Watts, to give voice to our praise. When people say, "Why don't we sing the good old hymns anymore?" they usually mean nineteenth-century or early gospel hymns—music from the past century or so. But for the richest treasury of church song, the "good old hymns" should really refer to texts such as those of Ambrose from the fourth century or tunes from medieval plainsong. These are gifts we have been given to join in the church's song of every time and place. To those, we add our own songs and remember that after we are no longer here, the song will go on.

Music as Real Presence

We value music, then, for its effect on our emotional and intellectual lives and for its power to create and build community, even across space and time. But in the experience of music we often sense something more, something that cannot be described in emotional, psychological, or social terms. Its aesthetic beauty and its textual sense call attention to music as music. But this artistic reality is also a translucence that allows illumination to pass through it. Music reaches to the center of our being and gives form and meaning to life, but it also gives a partial revelation: a glimpse of God.

In one sense, music reinforces the temporality of our humanness. Like all earthly things, music happens in time: it has a beginning, middle, and end, mirroring our passage through life's stages. In this temporal process, music conveys something about the nature of living. Through rhythm and form, it underlines our sense of our physical and chronological lives, an understanding that is purely musical in meaning. To say that music's temporality represents in sound life's temporality is not quite correct; rather, the experience of music in some inexplicable way illuminates for us a deeper awareness of our lives' wholeness and shape.

Music's temporality, ironically, also conveys timelessness. In the experience of music, we can momentarily transcend our finite life. As art perceived, music cannot be transparent to God. Listeners have expectations of sequential time in music, and when composers play with these expectations by changing rhythm, tempo, or length, music can produce an altered sense of temporality. Composers also use music's temporal nature through which to hint at eternity. Olivier Messiaen indicates extremely slow tempi in some of his organ works to portray a sense of God's infinity. A Taizé worship service includes singing that has no definite ending; the refrains, canons, or ostinati are sung over and over. Brother Roger of Taizé writes:

> Nothing is more conducive to a communion with the living God than a meditative common prayer with, as its high point, singing that never ends and that continues in the silence of one's heart when one is alone again. When the mystery of God becomes tangible through the simple beauty of symbols, when it is not smothered by too many words, then a common prayer, far from exuding monotony and boredom, awakens us to heaven's joy on earth.[12]

Brother Roger suggests we imbibe a sense of God's ineffable mystery in music's auditory beauty, a sense that lasts into our solitude. In worship, music's temporality can give an indelible vision of the eternal, that "singing that never ends."

When music puts our lives into form, helping us to better understand our humanness, this meaning has a deep reality, but it cannot be explained. In his argument that art has meaning beyond what reason can know, George Steiner speaks of its "real presence": "Music makes utterly substantive what I have sought to suggest of the real presence of meaning where that presence cannot be analytically shown or paraphrased. Music brings to our daily lives an immediate encounter with a logic of sense other than that of reason."[13] Steiner argues that this "real presence" reaches to the core of what it means to be human:

---

12. Brother Roger of Taizé, *Songs and Prayers from Taizé* (Chicago: GIA, 1991), 5.
13. George Steiner, *Real Presences* (Chicago: University of Chicago Press, 1989), 218.

> The energy that is music puts us in felt relation to the energy that is
> life....The translation of music into meaning, into meaning that is en-
> tirely musical, carries with it what somatic and spiritual cognizance we can
> have of the core-mystery that we are. And this energy of existence lies
> deeper than any biological or psychological determination.[14]

Through this mysterious sense of meaning arrived at somatically and
felt spiritually, music translucently communicates this "real presence of
meaning" to give us fuller understanding. Musical sound in harmony,
counterpoint, ornamentation, and rhythm shapes our humanity into
beauty, and we somehow see our place in God's larger reality. The
unique meaning and "energy of existence" that music brings is part of
its giftedness; our greater understanding of ourselves is Hyde's "increase" of the gift.

Steiner describes music's temporality as a kind of freedom from
time: "It liberates us from the enforcing beat of biological and physical-
mathematical clocks. The time which music 'takes,' and which it gives
as we perform or experience it, is the only free time granted us prior to
death."[15] As in my *St. Matthew Passion* experience, people sometimes
describe an altered sense of time in a concert or worship service, an experience in which "time stood still." Moments seem to be eternal: a long
performance seems to take no time at all. When one is truly immersed
in music, either as performer or listener, clock time has no power or
significance. Steiner's "free time" in the experience of music allows us
to temporarily transcend mortality. Music's ability to provide at least
momentary freedom from time is another expression of its increase
as gift.

The translucence of music opens to us glimpses of realities beyond ourselves and indeed glimpses of God's glory. Steiner argues that
"the aesthetic is the making formal of epiphany. There is a 'shining
through.'"[16] Steiner's argument suggests that music works as a
translucent lens that draws attention to itself as a filter of light, but
that also lets transcendent illumination pass through; in the process,
we hear the work's earthly attributes but also, through them, its inti-
mations of eternity. As I sang the *St. Matthew Passion* that day so long

---

14. Ibid., 196.
15. Ibid., 197.
16. Ibid., 226.

ago, I experienced the truth of what I could not know. In the dramatic Passion story set to music so that it became new for me, God shone through that night. Music provides that translucent vision of God's being and presence that cannot be revealed in any other way. Its translucence draws us to the divine.

Planning Worship Music as Gift for the Body of Christ

How do we, as church musicians planning worship, act as catalysts to enable this transcendent musical experience to occur? We cannot simply depend on the quality of translucence in any hymn or anthem. We need, rather, to think about how our choices may enhance social cohesion, affirm tradition, enlighten belief, and enable epiphany. We need to be aware of the profound possibilities available to us in our role as actors in a gift exchange between God and God's people.

I have some ideas. We must insure that the compositions we use are well crafted—whether hymns, preludes and postludes, voluntaries, chants, or anthems. It is not coincidental that my most memorable experience was the performance of Bach's *St. Matthew Passion;* both believers and nonbelievers view it as a great work. Bach's dramatic handling of the text testifies to his ability to master Baroque forms and text setting. He uses breathless rhythm and an upward motive to make more dramatic the questioning phrases as the crowd/chorus—when accused of denying Jesus—asks "Is it I?" He crafts the intertwining counterpoint and harmony with deft compositional skill. The interrelationship of solo, chorus, and orchestra demonstrates his mastery of the Baroque oratorio form. Bach incorporates texts and tunes of well-known, traditional Lutheran chorales, interspersed with parts of the biblical Passion story told by chorus and solos, the poetry in the arias commenting on the story. Bach's musical rhetoric complements these varied texts. A compendium of Baroque musical forms—fugue, recitative, *da capo* aria, chorales, concertato style—the work masterfully portrays the narrative and invites a believer's deeply felt response to it.

Bach's fine intertwining of music and text suggests another crucial quality of music as the translucent conveyer of the transcendent: the complementarity of text and music. When a hymn text used in worship is rich in meaning, and when text and tune are thoughtfully wedded, the worshipper is transported. A contemporary example is "Thine the

Amen," with text by Herb Brokering and hymn tune by Carl Schalk. The text, unusual in its lack of punctuation and verbs, is thoughtful and inspiring. The tune is, at first glance, simple in its stepwise motion and rhythmic regularity. Yet each musical line has a definite and satisfying arc shape: the first half of the first, second, and fourth lines is identical, but each ends differently. The third line begins a fifth higher than the others, but the hymn's climactic moment is at the highest melodic point, near the end of the last line. Both the tune's regular rhythm and the lines' initial repetition conform perfectly to the text. The stepwise motion of mostly eighth-notes, continuing to rise to the hymn's conclusion, supports the breathless continuity of the text to its ecstatic end. Text and tune combine so that by the last stanza we are filled with hope in the resurrection, and for that brief moment we are not afraid of our own mortality:

> Thine the glory in the night no more dying only light
> thine the river thine the tree then the Lamb eternally
> then the holy holy holy celebration jubilee
> thine the splendor thine the brightness only thee only thee.[17]

Selecting well-crafted music that complements the text heightens meaningful worship, but the church musician also needs to think about how music grounds church ritual. In the most effective worship, the text, the sounds of instrument and voice, and the participants' movement complement each other. During that first Holy Thursday experience in my Roman Catholic parish, as the priest washed the feet of ordinary people, we sang the Taizé *Ubi caritas*. I was struck by the holy moment: music and ritual joined in a vision of God's love for creation, the melodious gift of God's Son. The priest symbolically demonstrated charity as he washed parishioners' lowly feet while we sang, "Where there is charity and love, God is there." In the Taizé tradition, Latin is used as a unifying symbol—not as a common language as in the medieval church, but as a language foreign to all. Through the simple eight-measure ostinato, musician and nonmusician become equals as they join together in participation, and the added instruments and solo verses complete the sense of greater unity. As the group sings the

---

17. Herbert F. Brokering, "Thine the Amen," © 1983 Augsburg Publishing House, admin. Augsburg Fortress, in *With One Voice: A Lutheran Resource for Worship* (Minneapolis: Augsburg Fortress, 1995), #801.

phrase over and over, it becomes a mantra for individual prayer. Even while conducting the instrumentalists during the singing, I felt the power of the Triduum and all it means. For me, Holy Thursday has never been the same; I have not been the same since that transforming night.

In all these worship experiences, music became a translucent light to allow a glimpse of God's glory. Perhaps music can sometimes even be a sign of resurrection. Several years ago a colleague of mine, a music therapist who was working in a nursing home with an elderly woman suffering from advanced Alzheimer's disease, was videotaping the session for her class. The patient, who had been totally unresponsive and silent for some months, gave no sign that her mind was functioning anymore. But when my colleague began playing her guitar and singing hymns, suddenly the woman's face lit up; she recognized the melodies and began to sing along. When the woman's son watched the tape later, he was amazed. The woman on the videotape was the mother he remembered, one he had not seen for years and would not see again before she died. Researchers may have a physiological explanation for the woman's sudden responsiveness to music, a connection between the acoustical properties of sound and brain waves, which caused her dementia to momentarily disappear. But for me, this is a musical resurrection story: the dumb speak and the dead live again. Though this resurrection took place outside of worship, it serves as powerful reminder of how music's translucence can give a vision of what awaits in the life hereafter.

If, like Luther, we fully embrace the idea that music is God's gift, it becomes that which we receive from the greatest of Givers. The gift has intrinsic value, without the expectation that we, like the servants with their talents, will pragmatically put it to use and turn a material profit. Music does not need to pay us the dividend of making us better mathematicians or smarter thinkers or increasing our earning potential. By providing us a new, translucent understanding of the Divine Other in what may be a life-changing experience, music allows us to envision that which is humanly impossible; it allows us to imagine a new life in faith. Hyde writes: "The gift is not merely the witness or guardian to new life, but the creator."[18]

---

18. Hyde, *The Gift*, 45.

In the pressures of worship planning and choir rehearsals, we as church musicians sometimes forget what a gift we have in music—a gift we can use each week to praise God and to transform lives. Music fulfills its purpose in us when it transforms our lives in small or large ways, when its combined sound and sense allow us to commune with neighbors near or far, present or past, and when the experience of Bach's *St. Matthew Passion* or the Taizé *Ubi caritas* moves us into the presence of the holy. As a gift, music increases in us and between us. We encounter the glory of God in ways only available through the medium of art, which is human-made but God-given.

8

Passion

Deconstruction as Spiritual Quest

PAUL BEIDLER

Recently I attended the thesis defense of a philosophy student who had, impressively, undertaken both to systematize Friedrich Nietzsche's thought and to demonstrate, point by point, a correspondence between Nietzsche's main points and those made by Max Weber. He had clearly read each philosopher's major works, demonstrating Nietzsche's influence on Weber most convincingly. But in the end, he claimed that the thoughts of both philosophers could be traced back to arbitrary, irrational assumptions. At that point, I had questions for him: Is there any other way to do philosophy? Is there any philosophy that is not built on airy definitions and assertions? Is there an alternative to selecting assumptions more or less randomly and reasoning more or less cogently upon them? He apologized that he was unprepared to answer the question—he had never considered these foundational questions. And he looked uncomfortable. In fact, several of those present looked uncomfortable.

Not being a philosopher, I asked the question simply out of curiosity. My intention was not to be subversive. Without meaning to, however, I suppose I had "deconstructed" him. I reflected later that deconstruction always affects people as my questions had. The first time I taught an essay by Jacques Derrida, one of the students later told a colleague that she felt the ground had disappeared beneath her feet. It is a

202

common reaction, but in fact the reaction is *passion,* and we should not fear but rather study it. I want to emphasize not only the unexpectedness of the questions I asked but also their unwelcome optimism. Had anyone asked me how I would answer these questions, I would have said, "Sure. Deconstruction is such an alternative." I am glad no one asked, of course; my intention was not to distract attention away from Nietzsche and Weber but only to shift the conversation toward methodology. But I was struck by the effect of the question. Those present seemed rather complacently comfortable with the posited ultimate baselessness of philosophical reasoning in general, as well as the pedagogical value of arguments that demonstrate it. The prospect of an alternative, though, was frightening. It is actually scary to think there might be a critical discourse that is not inherently hypothetical and provisional; we have all been taught to strenuously assume there can be no such thing. What would such a discourse look like? What would its implications be? We who inhabit colleges of the church ought perhaps to be more ready than most to deal with such a possibility. But we are not.

I do not plan to argue here that deconstruction is less hypothetical and provisional than other philosophical discourses because its assumptions, unlike those of other styles of thought, are rooted solidly in reality. They are not. To pursue deconstruction is to acknowledge this. What I will try to demonstrate here is that deconstruction is reading. Its basis is not concepts or assumptions but the text itself, whose existence, while of course complex, is not in question. Jacques Derrida's work involves not debunking philosophy but reading it. And his readings often nonplus his readers. We are unprepared for them. There seems something obscene about Derrida's way of reading, just as there seemed something obscene about the question I asked our young philosopher. Surely I could not be so naïve as to be asking him whether a philosophical argument could be true. And yet I was asking precisely that.

Our topic in this volume is the arts, and Derrida approaches the arts differently from the kind of criticism we have come to expect. We expect philosophers to talk about things, but Derrida does not talk about: he reads. Derrida's texts are readings, but again, not in the sense that term usually implies. His texts, for example, are often more intimate and personal than we are comfortable with. He also experiments radically with form and style. Fair enough, as long as he does not call himself a philosopher, right? A culture critic—a "postmodernist," perhaps. But read his work more closely and you may find that it is too philosophical for your liking—too abstract and dry, and at the same time not serious enough. For example, in "Signature Event Context," one of his most important forays into the philosophy of language, Derrida discusses the logical priority of iterability. It is, as he observes toward the end, a "very *dry* discussion."[1] But the italics also point to the initials of the title, "S.E.C."—*sec* is the French word for "dry." Is that a joke, a demonstration of a serious philosophical point, or both? It is hard to tell. We want to be able to say exactly what kind of writer Derrida is, but he seems to defy categorization.

Furthermore, he is just not as cynical as we would like him to be. Ask, and you may be told that Derrida destroys the meaning and value of things. The young philosophy student I mentioned responded at one point to my question (I confess that I repeated it several times) by explaining that philosophy did in fact have real value—as if I had suggested it didn't. Of course, he was the one who had suggested it was all based upon arbitrary assumptions. What makes Derrida frustrating, and particularly relevant in a volume seeking to explore spirituality and the arts, is that his writings are as spiritual as they are artistic. He has this to say, for example, in *Demeure:*

> Any testimony testifies in essence to the miraculous and the extraordinary from the moment it must, by definition, appeal to an act of faith beyond any proof. When one testifies, even on the subject of the most ordinary and the most "normal" event, one asks the other to believe one at one's word as if it were a matter of a miracle.

The passage exemplifies the characteristic move of deconstruction: two mutually exclusive concepts, here truth and fiction, are shown to be dependent upon each other. The idea is that testimony only makes sense if we assume a coherent, continuous, miraculous self, a "self itself."[2] We can all, I think, relate to the narrator of the story Derrida is commenting on here, who says, in Derrida's expansive paraphrase, "At the moment of my attestation I am no longer the same as the witness who lived that and who remains irreplaceable." The self who testifies cannot be the same as the self who was present to that which must be testified,

---

1. Jacques Derrida, *Limited Inc,* ed. Gerald Graff and trans. Samuel Weber and Jeffrey Mehlman (Evanston, Ill.: Northwestern University Press, 1988), 20.

2. Jacques Derrida, *Demeure: Fiction and Testimony* (Stanford, Calif.: Stanford University Press, 2000), 75, 65. Literature critics and others who are curious about deconstruction, and those who wonder how deconstruction ties to religion, may find this little book the best to start with.

if only because of the profound act of testimony. Given what might be called the deconstruction of the self, the fact that the self that recognizes itself cannot be the self that is recognized, testimony is predicated on miracle, is it not? We might be less surprised if Derrida were to argue that true testimony cannot exist, but he does not argue that. Also, we would be wrong to read Derrida as denying the existence of the self here—the deconstruction of the self is simply something he reads with particular attention in Blanchot's story. Rather, Derrida suggests that all testimony, testimony *qua* testimony—if there is any such thing, and apparently there is—testifies to miracle. To read Derrida is to have both the unity and the coherence of one's most basic notions, such as truth and fiction, called into question. It is also to find one's faith in the miraculous strengthened to an almost uncomfortable degree. Not one's belief in individual miracles—one's faith in the miraculous. In the passage I have quoted, Derrida shows that every utterance, even the most mundane, is a testimony of faith. I am not sure most of us even want that kind of faith. And he does this not in some ponderous philosophical tome but in passing, in a reading of a story.

Derrida's topic in *Demeure* is passion. If you enjoy the arts, you probably do not seek triumphant aesthetic explanations, and you probably do not seek art that transparently conveys a message, either, though polemical art can be interestingly monstrous. You do not seek the truth because the truth is not the truth of art. You seek to experience, savor, and remember works that are deeply present. You seek a richness that opens the pores of your sensitivity. It is not clarity you seek, but something clearer: not the truth, but something truer. You seek passion. If you read criticism, you seek a discourse on passion that does not try to categorize it or reduce it to artistic greatness or historical significance. You want a discourse that will help you to orient yourself to passion, to open yourself to passion, and to respond with passion; you want criticism that is itself passionate. You want more than talk about art's translucence: you want language that participates in that translucence. Derrida's deconstruction is such a discourse of passion—and of resistance. Like Peter, who—after Jesus declares his coming death and resurrection—insists that it will never happen, we often resist passion.[3] We fear

---

3. *The New Oxford Annotated Bible, with the Apocryphal/Deuterocanonical Books,* ed. Bruce M. Metzger and Roland E. Murphy (New York: Oxford University Press, 1991), Matt. 16:21-23.

it, and it is important to be honest about that. Is there a philosophical relationship between passion and resistance?

Derrida has testified in an interview that his deepest interest is not in philosophy or in literature but in autobiography. The reason he gives is that "in a minimal autobiographical trait can be gathered the greatest potentiality of historical, theoretical, linguistic, philosophical culture."[4] But there's something obscene about autobiography, a flaunting of self that seems to require apology. When Wordsworth made himself the subject of his epic, he apologized throughout the work for having done so.[5] Similarly, Derrida has said that he writes to apologize for writing: "whenever I write, I say sorry to the other, and even to the intended readers, for the impropriety of writing."[6] I will confess to the same "obsessive desire"[7] in this essay: I intend here not to explain deconstruction but to perform it autobiographically. I do so in the hope of writing passionate criticism. An explanation would treat deconstruction as something outside me—a method or technique—but it is not that. This will be an essay on moments constitutive of my selfhood, on the momentness of those moments, and on the new sense of self that emerges from their reading. This is not an essay on deconstruction and religion but a testimony of faith, passion, and desire.

Myself

In Jeanette Winterson's beautiful novel *The Passion,* Henri says, "I have never been myself and it is the thought of that that makes it easier for me to say goodbye."[8] This notion of having "never been myself" makes sense to me. I cannot remember when my self-detachment began— when I left my self behind. I think it must have been very early—at the beginning of what Jacques Lacan calls the mirror phase, when the child apprehends its basic separation from the world. As far back as I can remember, I have always been easily stymied, and what I remember of

4. Jacques Derrida, *Acts of Literature,* ed. Derek Attridge (New York: Routledge, 1992), 34, 43.

5. William Wordsworth, *The Prelude, 1799, 1805, 1859,* ed. Jonathan Wordsworth (New York: Norton, 1979); see 13.386ff. in the 1805 version, for example.

6. *Derrida's Elsewhere,* directed by Safaa Fathy, First Run/Icarus Films, 1999.

7. Derrida, *Acts of Literature,* 34.

8. Jeanette Winterson, *The Passion* (New York: Grove, 1987), 33.

my reaction to life's prodding jabs is that I have stood detached, passively observing what was happening to and around me.

I did this partly because I was taught to. When I was in middle school, kids used to pick on me, and my mother's advice was to wait for them to get bored and stop. This was profoundly bad advice, but she offered it sincerely, and, more important, I took it eagerly. Of course the kids didn't get bored—they excitedly spread the news, and soon seventh-graders I didn't even know were waiting to join the fun. I suppose my detachment began around that time. I was over six feet tall from the awkward age of twelve, and my assailants kept getting smaller and smaller as the word spread that there was a gentle giant you could line up to pick on. It was as if there were a line of them, descending in stature from the middle-grown currently at work on me to the runts waiting patiently behind them for a turn. That is the way I remember it, though I know it could not actually have been so. Eventually, after being formally challenged, I decked the smallest kid in the school by the trophy case after gym class, surprising everyone, but especially myself. Being punched and goaded was not me, but fighting didn't seem like me, either, though it stopped the outward violence. What "me" meant was beginning to baffle me.

I jump now from that memory to my PhD dissertation defense fifteen years later, where I could hardly remember what I had written and submitted to the committee only two months before and could hardly understand the questions they were asking me. I had become a parent of a son since that submission, but still, you would think I would be able to remember and talk about something I had worked on for two years. But I could hardly remember. At the defense, I had the same feeling I had had years before in school when those boys lined up to work on me. I was detached, watching things happen to me, waiting. I had the same sense of not being in the moment, of there being no moment in which I could be present and active.

Examples of this seemingly unnatural detachment go way back. Another out-of-moment memory: I remember being in love with my kindergarten teacher, Mrs. Pierce, in Tucson, Arizona. (My mother thought she was a bimbo, and told me so—I forget when.) For some reason one day, I told Mrs. Pierce to shut up. I have no idea why, or what she had said, but I remember us all saying that very often at home—"shut up" was just something we said, laughingly, in fond response to friendly teasing. Why should not sign and signifier so conjoin? Anyway, Mrs. Pierce, who presumably had not yet made her personal peace with the arbitrariness of the sign, had me sit in the back of the room and wait while she called my mom to come and take me home. There must have been a closet at the back—I remember waiting for my mother and not being able to crawl back far enough, crawling back, under the coats, over the shoes, and back to the dark depths of a closet that seemed endless. And I sobbed—the eldest sibling, the first to leave home, was being sent back in shame. As I recall this event, the image of the boots and coats around and above me is blurred by my tears, so what I remember as vividly as life is actually wet raincoats and boots dripping mud, though of course it never rained in the Arizona desert, and no one wore coats. You could take that moment, profoundly true in its falseness, as emblematic of so many of my life's subsequent punctuating events—my collapsing, losing touch, finding in endurance a strength that is really a weakness, an inability to live in my life. What I see, as I look back, is a longing for attachment that was consistently stymied, but always because it had always already been stymied before.

My life is a consequence of my sensitivity to the cut, the severance, the structural break marked by the moment's deconstruction. The moments I have cited were memories of aching sadness, guilt, and shame for me: I wanted to have been fully there, fully present, participating in the moment, and yet was not. Derrida's way of looking at the moment helps me to read those memories differently. For Derrida "the instant is instantaneously, *at this very instant,* divided, destroyed by what it nonetheless makes possible—testimony."[9] To see this is to be free of the guilt: my suffering, my passion, was not my failure but my awareness of the structural dividedness of all experience.

Memory is a type of testimony, and so to recall an instant is to destroy it, to make it something it never was. Each of my memories is an instant: I remember each quite vividly, not as a time, a feeling that had duration, but as something instantaneous—like an emotional photograph. I do not remember my dissertation defense as a two-hour event in which I participated. Instead, I remember a particular instant. David Shaw asked me about Hegel's lectures on aesthetics. It was a plant—he had suggested months before that he thought my work would benefit from a consideration of Hegel. It was a hint, and I had sort of expected

---

9. Derrida, *Demeure,* 33.

the question while hoping it wouldn't come, because I had not read Hegel. In saying so, apologetically, to the committee—the rest of whom were unaware of the tacit agreement I had apparently made to read and then discuss Hegel in the defense—I heard myself denying or questioning Hegel's relevance to my topic, which was not what I wanted to be saying. I heard myself simultaneously repudiating and disappointing David Shaw, whose work I respected and with whom I had hoped to build a relationship. As I recall the moment, I feel it as a shattering. My words did not sound like mine. Things were not going as the committee and I had hoped. My supervisor, Peter Allen, told me later that it was, paradoxically, a poor defense of a good dissertation. We were not communicating.

In fact, I was not even there. "I" was at that point the father of a four-week-old infant who, it seemed, did nothing but scream. I was not, then, the one whom they saw—I was a ghost haunting my defense. The instant was not one: it was divided and destroyed. But that is the way instants are. One cannot conceive of an instant that is not somehow memorable. A moment is simply what is annihilated by testimony. Surely that is why we find freedom in confession.

The Instant

But let us look again at what Derrida says about instants and try to understand how they are structured. The deconstructive insight is that (a) one cannot sever the instant from the telling of it, and (b) in the telling, one must restrict oneself to the iterable, to sounds, words, and sentences that are constituted by their quotability, their ability to be repeated.[10] If I do not commit myself to repeating and maintaining tomorrow what I say now, I abandon my claim to the truth, and, as Derrida says, "truth is not a value one can renounce."[11] A barrier therefore severs me from the moment: I can re-member only what I can re-cognize, only what is repeatable. Experience is the experience of repetition.

Derrida does not say that there's no such thing as an instant, a presence in space and time. He says that the instant is divided by what it makes possible and by what makes *it* possible: testimony. The instant

---

10. On "iterability," see Derrida's "Signature Event Context," in *Limited Inc.*

11. Jacques Derrida and Maurizio Ferraris, *A Taste for the Secret,* trans. Giacomo Donis (Cambridge, U.K.: Polity, 2001), 10.

lies in something like what Ferdinand de Saussure calls the vague neb-
ula of pre-linguistic awareness—"In itself, thought is like a swirling
cloud, where no shape is intrinsically determinate"[12]—or in what Julia
Kristeva calls the *chora*, "a non-expressive totality": "Discrete quantities
of energy move through the body of the subject who is not yet constituted as such and, in the course of his development, they are arranged
according to the various constraints imposed on this body—always already involved in a semiotic process—by family and social structures."[13]
Kristeva shows how both the moment and the self are constituted and
structured by language, by the same split between signifier and signified
that structures the sign. But in re-membering the instant, I destroy it,
simply because I do so in and from another instant, the present instant
rather than the one I remember. Even in initially experiencing the instant, I experience only what I can re-cognize in it, severing that from
what I cannot.

This may begin to account for the one quality all my memories
have in common: things simply could not have been as I remember
them. In remembering, we destroy the instant, and we mistranslate it.
Derrida writes:

> The moment one is a witness and the moment one attests, bears witness,
> the instant one gives testimony, there must also be a temporal sequence—
> sentences, for example—and, above all, these sentences must promise their
> own repetition and thus their own quasi-technical reproducibility. When I
> commit myself to speaking the truth, I commit myself to repeating the
> same thing, an instant later, two instants later, the next day, and for eter-
> nity, in a certain way. But the repetition carries the instant outside itself.[14]

So in testifying to an instant, as I have done here to a few moments in
my life that seem constitutive of my identity, I destroy it. I cannot rip it
out of the nebulous, choric continuum without structuring it in an
absolute-truth field, without committing myself to repeating what I
say (that is, not changing my mind about it) and to the repeatability of
what I say, since the constitutive quality of the truth is that it bears repetition. So the instant either is not *(chora)* or is always (I testify to how

---

12. Ferdinand de Saussure, *Course in General Linguistics*, ed. Charles Bally and Albert Sechehaye, trans. Roy Harris (La Salle, Ill.: Open Court, 1972), 155.

13. Julia Kristeva, *Revolution in Poetic Language*, trans. Margaret Walker (New
York: Columbia University Press, 1984), 25.

14. Derrida, *Demeure*, 33.

it, in fact, then, now, and for always, *was*), and in neither case is it an instant. The instant thus divides: it is the liminal mark dividing nothing (oblivion) from the absolute (the way that it really was). Testimony instantaneously constitutes and destroys the instant. Testimony is thus in a sense an outrage. As Domino, the dwarf, demands of the rational and detached Henri in Winterson's *The Passion*, "What makes you think you can see anything clearly? What gives you the right to make a notebook and shake it at me in thirty years, if we are still alive, and say you've got the truth?"[15] And yet, conversely, the instant is that which is simultaneously constituted and destroyed by testimony.

What I want to do here is show the relevance of these structural characteristics of all instants to the instants that constitute who I am. And yet I cannot know who I am, as Derrida points out in *Derrida's Elsewhere*: "There are events that consist in saying 'I' or 'me' but that does not mean that the 'me' exists as such and should ever be perceived as being present. Who ever met a 'me'? Not me." I suppose you could say that what I want to be able to do is deconstruct myself—if you were comfortable with "deconstruct" as a transitive verb, which I am not (though Derrida himself seems to be). I want to show what this deconstructing of myself would look like, and at the same time I want to glean for myself and others the benefits of such a deconstruction, which can only be what John D. Caputo calls an affirmation.[16]

The Self

In question, then, is the relationship between the instant I remember and the structure of the instant *qua* instant. In other words, how do I read my memories now that I have read Derrida? That is the question, though at the same time it must be indefinitely postponed. First, we must see that the question cannot be limited to the instant's structure. Deconstruction proliferates: as I have shown with the Kristeva passage cited above, the self deconstructs the same way that the instant does. In *Demeure*, Derrida writes of

> the difference both null and uncrossable, real and fictional, actual and virtual, between the one who says "I" and the young man of whom he speaks and who is himself, whom he still remembers according to the synthesis of

---

15. Winterson, *The Passion*, 28.
16. John D. Caputo, *The Prayers and Tears of Jacques Derrida: Religion without Religion* (Bloomington: Indiana University Press, 1997), 3.

which we spoke earlier. The one who says and undersigns "I" today, now, cannot replace the other; he can no longer, therefore, replace himself, that is, the young man he has been. He can no longer replace him, substitute himself for him, a condition that is nonetheless stipulated for any normal and non-fictional testimony. He can no longer relive what has been lived. And thus, in a certain way, he no longer knows, he has a memory of what he no longer knows. . . . In other words, he testifies *for* a witness, in a different sense this time, *in the place* of the witness he cannot be *for* this other witness that the young man was, and who is yet himself.[17]

What Derrida is writing about here is the impossibility of testimony, of confession, even of responsibility. That impossibility will of course require a response, but first we must understand it. This deconstruction of the self, not an action taken by a "deconstructionist" but something always already at play in every subject—something that is, in its single gesture, simultaneously *constitutive* and *destructive* (hence, *deconstructive*)—is structurally identical to the deconstruction of the instant. And each deconstruction pivots on testimony: a self that cannot say "I" is a choric, pre-mirror-phase no-self devoid of agency, and yet when I say "I," when I testify to myself, I ground it as an absolute entity, despite the fact that if I were merely that, I would have no cause, desire, or ability to testify. So I am always already no longer that to or of whom I testify. I am a self different from all other selves, to be sure, but deconstruction is the structure of the self that I am at each de-constitutive instant of my being. It is the structure of each of us, the truth from which each thought, argument, action, and truth is a turning away.

So instants and selves deconstruct. When I come back to the moment of being flummoxed at my thesis defense, what do I have? Certainly I have a moment in context, which is already helpful: I have a moment not so different from other moments as I might have thought. For most of my life, as I say, I have felt myself unusually subject to moments like the one I described of not having read Hegel at my thesis defense. I have tended to experience myself as subject, like the hero of Tennyson's *The Princess,* to periodic and parodic "weird seizures": "I seemed to move among a world of ghosts, / And feel myself the shadow of a dream."[18] But to read deconstruction is to see that such seizures,

---

17. Derrida, *Demeure,* 65–66.
18. *Tennyson: A Selected Edition,* ed. Christopher Ricks (Berkeley: University of California Press, 1989), 1:14–18.

weird as they may be, better represent the structure of the moment *qua* moment than other more comfortable moments do. The instants I have narrated here were traumatic for me, but they were true to their momentness. Beating my dad at ping-pong the other day, probably for the first time in my life, felt great. I relished the illusion of full presence. But even as it was happening, I was remembering vividly the many times I had been beaten. I remembered the feeling of being, like Thackeray's Pendennis, my own worst enemy, of being unable to do what I wanted to with my body, of being defeated first by my own mind. The self that I was in those moments of defeat, "working a kind of repeated severance from the originary severance," echoed the truth of all selves at all moments.[19] Those, in an odd way, were my instants of communion, my moments of awareness of the structure of experience.

Passions

The refrain repeated throughout Winterson's novel is her description of passion: "It is somewhere between fear and sex." Certainly, Peter's fear of Christ's passion to come is naïve, and he is soundly rebuked for it, but Winterson's point, that it is also naïve to separate passion from fear, is also important. My moments have been moments of not-very-Christlike resistance, and my resistance, not the deconstruction, made them painful. What would it have been like to fully accept the deconstruction of the self and of the moment, not to resist their structural natures? I cannot say. I have come to think of those deconstructive

---

19. Jacques Derrida, "Passions: An Oblique Offering," in David Wood, ed., *Derrida: A Critical Reader* (Oxford: Blackwell, 1992), 12. This essay, one of Derrida's recent discussions of deconstruction in its wider context, discusses clarity, responsibility, the thesis, the ethics of writing, non-response, and some common complaints about deconstruction. My readers may be interested in consulting this work, in which Derrida disowns both those who see deconstruction as "a modern form of immorality, of amorality, or of irresponsibility" and those determined to construct "a remoralization of deconstruction" (15). He both refuses the role of Christ many in the academy have bestowed upon him ("I am not taking the insane risk and adopting the odious attitude of treating all these thinkers as disciples" [18]) and describes the passion of refusing to respond, of being unable to respond, to his stupid detractors: "So many dogmatic naïvetés that one will never discourage, but all the more reason not to respond"(20); "It is impossible to respond here.... This aporia without end paralyzes us because it binds us doubly.... In one and the same place, on the same apparatus, I have my two hands tied or nailed down" (22). The essay ends with "the absolute solitude of a passion without martyrdom" (31).

moments as my *passions,* and I follow Derrida and Winterson in retaining all the various senses of the word "passion": passing through, passing on, being passive, loving intensely, suffering deeply, sacrificing oneself.[20] Each author synthesizes passion in ways that surprise, frustrate, and terrify us. Deconstruction is passion, Derrida says—"one might be able to reduce 'différance' to another name for passion," he writes in *Demeure,* and by *passion* he certainly means to reference Christ on the cross (Acts 1:3): "Finally, and above all 'passion' implies the endurance of an indeterminate or undecidable limit where something, some X— for example, literature—must bear or tolerate everything, *suffer everything precisely because it is not itself,* because it has no essence but only functions."[21] The truth depends upon this passion that I resist. Testimony is a fiction—it cannot be true. But that sounds negative. Another way to say the same thing is to say that testimony is the truth of fiction:

> Without the *possibility* of this fiction, without the spectral virtuality of this simulacrum and as a result of this lie or this fragmentation of the true, no truthful testimony would be possible. Consequently, the possibility of literary fiction haunts so-called truthful, reasonable, serious, real testimony as its proper possibility. This haunting is perhaps the passion itself, the passionate place of literary writing, as the project to say everything—and wherever it is auto-biographical, that is to say, everywhere, and everywhere autobio-thanatographical.[22]

There is a lot in this passage. Derrida makes four contiguous claims: (1) truth is haunted by fiction; (2) that haunting is the passion; (3) that passion is the place of literature, the purpose of which is to say everything; and (4) literature, which occupies the place of passion, is not just autobiographical but "autobiothanatographical"—an image of the death that constitutes my life. The passion of literature: the passion of passing between the positions of author, character, and narrator in fiction, and the passion of truth into fiction, each of which always haunts the other.

I can now draw several conclusions. (1) Each of my "weird seizures" is more than a lapse of presence—it is a moment that is structurally translucent, or true to itself as moment. (2) Each "weird seizure" is therefore a nexus of passion. (3) I experienced each moment of seizure

---

20. Derrida, *Demeure,* 26–28.
21. Ibid., 27–28.
22. Ibid., 72.

not as passion but as trauma. I have mentioned not having read Hegel at my dissertation defense: I still haven't—I am still resisting. But not so traumatically now. Each sentence I write, I promise, will be as true as I can make it each time you read it, but I write in the name of the truth of passion and the passion of truth. I write now, I hope, in more passive, more passionate resistance. But I find that one more question must be answered—I cannot stop here. "Trust me—I am telling you stories."[23]

Iterability

Winterson's Henri, whose passion turns out to be profoundly inauthentic, says to himself, "You cannot make sense of your passion for life in the face of death, you can only give up your passion. Only then can you begin to survive."[24] And that is what he does—he gives it up. Supposing I do not want to do that, what am I to do? Having acknowledged that being is contingent, a consequence of iterability, how am I to be? Deconstruction yields no answer to this question, no solution to the problem. I remember often being tempted to blame someone or something—myself, my upbringing, some oppressor—for each traumatic defeat. But I resisted. The reason is that I thought of attachment, communion, as a natural, prior, authentic state that, somehow, I had lost—this is a way of thinking that still seems the most natural way for me to think. I am a victim of my own unnatural nostalgia for origins, even after having recognized that in fact there is no word, no self, no thing that cannot be copied, no way to imagine a word, self, or thing that cannot be copied, and that it is only as original first copy that I emerge: I am my iterability, and nothing besides. Resistance is futile. No matter how deep my journey of self-discovery may lead, I will find nothing that cannot be copied because to find something is to *re*-cognize it. Discovery is *re*cognition. To see this is to be "interpellated," or hailed,[25] not by ideology but by the truth. The state of affairs seems to require a response from me, and resistance seems to me an inappropriate response to the, or any, truth. But how am I to be?

---

23. Winterson, *The Passion*, 40.
24. Ibid., 82.
25. Louis Althusser, *Lenin and Philosophy and Other Essays*, trans. Ben Brewster (London: NLB, 1971), 162.

What is to be my relationship to this iterability, this arbitrary, inexplicable, automatic, and instantaneous miracle of which being is only an effect? Like the self or the instant, iterability cannot be thought. No matter what or how I may think about iterability, my thoughts are iterable. They are consequences of the iterability that seems a state of all things. So here's my answer, and it is a religious one. One cannot see or experience iterability but only infer it as the one quality all things everywhere have in common, the one quality they all share. One is free to infer this or to resist. My tendency is to resist inferring the priority of iterability, but once I infer it, I can no longer ignore it. I can only be grateful for the unbelievable gift of iterability, since everything I see, think, write, and have become is contingent upon it, and to be coy about my enthusiasm would be dishonest. I *like* deconstruction. Derrida affirms this necessary affirmation himself: "In deconstruction there is a movement of sensitization to the multiplicity of levels of structure; at every instant, there are dislocations within the instant. But this, for me, instead of cooling and disintensifying experience, intensifies it."[26]

And if we are to think in terms of gratitude, we must acknowledge, with Derrida, the special place of the arts. Art acknowledges the passion in all things. It resists resistance. Deconstruction, then, is the pleasure we call desire: "We write autobiographies because we are driven by the desire of this meeting with a 'me' which finally will be what it is" (in *Derrida's Elsewhere*). My autobiography must be the narrative of how, in response to deconstruction, I have become, and I must savor it.

I will risk any clarity I may have brought to the implications of Derrida's writings by introducing another theorist briefly at the end. I need to do so because I want to further explore the question of response, or responsibility—or an ethical response to deconstruction. Lacan is difficult to read, but he is very good on what he calls "intersubjectivity," or the syntax of our orientation vis-à-vis texts and other people. Lacan shows, in the famous seminar on Poe (1956), that language speaks us: the letter, once we encounter it, elicits a response. Derrida disagreed with Lacan on several points, but that disagreement should not obscure the fact that Lacan's analysis can shed much-needed light on our responses to deconstruction. It is also a powerful reading of the truth in fiction. In Edgar Allen Poe's "The Purloined Letter," a letter has been stolen. It is eventually recovered in the last place one

---

26. Derrida and Ferraris, *A Taste for the Secret*, 88.

would expect to find it. And every time the letter changes hands, the whole balance of power shifts. Lacan finds that there are three ways one can respond to the letter of iterability and the iterability of the letter, and I want to argue that there are corresponding responses to deconstruction. My main question in this essay is how I am to respond, and it helps to be clear about the possibilities.

Lacan writes:

> Thus three moments, structuring three glances, borne by three subjects, incarnated each time by different characters:
> The first is a glance that sees nothing: the King and the police.
> The second, a glance which sees that the first sees nothing and deludes itself as to the secrecy of what it hides: the Queen, then the Minister.
> The third sees that the first two glances leave what should be hidden exposed to whoever would seize it: the Minister, and finally Dupin.[27]

Similarly, when hailed by the reality of deconstruction, one can act in three ways. First, one can occupy the place of the King and the police Prefect and remain willfully blind to the letter—to deconstruction, or to the priority of iterability, in my analogy (glance 1). Students at the onset of their first course in theory often fall into this category. Second, one can also, like the Queen, see that others are neglecting deconstruction and hope the neglect will be contagious and permanent (glance 2). These readers see the letter (deconstruction) as a threat. It is common in some circles today to assume that deconstruction is a negative thing, and I can see why. The worry, I think, is that I might come to see myself as merely a poor copy, a simulacrum, of who I *could* or *ought* to be and that this ontological lapse will effect a moral one. It is hard, sometimes, to see how one's moral situation could be improved by one's observing that there are no originals, only bad imitations.[28] Third, one can, like the Minister and Dupin in Poe's story, trumpet the glory of one's possession, as is still sometimes done with deconstruction (glance 3). In this category are the would-be "deconstructionists," but also those for

---

27. John P. Muller and William J. Richardson, eds., *The Purloined Poe: Lacan, Derrida, and Psychoanalytic Reading* (Baltimore: Johns Hopkins University Press, 1988), 32.

28. The truth is that iterability is not relative—nothing, no person, thing, or entity, is less iterable than I. Far from leaving me an abandoned orphan in the world, however, as I have testified above, my iterability is good news—it actually frees me to explore a world of iterable gifts whose delicate, precious contingency equals my own.

whom "deconstruct" is just a pretentious synonym for "analyze." Each position in Lacan's triangle of the three ostriches is unstable. The possessor of deconstruction, for example, becomes the blind King in the presence of someone who has read Derrida more carefully. Within this intersubjective framework, each of us determines and is determined by our own ever-shifting relationship to the structure of the letter, and it is easy to feel trapped.

My point in this essay is similar to Derrida's in his reading of Lacan's seminar:[29] there is at least one other position, one other way to respond, a way that Lacan could not find in Poe and that generations have failed to find in Derrida. My own response to the deconstruction of the subject, as I have said (though it is not a natural or easy response), is gratitude. My praxis, as I negotiate the inter- and intra-subjectivity of deconstruction, is to try to accept myself provisionally as provisional so as to deepen my awareness of deconstruction and of each detail of my finite, material life in this awareness. The question, for me, as I look at the arts or view myself, is not what is original or authentic but rather how to read each manifestation of repetition, each variation, each inversion that I encounter, as a gift of iterability. In foregrounding the passion that structures everything, the arts are particularly gift-like. And when Derrida shows that "the gift is the impossible," he means not to deny the gift but to identify the gift with impossibility, the impossibility of the origin and therefore the originality of iterability, which cannot be copied.[30] Each repetition, myself included, is a tribute to iterability, an expression of gratitude to it, an affirmation—"the affirmation of affirmation, the 'yes' to the originary 'yes.'"[31] Deconstruction must be affirmation, implicitly or otherwise. To deny this seems to me both dishonest and quixotic.

---

29. Derrida is quite right about Lacan's refusal to deal with Poe's narrator in his schema, and his revelation of Lacan's simultaneous plagiarism and sexism seems to me indisputable. Derrida does not dispute Lacan's search for the truth in fiction, however, but rather reads Lacan so as to complicate that search. Lacan's allegory of intersubjectivity remains impressive, and Derrida's adjustment to the model (the narrator makes Lacan's figure not a closed triangle but an open square) only adds to its value (Jacques Derrida, "The Purveyor of Truth," from *The Post Card: From Socrates to Freud and Beyond* [Chicago: University of Chicago Press, 1987] and excerpted in *The Purloined Poe*).

30. Jacques Derrida, *Given Time. 1, Counterfeit Money*, trans. Peggy Kamuf (Chicago: University of Chicago Press, 1992), 7.

31. Jacques Derrida, *Archive Fever: A Freudian Impression*, trans. Erik Prenowitz (Chicago: University of Chicago Press, 1995), 74.

And so what about that little boy, who was (not) me, sniveling on the boots at the back of that Tucson classroom? That boy was in love, attached. He would have done anything for that teacher, and he thought of himself as set apart, as one of her special ones. But he could not see her as one who might not have been herself that day. He could not see her as a woman whose body, through no fault of her own, happened to fit a certain five-year-old's image of the ideal. He was not capable of it. Nor was she, it seems, capable of seeing in the words "shut up!" anything but their literal "meaning." Finally, he was apparently incapable of taking her provisionally, of taking her reaction in stride, of seeing it not as it was but as a copy of something better, as a poor affirmation of something true and real. The boy lacked faith. Resisting deconstruction made his passions into seizures. He thought things should be otherwise than they are. He could not see those moments of humiliation as echoes of "the originary severance." He lacked faith. And who does not?

Deconstruction is not nihilism, relativism, skepticism, or any other ism. In fact, though many of us wish to renounce these isms of our time, I would argue that deconstruction is one of the only really rigorous, scholarly denials of them on the current intellectual stage. Deconstruction is religious discourse. Deconstruction reads the ecstatic passion of full presence in the world. Deconstruction is a surrendering to and an affirmation of the radical contingency of all experience. It is reading, an opening up to the openness that is all-pervasive. It is a reading, a feeling, a glowing of which we only become aware when we turn away from clarity and objectivity and seek solace in the translucence of the arts. Deconstruction is reality, since it is always already at play, and since it also structures us, it is our communion with reality. Ultimately, deconstruction is prayer.

"The Word First Gathered Chaos Up"

Carol Gilbertson

Academy

Karen Black

1. The Word first gathered chaos up, dividing land and sea. Created things gazed toward the sun, and cells began to thrive. Our language follows God's first word, and reaches toward the light. We marvel at the power of words to probe our deepest thought. Let alphabets seed into words, let words sprout sentences. We echo love in cadences that sing of God's rich earth.

2. Recall by heart the gospel words, tell tales that capture love. Teach children how to ponder texts, and syncopate our sighs. We language to articulate earth's wrongs, turns Babel to a symphony of varied human tongues. Let alphabets seed into words, let words sprout sentences. We echo love in cadences that sing of God's rich earth.

3. In poetry we find a voice to grope our way toward prayer. God's language in our rhythmic lines can share laughter deepens human life. Let language from rough clay; a canvas shows our folks sit down to eat. We chords and melodies we make light our reverent hearts.

4. The passion of our lives takes shape in syllables of love. Recounting stories, sharing snowflakes form, let pastures bloom, let celebrate the arts we have to signal God's good gifts.

220